GLOSSARY OF LIBRARY AND INFORMATION SCIENCE

GLOSSARY OF LIBRARY AND INFORMATION SCIENCE

By

Dr. Pankaj Kumar Singh

Librarian & H.O.D.
Dept. of Library & Information Science
D.S.N. (P.G.) College
Unnao - 209 801 (U.P.)
(India)

DISCOVERY PUBLISHING HOUSE PVT. LTD.
NEW DELHI-110 002

Published by:
Namit Wasan
DISCOVERY PUBLISHING HOUSE PVT. LTD.
4383/4B, Ansari Road, Darya Ganj
New Delhi-110 002 (India)
Phone : +91-11-23279245; 23253475; 43596065
E-mail : discoverybooksindia@gmail.com
discoverypublishinghouse@gmail.com
namitwasan9@gmail.com
web : www.discoverypublishinggroup.com

***Reprinted:* 2019**

***First Edition:* 2014**

ISBN: 978-93-5056-422-6

Glossary of Library and Information Science

Printed at:
Infinity Imaging Systems
Delhi

Preface

Dramatic developments in information technology have changed the ways library information is being organized and disseminated around the world. Newer and increasing numbers of terms, as well as terms that are already used in related fields have become part of the daily vocabulary of libraries and information services environments.

The Glossary of Library and Information Science presents a thorough yet concise book to the specific words that describe the materials, processes and systems relevant to the field of librarianship. This glossary defines common library terms and serves as a quick reference source for library users. Many of the new terms that have been incorporated to librarianship are consolidated in this book as well as new terms created as a result of developments in technology. Written by an expert author from the LIS world, this helpful book will become an essential part of every library's and librarian's reference collection and will also be a blessing for LIS students and recent graduates. We welcome corrections and suggestions from all users.

–Author

Contents

A

A Repetition

A style of French book-binding in which a single design element is repeated uniformly over the entire surface of the cover.

A Side

In the music recording industry, the side (tune) of a two-sided audio-recording designated for promotion, based on its perceived potential for commercial success. Compare with B side.

A&I

Abstracting and Indexing.

A.E.G.

An Abbreviation of *All Edges Gilt*.

A.E.M.

An abbreviation of *all edges marbled*. Marbling applied to the fore-edge and the top and bottom edges of a volume.

A.K.A.

An Abbreviation of *Also Known As*.

A.L.S.

Autograph Letter Signed.

AACR

Anglo-American Cataloguing Rules.

AACR2 2002

Anglo-American Cataloguing Rules.

AACR2-e

Anglo-American Cataloguing Rules.

AACR2R

Anglo-American Cataloguing Rules.

AAHSL

Association of Academic Health Sciences Libraries.

AALL

American Association of Law Libraries.

AAMES

Asian, African, and Middle Eastern Section.

AAP

Association of American Publishers.

AAS

American Antiquarian Society.

AASL

American Association of School Librarians.

AAT
Art and Architecture Thesaurus.

AAUP
American Association of University Professors and Association of American University Presses.

ABA
American Booksellers Association.

ABAA
Antiquarian Booksellers Association of America.

ABC Book
Abecedary and Alphabet Book.

Abecedarium
Abecedary.

Abecedarius
Acrostic.

Aberrant Copy
A copy of a book containing obvious printing and/or binding errors that are more serious than minor defects.

Aberrant Date
In archives, a date that falls outside the chronological sequence of dates pertaining to the majority of the documents in the record unit described.

ABF
Association des Biblio-thécaires Français.

ABPC
American Book Prices Current.

Abridged Decimal Classification (ADC)
A logical truncation of the notational and structural hierarchy of the full edition of Dewey Decimal Classification, developed for general collections of 20,000 titles or less.

Abridged
Abridgment.

Absolute Humidity
Humidity.

Absorbed Title
Absorption.

Absorbency
The capacity of paper to absorb and retain moisture, which varies with type of paper and is of particular importance in printing processes that use liquid ink.

Abstracting and Indexing (A&I)
A category of database that provides bibliographic citations and abstracts of the literature of a discipline or subject area, as distinct from a retrieval service that provides information sources in full-text.

Abstracting Journal
A journal that specialises in providing summaries of articles and other documents published within the scope of a specific academic disciline or field of study. Synonymous with *abstract journal*. Compare with abstracting service.

Abstracting
The preparation of a brief, objective statement of the content of a written work to enable the researcher to quickly determine whether reading the entire text might satisfy the specific information need. Abstracting is usually limited to the literature of a specific discipline or group

of related disciplines and is performed by an individual or commercial entity, such as an indexing and abstracting service, that provides abstracts regularly to a list of subscribers.

ACA

Academy of Certified Archivists and Association of Canadian Archivists.

ACACC

Association of Canadian Map Libraries and Archives.

Academic Press

University press.

Academic Status

Recognition given by an institution of higher education that the librarians in its employ are considered members of the teaching or research staff but are *not* entitled to ranks, titles, rights, and benefits equivalent to those of faculty. The Association of College and Research Libraries (ACRL) has published Guidelines for Academic Status for College and University Librarians. Compare with faculty status.

Academy Aperture

Academy format.

Access Time

The amount of time a computer takes to retrieve requested data from an electronic storage medium to a user who follows correct procedures. In online retrieval, the speed of the computer's Internet connection is an important factor, but even with a fast connection access time may be slower during periods of peak use.

Access

The right of entry to a library or its collections. All public libraries and most academic libraries in the United States are open to the general public, but access to certain areas such as closed stacks, rare books, and special collections may be restricted. In a more general sense, the right or opportunity to use a resource that may not be openly and freely available to everyone.

Accessibility

The ease with which a person may enter a library, gain access to its online systems, use its resources, and obtain needed information regardless of format. In a more general sense, the quality of being able to be located and used by a person. In the Web environment, the quality of being usable by everyone regardless of disability.

Accession List

Accession record.

Accessions

Accession.

Acclimatisation

The process of allowing archival records and other materials to adapt to environmental changes, especially when removed from cold storage for use at room temperature. Because materials can take hours to adapt to normal room temperature, the Society of American Archivists does not recommend cold storage as a practical solution for preserving frequently consulted items.

Accounts Binding

Stationery binding.

Accreditation Action

One of seven possible decisions by the *Committee on Accreditation* affecting the accreditation status of a library and information studies programme under the *Standards for Accreditation of Master's Programmes in Library and Information Studies,* conveyed to the dean of the programme and to the institution's chief executive officer in a formal Decision Document. The actions are:

- *Precandidacy Granted*: The program's and institution's commitment to achieving ALA accreditation is accepted.
- *Candidacy Granted*: The programme is ready to begin the two-year process culminating in the Programme Presentation document, comprehensive review, and COA accreditation decision.
- *Initially Accredited*: The programme is accredited for the first time.
- *Accreditation Continued*: The programme continues to demonstrate conformity to ALA *Standards.*
- *Conditionally Accredited*: The programme needs significant and immediate improvement to maintain conformity to ALA *Standards.*
- *Accreditation With-drawn*: The programme is no longer accredited by the ALA, as of the date specified by the COA.
- *Initial Accreditation Denied*: The programme or institution may file an appeal.

The Committee on Accreditation may withdraw accreditation for serious lack of conformity to the *Standards,* for failure to participate in the evaluation process, or for not meeting financial obligations to the COA.

Acetate Film

Cellulose acetate.

Acid Barrier

A sheet of acidfree or buffered paper, or polyester film, placed loose between an acidic component of a book, such as a bookplate, and the adjacent leaf or board to prevent acid migration.

ACL

Association of Christian Librarians.

ACMLA

Association of Canadian Map Libraries and Archives.

ACP

Association of Canadian Publishers.

Acquisition Number

A unique number used by the acquisitions department of a library to identify a specific bibliographic item on a purchase order. Some libraries use a standard number such as the ISBN or ISSN as the acquisition number.

ACRL Publications

Choice: Current Reviews for Academic Libraries.

- College and Research Libraries (C&RL).
- College and Research Libraries News.
- RBM: A Journal of Rare Books, Manuscripts, and Cultural Heritage.

ACRL
Association of College and Research Libraries.

Acrobat
Adobe Acrobat.

Ad Loc
An abbreviation of the Latin phrase *ad locum*, meaning "at the place [cited]."

ADA
Americans with Disabilities Act.

ADC
Abridged Decimal Classification.

Adjacency
Proximity.

Adjustable Shelving
Fixed shelving.

Administrative Value
Archival value.

ADS
Autograph Document Signed.

Adultliteracy
Literacy.

Advance Sheet
Advance copy.

Advanced Search
Search mode.

AECT
Association for Educational Communications and Technology.

AEP
Association of Educational Publishers.

Aerial Map
Photomap.

Aerial Mosaic
Photomosaic.

AFAS
African American Studies Librarians.

Affiliate
A separately administered organisation closely connected with another by formal agreement and mutual interest, for example, the various organisations affiliated with *American Library Association* (ALA). Also refers to the process of forming such a link.

AFI
American Film Institute.

A-G Canada Ltd.
Auto-Graphics, Inc.

AG
Authors Guild.

AH
Alternate History.

AI
Artificial Intelligence.

AIC
American Institute for Conservation of Historic and Artistic Works.

AIGA
American Institute of Graphic Arts.

AIIP
Association of Independent Information Professionals.

AILA
American Indian Library Association.

ALC
Americans for Libraries Council.

All Across
All along.

All On
All along.

All Over
A style of binding in which the entire surface of both covers is decorated, as opposed to design appearing on the front or back cover only, in the centers and/or corners, or around the edges.

All Through
Letter-by-letter.

Allied Professional Association
ALA Allied Professional Association.

Alligator
Leather made from the skin of a reptile, not as widely used in bookbinding as it once was for shoes and fashion accessories. In England, the material is known in the binding trade as *crocodile.*

All-rag
Rag paper.

ALPSP
Association of Learned and Professional Society Publishers.

ALSC
Association for Library Service to Children.

Alt Text
Alt tag.

ALTA
American Literary Translators Association.

ALTAFF
Association for Library Trustees, Advocates, Friends and Foundations.

Alternate Delivery
Shipment by a publisher or vendor of materials ordered by a library via a commercial delivery service rather than the U.S., Postal Service.

AMC Format
An abbreviation of Archival and Manuscripts Control format.

AMIA
Association of Moving Image Archivists.

Amnesty
Grace period.

Anacronym
A portmanteau word made by combining anachronistic with acronym. An acronym so old that few people recall what its letters stand for.

Anaglyphic Map
Anaglyph.

Analytic Classification
Hierarchical classification.

Analytics
Analytical entry.

ANSCR
Alpha-Numeric System for Classification of Recordings.

ANSI
American National Standards Institute.

ANSS
Anthropology and Sociology Section.

Antiphonary
Antiphonal.

Antiphoner
Antiphonal.

Antiplagiarism Programme
Plagiarism detection software.

Antique Map
Old map.

App
Application.

Archival Paper
A grade of paper that is permanent and highly durable, particularly with respect to fading and physical deterioration caused by acidity, used for printing materials of archival quality.

Archives Policy
A formal written statement defining the authority under which an archives operates, the scope of its activities and the range of services it provides. Compare with access policy.

ARIST
Annual Review of Information Science and Technology.

Aristonym
A surname used as, or derived from, a formal title of nobility.

ARL
Association of Research Libraries.

ARLIS/NA
Art Libraries Society/North America.

ARMA
Association for Information Management Professionals.

Armed Forces Library
Military library.

Armorial Binding
A binding, usually in leather, decorated with a coat of arms or other heraldic device to signify the royal or noble lineage of its original owner.

Armorial Bookplate
A bookplate bearing a heraldic device, such as a coat of arms, originally serving to identify the family of the owner.

ARSC
Association for Recorded Sound Collections.

ARSL
Association for Rural and Small Libraries.

Art Print
Print.

Artificial Leather
Imitation leather.

Artistic Control
Creative control.

ARTS
ARTS Section.

As New
Mint.

As Usual
In the antiquarian book trade, a volume which has one or more of the normal defects found in exlibrary books, such as library property stamps and other markings, spine labels, pockets, missing endpapers, etc.

AS
Acquisitions Section.

ASCAP
Pronounced "as cap."

ASCLA
Association of Specialised and Cooperative Library Agencies.

ASERL
Association of Southeastern Research Libraries.

ASI
American Society of Indexers.

Aslib
Association for Information Management.

ASPA
Association of Specialised and Professional Accreditors.

ASPP
American Society of Picture Professionals.

ASRS
Automated storage and retrieval system.

Assistive Technology
Adaptive technology.

Associative Relation
A semantic relation in which two words or phrases are conceptually connected, sometimes within a specific context, but are not related hierarchically, for example, the terms 'library extension' and 'library outreach.'

Asyndetic
Lacking crossreferences. Compare with syndetic structure.

ATA
American Translators Association.

ATG
Against the Grain.

ATLA
American Theological Library Association.

Auction Gallery
Book auction.

Audiodisc
Phonograph record.

Audiorecording
A generic term for any medium on which sounds are recorded for mechanical or electronic playback, including phonograph records, audiotape, and compact disc. Synonymous with sound recording.

Audiotape
A continuous strip of thin magnetic tape on which sounds can be recorded as electrical signals and converted back into sound with the proper playback equipment. The most common size in libraries is one-fourth inch wide, stored on audiocassette. Synonymous with *tape recording.*

Audiovisual (AV)
A work in a medium that combines sound and visual images, for example, a motion picture or videorecording with a sound track, or a slide presentation synchronised with audiotape. Directory information for products and services provided by the audiovisual industry is available in *AV Market Place (AVMP),* published annually by Information Today, Inc. Also spelled *audio-visual* and abbreviated *a-v.*

Audit Trail
Information contained in available records that enables a transaction to be tracked from beginning to end, facilitating review of whether it was executed according to established policies and standards. Such information typically includes time of transaction, names

of parties involved, and actions taken.

In computing, an activity log of who has accessed, or attempted to access, a computer system and what operations were performed during a given period of time, useful for recovering lost transactions, maintaining security, and detecting misuse. An audit trail component is included in most accounting systems and database management systems.

Audit
An official examination of the accounts or records of an individual, company, organisation, or institution to determine if they are correct. Also, to conduct such an examination, usually on a regular basis.

AUP
Acceptable Use Policy.

Author-publisher
A writer, photographer, composer, etc., who self-publishes his or her own works.

Author-title Added Entry
Name-title added entry.

Authorware
Courseware.

Autograph Document Signed (ADS)
A document written and signed by its author.

Autograph Letter Signed (ALS)
A letter handwritten by the person who signed it, as opposed to a manuscript letter written by someone other than the signer.

Autograph Note Signed (ANS)
A note hand written by the person who signed it. To see examples, try a keywords search on the term in *Google Images*.

Autograph Score
An original music score written entirely in the hand of the composer, often highly prised by museums and other collectors.

Autograph
An original manuscript written entirely in the hand of the author or dictated by the author, often highly prised by rare book collectors. Also refers to a person's own signature.

Autographed Copy
A copy of a book or other published work signed by the author. Autographed copies may be of considerable value to collectors if the author is very well known and signed copies rare, as in the case of a small limited edition. Compare with inscribed copy.

Autographed Edition
An edition of a work in which all the copies are personally signed by the author, possible only in comparatively small editions.

Autonym
A person's own name. Also refers to a work published under the real name of its author, rather than a pseudonym or allonym.

Auxiliary Facility
A secondary library facility, often housing technical services and/or low use and archival materials to alleviate space constraints in the

main building. High density shelving may be installed to maximize storage capacity. When used to store manuscripts and rare and fragile materials, an auxiliary facility may be equipped with conservation level environmental controls.

Auxiliary Schedule
In library classification, a separate list of classes that serves only to subdivide the classes listed in the main schedules, for example, the standard subdivisions listed in Table 1 of Dewey Decimal Classification.

AV
Audiovisual.

Avantgarde Film
Experimental film.

AVIAC
Automation Vendors Information Advisory Committee.

AVSL
Association of Vision Science Librarians.

Award
Library award and literary award.

B

B&W
Black and white.

Back Number
Back issue.

Back Title
Spine title.

Backlining
Lining.

Backslanted
A typeface or handwriting that inclines to the left of center.

Balance Stripe
Magnetic stripe.

Bar Graph
Histogram.

Basic Search
Search mode.

Bastard Title
Half title.

Bâtarde
Bastarda.

BBC
British Broadcasting Corporation.

BBFC
British Board of Film Classification.

BBR
The Boston Book Review.

BBS
Bulletin board system.

BCALA
Black Caucus of the American Library Association.

BCCB
Bulletin of the Center for Children's Books.

BCL
Books for College Libraries.

BD
Bluray.

BEA
BookExpo America.

Belles Lettres
A French phrase meaning "beautiful letters", referring to polite, refined literature and to the aesthetics of literary studies.

Belpré Award
Pura Belpré Award.

Bequest
A gift of tangible property by will. Library and archival collections are enriched by such gifts, which are often acknowledged by the use of special bookplates, plaques, and memorial names, depending on the size of the gift.

BES
Buildings and Equipment Section.

BFI
British Film Institute.

BI
Bibliographic instruction and business intelligence.

Biannual
Issued twice each year. Also refers to a publication issued twice a year.

BIBCO
Programme for Cooperative Catalogueing (PCC).

Bible Style
A general term for any flexible leather binding that has rounded corners, especially one of dark colour.

Biblioclast
A person who destroys or mutilates books, for one reason or another. Fortunately for bibliophiles, this form of aberrant behaviour occurs infrequently.

Bibliognost
A person who has a profound knowledge of books, bibliography, etc.

Bibliogony
Of or relating to the production of books in all their forms. Synonymous with *bibliogenesis*.

Bibliographee
A person concerning whom a bibliography is compiled, as in a list of references at the end of a biographical essay or booklength biography.

Biblioklept
A thief who steals books. A bibliokleptomaniac is a person suffering from a compulsion to steal books. When library collections are targeted, biblioklepts are considered problem patrons.

Bibliology
The historical and scientific study and description of books as physical objects, from their origins in human society to the present, including knowledge of the processes and materials involved in making them. Compare with codicology.

Bibliomancy
The art of divination through the use of books or verses of the Bible or some other sacred text. Also, the practice of opening the Bible, or a book of verses or aphorisms such as the *I Ching*, without previously marking the page, to discover meaning or significance in the passage found.

Biblionarcissism
The art of convincing others that one is more knowledgeable about books or bookish than one really is, a term attributed to Tom Raabe,

author of *Biblioholism: The Literary Addiction.*

Bibliopegy
The fine art of binding books by hand, performed by a bookbinder or *bibliopegist.*

Bibliophilately
The collection and study of library related postage stamps, usually as a hobby

Bibliophile
A person who loves and treasures books and is sufficiently knowledgeable to be able to distinguish editions by their characteristics and qualities. Most bibliophiles are book collectors. The opposite of bibliophobe. Synonymous with *booklover* and *bibliophilist*. Compare with biblioholism and bibliomania.

Bibliophilist
Bibliophile.

Bibliophobia
An irrational fear or dread of books so intense that the afflicted person, known as a *bibliophobe,* avoids them whenever possible. The opposite of bibliophily.

Bibliopole
A bookseller, especially one who deals in rare books and editions.

Bibliopsychology
The psychological study of the interrelationships between authors, books, and readers.

Bibliotaph
A person who hoards books and hides them from others, even to the extent of keeping them under lock and key.

Bibliotheca
From the Greek *biblion* and *theke.* A library or collection of books. Also refers to a list or catalogue of books, especially one prepared by a bibliographer.

BICI
Book Item and Contribution Identifier.

Biennial
Issued every two years. Also refers to a serial publication issued every two years. Compare with semiannual.

Bilinear Script
Majuscule.

Bill and Melinda Gates Foundation Access to Learning Award
Access to Learning Award.

Bimonthly
Issued in alternate months. Also refers to a serial issued every other month. Compare with semimonthly.

Binder's Ticket
A small printed or engraved paper label affixed to a book, usually on the lower inside corner of the front or rear paste-down, bearing the name or mark and location of the binder.

Binder's Title
The title stamped or lettered on the spine of a bound volume by the binder, as distinct from the cover title on the publisher's edition and the title printed on the title page.

Binding Copy
A worn book in such poor condition that it needs to be rebound

and is worth the expense of re-binding.

Biopredation
Damage to books or other library materials caused by living organisms, such as insects or mold.

BIP
Books in Print.

Birthday Book
A type of book popular during the Victorian period in which a quotation from a work by a well known writer is given for each day of the year, with space left blank for autographs.

BISG
Book Industry Study Group.

Biweekly
Issued every two weeks. Also refers to a serial issued at two-week intervals. Used synonymously with semimonthly. Compare with semiweekly.

Black Face
Boldface.

Black Letter
Gothic.

Blanking
In binding, the application of a heated brass stamp to the cloth cover of a book to create a glossy impression to serve as a base for lettering or for a stamped decoration.

BLB
Big Little Book.

Blind Folio
A leaf in a manuscript or book included in the foliation but not given a folio number. Compare with blind page.

Blind Page
A page in a book, usually the half title, title page, dedication, or a blank page, included in the pagination but not given a page number. Compare with blind folio.

Blind Reference
A cross reference in an index or catalogue directing the reader to a heading that does *not* exist in the same index or catalogue.

Block Quotation
Quotation.

Blog
Weblog.

BMI
Book Manufacturer's Institute.

BNB
British National Bibliography.

BNC
Library and Archives Canada.

BNF
Bibliothèque Nationale de France.

BO
Back order.

Body Matter
The text of a work to be printed, as distinct from any display matter.

Body Type
Text type.

Bold
Boldface.

Bond Measure
Library bond.

Book Award
Literary award.

Book Band
A strip of printed paper placed around the jacketed cover of a book to call attention to a special characteristic, such as availability at a reduced price, receipt of an award, or special loan status.

Book Block
All the sections of a book sewn or glued together, plus the endpapers and any other leaves added by the binder, before the cover is applied. Compare with text block.

Book Box
A container made of rigid, solid material, usually rectangular in shape, designed to hold a book and keep it tightly covered on all sides.

Book Catalogue
A library catalogue in the form of a bound or loose leaf book, whether handwritten, printed, or computer generated, practical only for small collections.

Book Cloth
Cloth.

Book Detection System
Security gate.

Book Format
Book size.

Book Jacket
Dust jacket.

Book Label
A card, strip, etc., smaller than a bookplate, usually made of paper, affixed to the inside of a book, in most cases to indicate ownership.

Book Light
A very small electric light designed to attach, usually by means of a clip, to the cover of a book for reading in dark places without disturbing others.

Book List
A selected list of books, usually on a specific topic or in a particular genre, arranged in some kind of order that may include brief descriptive annotations, used mainly in readers' advisory.

Book Louse
Book lice.

Book Mark
Book number.

Book Mite
Book lice.

Book Prize
Literary award.

Book Rate
Media mail.

Book Repair
Repair.

Book Return
Book drop.

Book Review
Review.

Book Scorpion
A species of small stingless arachnid, also known as the *false scorpion,* that diets on tiny insects such as book lice that damage books by feeding on paper and bindings.

Book Scout
A person in the business of scouring obscure or remote bookshops,

secondhand stores, and book sales in search of books and editions desired by librarians, private collectors, and antiquarian booksellers.

Book Shoe

An inexpensive sleeve made to measure from thin card stock, cut and folded to fit unobtrusively around a book to protect and support the binding while it rests on the shelf, leaving the spine and head exposed to allow the volume to be easily removed and reinserted without damage.

Book Signing

An event scheduled at a retail bookstore or library at which the author and/or illustrator of a new book is available to autograph copies of his or her work, sometimes scheduled in conjunction with a book talk or a reading from the text.

Book Stamp

A wood, metal, or rubber stamp used to make an inked impression on the cover, edge, endpaper, or title page of a book, usually as a mark of ownership.

Book Stock

The total number of books in a library's collections, subject to growth through acquisition and to diminution through loss, damage, theft, weeding, etc., Synonymous with *book collection.*

Book Stop

A narrow ridge or ledge along the lower edge of the sloping top of a dictionary stand, atlas case, or lectern allowing an open book or sheaf of papers to rest at an angle convenient for reading without sliding off.

Book Support

Bookend.

Book Talk

An event, usually scheduled in a library, bookstore, or educational institution, at which the author, a librarian, or other interested person discusses a book and reads excerpts from it to encourage readership and promote reading in general. Also spelled *booktalk.*

Book Truck

A wheeled metal or wooden cart with two or three shelves, used by a page or other library staff member for transporting books and other materials from one area of the library to another, available in various sizes from library suppliers.

Book Week

Children's Book Week.

Book Wheel

A form of movable lectern used in the Middle Ages, consisting of a bookrest of a size sufficient to accommodate more than one open book, which could be rotated by the user to bring each volume into reading position.

Booklet

A book of small size or containing little text. Also used synonymously with pamphlet.

Booklover

Bibliophile.

Bookman

A man in the business of publishing, making, or selling books. Also, a man of literary or scholarly inclination who is familiar with books.

Bookmarker
Bookmark.

Book-on-tape
Audiobook.

Bookrest
A portable device similar to the music rest on a piano, designed to be placed on a desk or table to hold a book at an angle convenient for reading. Bookrests are also available in metal for attachment to indoor exercise machines and in the form of a soft cushion for laptop use or bedtime reading.

Books-by-mail
Circulation of library materials via the postal system to registered borrowers who request items by telephone or post, usually from a mail-order catalogue, a service provided by public libraries serving rural areas and homebound patrons.

Bookshop
Bookstore.

Bookstall
A small open-air retail book outlet, usually found in airports and railway stations and at fairs and markets. In France, quay-side book-stalls have been an important part of Parisian culture for centuries.

Borrowing
Period loan period.

Borrowing Library
A library or institution that requests and receives materials from another library, usually on interlibrary loan. Compare with lending library.

Bounding Lines
In manuscripts, marginal lines hand ruled to guide justification of the text and its decoration as in this example.

Bowker
Founded in New York City in 1872, Bowker specializes in publishing reference works on libraries, publishing, and the book trade. Now affiliated with ProQuest, the company is known for its long-standing reference serials (*Books in Print, Children's Books in Print, Magazines for Libraries, Ulrich's International Periodicals Directory*, etc.). Bowker has also served as the official ISBN agency for the United States since 1968. Click here to connect to the Bowker homepage.

Bowker, Richard Rogers (1848-1933)
A literary editor who, with Frederick Leypoldt and Melvil Dewey, founded in 1876 the publication *Library Journal*. In the same year, he helped found the American Library Association and with Leypoldt began publication of *American Catalogue*, a comprehensive index of books published in the United States. In 1879, he purchased *Publishers Weekly*, which Leypoldt had created in 1873, assuming editorial control of the trade journal after Leypoldt's death in 1884. During this period,

Bowker also helped found a liberal movement within the Republican Party known as the "Mugwumps" who were instrumental in preventing the nomination of Ulysess S. Grant for a third term. In 1880, he traveled to England to start the British edition of *Harper's Magazine*.

Bowker is also known for his interest in international copyright law and his success as a businessman. In 1911, he consolidated his business and publishing interests in the R.R. Bowker Co., a leading publisher of reference books on libraries and the publishing industry. Bowker remained an active member of the ALA throughout his life but refused its presidency three times because he felt the position should be held by a librarian. He finally accepted the title Honorary President when he was in his seventies. Although he eventually lost his sight, in his later years he published a book of essays titled *The Arts of Life* and two volumes of verse.

Boxed-in
Box.

B-picture
B-movie.

Brass
Blocking.

BRASS
Business Reference and Services Section.

Break
Gap and non-gap break.

Bricks-and-mortar
The traditional library, functioning for millennia as a physical repository for the permanent storage of tangible items, as opposed to the modern concept of the library as an institution dedicated to providing access to information maintained onsite or remotely, in print or non-print formats. The opposite of *library without walls*.

Brief Record
An abbreviated display of a bibliographic record in an online catalogue or database, omitting data elements contained in some of the less essential fields and subfields, in contrast to the full record providing a complete bibliographic description of the item. In most catalogues and bibliographic databases, search results can be displayed in both formats.

Brief
An outline of the evidence and arguments supporting one side of an argument. In a more general sense, any concise statement in written form. In law, a summary statement of the main points of an oral or written argument presented in court. Also refers to a letter of authority, especially one sent by the pope to the members of a Roman Catholic religious community.

Bright Copy
A copy of an older book that is as fresh and new as the day it was published, a condition likely to command a higher price in the market for antiquarian and used books than a copy of the same edition showing signs of wear.

Briticise
To convert to British English the style and spelling of a work written in American English. Compare with americanise.

Broadsheet
A long, narrow unfolded sheet of paper printed on one or both sides, used mainly for advertising purposes and formerly to disseminate religious or political views.

Broadway
In theatrical production, the premier showcase in the United States for presenting live shows, comprising about 40 professional theaters, each seating an audience of at least 500, located on or adjacent to Broadway Avenue between 41st Street and 53rd Street in New York City—comparable to London's West End theatre district. Also called the *Great White Way*. Compare with Off-Broadway.

Brocade Paper
A type of decorated paper in which an embossed pattern is pressed into coloured or uncoloured paper in real or imitation gold or silver foil, using thick copper plates or cylinders bearing the design in positive or negative relief.

Brochure
From the French word *brocher*. An independent non-serial publication consisting of a few leaves of printed material stitched together but not bound, usually issued in paper covers. Considered ephemera in most libraries, brochures are not catalogued separately unless they are of historical interest or issued by a government agency and selected for inclusion in a government documents collection. Used synonymously with pamphlet.

Brodart
A commercial company that supplies books, furniture, equipment, supplies, and automation services to libraries of all kinds, largely through its printed trade catalogue.

Broken Hinge
A book in which the reinforcing material along the fold separating the two halves of one of the endpapers has torn, leaving the text block detached from the cover, a condition that can be repaired without rebinding. Compare with detached board.

Broken Link
A link in an HTML document that is not functioning properly, usually because the link address is incorrect or the Web site is no longer available or has been moved to another server without providing a forwarding address. When a broken link is selected in a Web document, an error message appears on the screen. The tendency of links in a hypertext document to become non-functional over time is known colloquially as *link rot*.

Broken Spine
A book from which the material covering the binding edge of the text block has become detached from at least one of the boards along the joint, a condition that often requires rebinding, espe-

cially if the text block has split along the length of the binding edge.

Broken Up
A book disassembled to enable its parts to be sold separately. Copies of the *Gutenberg Bible* have been broken up, and the leaves sold separately.

Browsability
The ease with which a library catalogue, index, bibliographic database, or other list of resources can be searched in a casual, unsystematic manner. A printed index is often more *browsable* than its online counterpart because the page format makes it easy for the eye to scan a list of headings in search of related information.

Browser Cache
The portion of micro-computer memory reserved by Web browser software for storing the contents of Web pages previously visited by the user, reducing the amount of time required to revisit a page using the same machine.

Browser
A person who searches a library collection, catalogue, index, bibliography, bibliographic database, or other list of resources in a casual, unsystematic manner. Also refers to a type of application software called a Web browser, designed to facilitate searching for information available on the Internet.

Browsing Collection
A collection of current issues of periodicals, recently added books, and general interest materials, usually housed in a designated room or space near the entrance to an academic library, to induce library patrons to read outside their focused disciplinary interests or curriculum requirements. Some libraries have enhanced these areas by the addition of a cafe or beverage dispensers and comfortable seating. In an increasingly online environment, the future of browsing collections remains uncertain.

BSA
Bibliographical Society of America.

BT (or B)
Broader term.

BTSB
Bound to Stay Bound.

Buckram
A strong, durable book cloth consisting of a heavy woven base in cotton, linen, or jute filled with starch or impregnated with pyroxylin, used to cover volumes for which heavy use is anticipated.

Budget
The total amount of funds available to meet a library's expenditures over a fixed period of time. In most budgets, funds are allocated by category of expenditure, called *lines*. In chronically underfunded libraries and library systems, budgeting can be a major source of frustration for librarians and library administration.

Buffering
In papermaking, the addition of an alkaline substance such as calcium

carbonate or magnesium carbonate to the pulped fibre to neutralise any acid that may develop as paper ages or that is introduced through acid migration or exposure to atmospheric pollution. Extent of buffering is indicated as a percentage of the paper weight, usually no more than 2-3 per cent.

Bug

In computing, a slang term for a persistent error in software or hardware. Once it has been located, a software bug can be corrected by altering the programme, a process known as *debugging*. To correct a hardware bug, it is usually necessary to reconfigure circuitry. Compare with glitch.

Also refers to an electronic eavesdropping device installed in a telephone receiver, or in some other hidden location, usually for the purpose of espionage.

Buildings and Equipment Section (BES)

The section of the *Library Leadership and Management Association* (LLAMA) within the *American Library Association* (ALA) responsible for matters concerning physical structures for housing all types of libraries, including site selection; planning and architecture; construction and renovation; interior design and organisation; furniture and equipment; heating, ventilation, air conditioning, and lighting; maintenance of library property; and bookmobile planning and design.

Built Number

In Dewey Decimal Classification, a class number constructed according to add instructions stated or implied in the schedules or tables. Number building is employed only when there is no existing class in the schedules that precisely represents the subject of the work.

Bulk

The thickness of a book without its cover, normally less after binding than in its unbound state. Also, the thickness of a sheet of paper in relation to its weight, as measured in thousandths of an inch. The thickness of printing papers is also measured in pages per inch. Publishers sometimes "bulk" a short text by printing it on thick, low density paper. India paper and bible paper are used to *reduce* the bulk of a large volume.

Bulk Dates

In archives, the earliest and latest dates of the majority of the materials in a collection, indicative of its chronological or period strength, especially when the researcher is likely to be misled by the inclusive dates.

Bulk Lending

The lending of a large volume of materials by one library to another, usually for a period of time longer than the normal borrowing period. Books published in large print and audiobooks are sometimes loaned in bulk to the branch libraries within a public library system, or even outside the system.

Bulk Subscription

A subscription for a substantial

number of copies of the same serial title, sent to a single address for subsequent distribution.

Bull
Narrowly speaking, a document, letter, edict, or decree issued by the pope, to which his official seal is affixed. Also refers to any statement of belief or doctrine, whether ecclesiastical or not.

Bumped
The condition of a binding that has at least one corner bent, compressed, or rounded by forceful contact with a hard surface, such as the floor in a fall from a bookshelf.

Bureau
An office or department within an organisation or government agency, responsible for collecting and disseminating information, usually on a specific topic, in a particular field, or of a certain type, for example, demographic information in the case of the U.S., Census Bureau.

Burlesque
From the Italian word *burla*, meaning "mockery." A crude form of satire in which the style of a work, or of an entire genre, is ridiculed by trivializing a serious subject or dignifying a trivial one, usually in the form of a stage performance. The purpose is to amuse and entertain, rather than to inform. Compare with parody.

Burnish
In bookbinding, to rub the coloured or gilt edges of a volume with a smooth hard tool, called a *burnisher*, until the surface gleams elegantly in the light. Left unburnished, a gilt edge is antique. In the production of medieval manuscripts, a dog's tooth, smooth piece of bone, or agate mounted in a handle was used by the illuminator to polish to a brilliant shine the metallic leaf applied to the gilded portions of an initial letter, decorative border, or miniature.

Burnisher
Burnish.

Burnout
Physical and mental exhaustion caused by working hard for too long, sometimes out of excessive devotion to a demanding project. When overwork is chronic in a workplace, the effect on staff morale may be felt in high rates of absenteeism and turnover and in the deterioration of quality of service. Also spelled *burn-out*.

Buy-out
In publishing and the recording industry, the outright purchase of all legal rights in a work or property from the copyright holder for an agreed sum, as distinct from the payment of royalties over a period of time.

Buzzword
A trendy or stylish word or phrase, often connected with a specialised field, used more to create an impression than for purposes of elucidation.

B-word
Biblio.

Byline

A line of type usually printed at the beginning or end of a newspaper or magazine article to indicate its authorship.

Byte

The common unit of computer storage used in digital computers of all types and sizes, composed of eight binary digits called bits. Hardware specifications for computers (microcomputers to mainframes) are indicated in bytes. Each unique sequence of 8 bits can encode a single character, for a total of 256 possible characters. In ASCII text, the characters are alphanumeric. Disagreement exists about the origin of the term. It may be an abbreviation of *binary table* or *binary term* or derived from the expression "by eights."

1 byte = 8 bits

1 kilobyte (K) = 1,024 bytes

1 megabyte (MB) = 1,024 kilobytes or approximately 1 million bytes

1 gigabyte (GB) = 1,024 megabytes or approximately 1 billion bytes

Text and image files are usually measured in kilobytes, portable storage and program files in megabytes, and hard disk capacity in gigabytes.

C

Cable Modem
A modem designed to operate over cable television lines, instead of telephone lines, providing faster data transmission because the coaxial cable used by cable TV companies has higher bandwidth. With millions of homes in the United States already wired for cable TV, Internet access via cable modem is growing.

Cache
A small section of dedicated high-speed memory built into a microcomputer to improve system performance by providing temporary storage for blocks of data and instructions that would otherwise be retrieved from slower memory. As a general rule, the larger the cache, the greater the enhancement of performance and speed.

CACUL
Canadian Association of College and University Libraries.

Cadastral Map
From the Latin *capitastrum*, meaning 'register of the poll tax.' A map showing boundaries and subdivisions made to record ownership and rights in land and to describe and establish the value of property, usually for the purpose of tax assessment. A cadastral map may also show culture, drainage, and other features that have a bearing on land use and value.

Cadel
A large capital letter composed of sweeping pen strokes creatively embellished with wide parallel calligraphic flourishes and occasional cross-strokes, giving the letterform the appearance of a versal. Cadels were an exaggerated form of gothic *littera bastarda*, used in medieval manuscripts from the 13th to the 15th century.

CALA
Chinese American Librarians Association.

Caldecott Medal
A literary award given annually since 1938 under the auspices of the American Library Association to the illustrator of the most distinguished children's picture book published in the United States during the preceding year. Donated by the family of Frederic G.

Melcher, the medal is named in honour of the Victorian children's book illustrator Randolph Caldecott. The ALSC maintains the *Caldecott Medal Home Page*.

CALEA
Communications Assistance for Law Enforcement Act.

Calendar Year
The one-year period beginning on January 1 and ending on December 31. Most journal subscriptions run for a single calendar year, although some publishers offer a financial incentive to subscribe or renew for multiple years. Compare with publication year.

Call Slip
A brief form that the user must fill out to request an item from the closed stacks of a library or archives, or from some other non-public storage area, usually retrieved by hand by a staff member called a page, although automated and semi-automated retrieval systems are used in some large libraries. Synonymous with *request slip*.

Camcorder
A self-contained electronic device, introduced by Sony in 1983, that combines the capabilities of a video camera and videocassette recorder (VCR) in the same portable unit. Newer camcorders record video images and sound in digital format and are considerably smaller in size than earlier analog models.

Cameo Binding
A style of bookbinding popular in Italy from about 1500-1560 in which the centres of the boards forming the cover are stamped in relief in imitation of a coin or medallion. The decoration may be left blind or embellished with ink, silver, or gold leaf.

Cameo Stamp
In binding, a metal tool of oval shape engraved with a design, usually in the form of a picture, used from the 11th to 16th century in blind tooling to make an impression resembling cameo jewelry on the side of a leather-bound book.

Cameo
A typeface used for special effect in which the normal method of printing is reversed, the characters appearing in white against a solid or shaded background, instead of in black against a light background. Compare with outline letter.

Camera Lucida Work
Latin for 'lit chamber.' A drawing made by tracing the image of an object or scene as it appears when reflected onto a drawing surface from the mirror of a camera lucida, a portable optical device widely used by artists up to the early 1800s to achieve accuracy and facilitate enlargement or reduction. Also refers to paintings and other works made from such drawings.

Camera Microfilm
In reprography, an image of an original source document, made with a camera on high-quality film usually retained by the producer

for the purpose of making second-generation archival print masters from which third-generation distribution or service copies are made. Synonymous with *first generation* and *master negative.*

Camera Obscura Work
Latin for 'darkened chamber.' A drawing made by tracing the image of an object or scene as it appears when projected through the aperture of a camera obscura, a simple optical device available to artists from the 1500s on. Also refers to paintings and other works made from such drawings.

Camera-ready Copy (CRC)
In printing, copy typed using word processing software, or produced by some other means, that has been fully edited and is ready to be photographed for platemaking without having to be typeset. Synonymous with *camera copy.*

Campaign
In medieval manuscript production, a single phase of work on a manuscript made in more than one phase over a period to time. The text was usually copied first, followed by the under-drawing of decorated initial letters and miniatures, then by gilding and painting, and finally binding.

Canadian Association for School Libraries (CASL)
A division of the Canadian Library Association (CLA) formed in 2004 by the merger of the Association for Teacher-Librarianship in Canada (ATLC) and the Canadian School Librarianship Association (CSLA), CASL is devoted to providing a national voice for school libraries in Canada, promoting excellence in school libraries, and facilitating the professional growth of school librarians. CASL sponsors conferences in conjunction with CLA and with provincial and territorial library associations.

Canadian Association of Public Libraries (CAPL)
The division of the Canadian Library Association (CLA) charged with enhancing public library service throughout Canada, CAPL holds an annual meeting in conjunction with the annual CLA conference and publishes the *CAPL Newsletter.*

Canadian Bookbinders and Book Artists Guild (CBBAG)
Founded in 1983, CBBAG is a non-profit association of craftspeople working in the hand book arts, including papermakers, paper decorators, bookbinders, book restorers, and paper conservators, both amateur and professional. CBBAG seeks to provide access to education in the book arts, promotes greater awareness of the book arts, and advocates high standards of excellence in the book arts through exhibitions, workshops, lectures and programme meetings, and publications. CBBAG sponsors an annual book arts fair and publishes the *CBBAG Newsletter.*

Canadian Booksellers Association (CBA)
A non-profit national trade association devoted to promoting the

current and future interests of the bookselling industry in Canada and to meeting the needs of Canadian booksellers. Its members include over 1200 book-stores and over 350 publishers across Canada. CBA publishes the trade journal *Canadian Bookseller* in nine issues per year.

Canadian Intellectual Property Office (CIPO)

The special operating agency (SOA) associated with Industry Canada that is responsible for administering the greater part of the intellectual property system in Canada. CIPO is responsible for administering patents, trademarks, copyrights, and the legal protections for industrial designs and integrated circuit topographies.

Canadian Library Trustees Association (CLTA)

The division of the Canadian Library Association (CLA) charged with providing a national voice for public library trustees in Canada, CLTA holds an annual meeting in conjunction with the annual CLA conference.

Canadian Publishers' Council (CPC)

Founded in 1910, CPC is a trade association representing the interests of Canadian publishers of English-language books and media for schools, colleges and universities, professional and reference markets, and the retail and library sectors. Located in Toronto, CPC also represents the Canadian publishing industry internationally and maintains a liaison with the Association of American Publishers.

Cancel

A new leaf or leaves printed to replace part of a book or other publication when changes are required in the text or illustrations, usually before binding but after the work has gone to press, more common in the 17th and 18th centuries than today because as printing developed, the frequency of printing errors declined.

Canceled

Said of a regular order, continuation order, or periodical subscription terminated for some reason by the library or the seller. A non-serial item may be reordered if it is still available. Library holdings of a canceled serial title are noted in the catalogue record in a closed entry. Serial cancellations have increased in recent years, particularly in academic libraries, due to the rising cost of print subscriptions and the availability of full-text in bibliographic databases. Compare with discontinued.

Cancellation Period

The period of time a library allows a publisher, jobber, or other vendor for shipment of a book or item before the order is automatically canceled, usually 90 to 180 days. The item may subsequently be reordered from the same vendor or a different source.

Cancellation

In the context of medieval manuscripts, a superimposed 'x' used to indicate a correction by crossing out one or more letters; a form of deletion.

Candid Photograph

A photograph in which spontaneity and naturalness, rather than technique, are over-riding considerations. The subject is generally unposed and the shot unplanned, taken unobtrusively with an unhidden camera by a person immersed in an event that is often private, involving people in close relation to each other or engaged in unrehearsed activity. Henri-Cartier Bresson is considered a master of candid photography. Some candid photographs have become iconic documents.

Candidate

A person whose application for employment has been accepted and who is being seriously considered for a position. Also refers to a person taking an examination, running for an elected office, considered for an award or degree, or destined for a particular purpose or fate.

Canned

A performance that is prerecorded or filmed, derived from the expression 'in the can' in reference to the metal containers used for storing film and recording tape.

Canon

In literature, the accepted list of works by a given author considered by scholars to be authentic, for example, the 37 plays of William Shakespeare. Also refers to the approved list of works included in the Bible. In the most general sense, a criterion or standard of judgment applied for the purpose of evaluation. Compare with apocryphal.

Canon Tables

A system of indexing the canonical Gospels devised in the 4th century by Eusebius of Caesarea, in which the concordance of passages numbered in the text is displayed in four parallel columns, usually placed at the beginning of a Gospel book, Bible, or New Testament. Popular during the early Middle Ages, canon tables were usually given architectural treatment in manuscript decoration. Some designs include the symbols of the four evangelists, Matthew, Mark, Luke, and John.

Canonical Order

The arrangement of headings, parts, divisions, or items in an order established by law or tradition, for example, the sequence of the books of the Bible.

Canto

A major subdivision of a long narrative or epic poem serving the same function as a chapter in a novel. Cantos are traditionally numbered in roman numerals. Examples of works divided in this way are Dante's *Divina Commedia*, Spenser's *Faerie Queene*, and Byron's *Don Juan*.

CAO

Chief Academic Officer.

Caoutchouc Binding

The precursor of modern perfect

binding. In 1836, William Hancock was granted a patent for a binding method in which single leaves, produced by trimming away the back folds of the sections, were attached directly to the cover without the use of thread by applying to the binding edge a layer of rubber solution made from the latex of various tropical plants. This form of adhesive binding did not wear well—spines cracked and pages fell out. Also called *gutta percha* and *rubberback*.

Cap Line
In typography, the imaginary horizontal line connecting the tops of the uppercase letters of a type font, often, but not necessarily, the same as the ascender line. Compare with mean line.

Caper
A fictional work in which the plot centres on the planning and eventual execution of a single daring crime, escape, race, etc., such as the robbery of a bank vault or museum collection so well protected that the operation requires meticulous organisaton and perfect timing, usually undertaken by two buddies or a gang whose diverse skills are essential, although their interpersonal relations may be less than cordial. Suspense centres on whether and how the plan will succeed, what happens to the plunder, and whether the perpetrators are caught.

Capital Expenditure
In budgeting, an allocation made on a one-time basis, usually for the construction of new facilities, the renovation or expansion existing facilities, or a major upgrade of automation equipment or systems, as opposed to the operating budget allocated annually or biennially to meet the ongoing expenses incurred in running a library or library system.

Capital Improvement
The acquisition of a long-term asset, such as a new or renovated facility, initial book stock, or new equipment, furnishings, or vehicle(s), funded on a one-time basis from a budget for capital expenditures, as distinct from the ongoing purchase of library materials, payment of salaries and wages, routine repair and replacement of existing equipment and furnishings, and regular maintenance of facilities, funded from the operating budget.

Capital Letter
A large letter of the roman alphabet that prior to the 4th century A.D. consisted of capitals only. The name is derived from the lapidary Roman letterforms incised with a chisel at the top of architectural columns and on other stone monuments. Also, any letter written or printed in a form larger and usually different from that of the corresponding small letter. Abbreviated *cap*. Synonymous with uppercase. Compare with majuscule.

Capitalisaton
The writing or printing of a letter, word, or words in uppercase

rather than lowercase. Also refers to the conventions in a language with respect to words written or printed with certain letters in uppercase. For example, in English the first letter of the first word of a paragraph, and of each of the parts of a proper name, is normally *capitalised.*

CAPL
Canadian Association of Public Libraries.

Caps
Capital letter.

Capsa
A box of cylindrical shape used in libraries of antiquity for storing scrolls in an upright position.

Caption Title
A title printed at the beginning of a chapter, section, or other major division of a book, or at the beginning of the first page of the text, which, in the absence of a title page, is sometimes used as the title of the whole in creating the bibliographic description. The cataloger usually adds *Caption title:* as a note in the bibliographic record to indicate its source. In a musical score, the title that appears immediately above the opening bars may be used as the caption title. Synonymous with *head title*. Compare with drop-down title.

CAR
Computer-Aided Retrieval.

Carbon Copy
A copy of a document made at the same time as the original by the use of thin paper coated on one side with a mixture of dark waxy pigment easily transferred to a second blank sheet under the pressure of pen or typewriter. Multiple copies can be made by alternating sheets of carbon paper with regular paper, but succeeding copies become fainter because each additional layer absorbs some of the pressure. The technique can be messy if the pigment is easily smudged.

Carbon Print
The result of a photographic process patented by Joseph Wilson Swann in 1864 and popular until about 1910, in which a thin sheet of paper coated with a layer of light-sensitive gelatin containing a permanent pigment is exposed to ultraviolet light under a negative. The resulting image is transferred under pressure to a second sheet of gelatin-coated paper, then washed in water to set the gelatin, producing a permanent print with a raised surface where the image is darkest. The most commonly used pigments are carbon black and sepia, but a wide range of tints can be used. Because carbon prints contain no silver, they are highly resistant to fading, making them especially suitable for book illustration and commercial editions of photographic prints.

Carborundum Print
A collagraph print made by a process invented in the 20th century in which the printing plate is coated with a layer of carborundum, an abrasive powder of

silicon carbide, mixed with resin, varnish, glue, or some other adhesive that hardens on the surface. The plate can then be worked to create an image in the same way as a mezzotint.

Card
A small, flat, rectangular piece of thin paperboard or stiff paper, specifically designed to convey a message or other information. When printed, cards may include graphic design. The category includes such ephemera as advertising cards, business cards, trade cards, collecting cards, comic cards, dance cards, greeting cards, membership cards, playing cards, postcards, sports cards, and visiting cards.

Card Catalogue
A list of the holdings of a library, printed, typed, or handwritten on catalogue cards, each representing a single bibliographic item in the collection. Catalogue cards are normally filed in a single alphabetical sequence or in separate sections by author, title, and subject in the long narrow drawers of a specially designed filing cabinet, usually constructed of wood. Most large- and medium-sized libraries in the United States have converted their card catalogs to machine-readable format. Also spelled *card catalogue*. Compare with online catalogue.

Caricature
A deliberately distorted picture of a person, or a critical or facetious imitation of a performance or literary style, achieved by grossly exaggerating certain features or mannerisms peculiar to the object of satire or ridicule. The Lilly Library at Indiana University provides *America in Caricature, 1765-1865*, an online exhibition of political cartoons.

Caricature Publication
A magazine or newspaper designed to imitate another publication with openly satirical intent. Published fortnightly from 1825 to 1826, the *Glasgow/Northern Looking Glass*, satirising political and social life in 19th-century Scotland, is an early example of a caricature publication.

Carousel
A detachable, circular slotted container, usually made of plastic, in which dozens of slides can be queued for sequential viewing on a specially designed slide projector. Although carousels are bulky, they can also be used to store slides when not in use.

Carousel Book
A type of tunnel book that opens in a circle to reveal, in three dimensions, several scenes in the story.

Carpet Page
A page in a medieval manuscript or early printed book that bears little or no text but is covered with elaborate decoration, sometimes with the Christian cross incorporated into the overall design. The term is derived from its resemblance to hand-knotted carpets imported from the East. Michelle

Brown notes in *Under-standing Illuminated Manuscripts* that this style of ornamentation, popular with the scribes of Ireland and Britain from about A.D. 550 to 900, was used to separate the major divisions of Gospel books and Bibles and may have been of Coptic origin.

Carrel
Originally, a small stall or pew in a medieval cloister containing a desk for reading, writing, and semiprivate study. In modern libraries, a small room or alcove in the stacks designed for individual study. Also refers to a free-standing desk with low partitions at back and sides to provide some degree of privacy, with a shelf across the back facing the reader. Newer study carrels have built-in illumination and may be wired to provide network access for patrons using laptops.

Carrier's Address
A verse in the form of a broadside or pamphlet, sometimes recapping the previous year's major events, distributed to clients at the beginning of a new year by newspaper carriers or other trades people in hope of a gratuity.

Carta Lustra
A form of tracing paper, probably made from kid parchment, that may have been used in medieval book production to transfer designs from a finished exemplar to a manuscript in process.

Cartobibliography
A systematic list of references to maps and/or works about maps arranged in some kind of order, with or without annotations, usually related to a particular location, region, subject, person, or time period. Also, the branch of bibliography pertaining to cartographic materials and mapping. The Libraries of Memorial University of Newfoundland provide the searchable *Newfoundland and Labrador Maps Bibliography*. The Sir George Fordham Award for Cartobibliography is given every three years by the Royal Geographical Society for distinguished contributions to the field.

Cartogram
A simplified map on which the size, outline, or location of geographic features is altered or exaggerated to illustrate a concept or a set of quantitative data for which the base is not necessarily true to scale. An *area proportional to (APT) map* is a cartogram on which surface extent is relative to the amount of map data for a feature, rather than the geographic extent of the base to which the feature is related.

Cartographic Materials
Any systematic representation of part or all of the surface of the earth or another celestial body on any scale. The category includes two- and three-dimensional maps and plans; nautical, aeronautical, and celestial charts; atlases; globes and planetaria; block diagrams, sections, and profiles; views; remote sensing images; cartograms; etc. Most cartographic materials are visual representations, but spa-

tial data sets are a notable exception. In the bibliographic record representing a cartographic item, the characteristics of the material are described in the material specific details area (MSD).

Cartography
The art and science of making maps, charts, and other cartographic materials. Broadly speaking, the term includes all the steps required to produce a map but mapmakers often apply the term only to map-finishing operations.

Cartonnage
Pieces of papyrus glued and tightly pressed together to form rigid sheets, used as boards in early bookbinding. The same material was used in ancient Egypt for making mummy cases.

Cartouche
A frame or panel, often in the form of a scroll, drawn or printed on a map or chart, usually as an inset, enclosing the title or subject of the work, name of cartographer, scale, and other descriptive information. On older maps, the cartouche often includes decorative elements, ranging from simple ornamentation to elaborate embellishment. The presence of a coat of arms signified land ownership.

Cartulary
The room or place where the official papers or records of a medieval monastery, landowner, or corporation were kept. Also refers to the register in which they were listed, synonymous in the latter sense with chartulary.

Cascading Style Sheets (CSS)
A feature added to HTML code that allows Web site developers to automatically apply the same layout to multiple documents. The appearance of design elements is determined by one or more templates called *style sheets* linked to or embedded in the HTML document, rather than specified in the source code of each document. By governing style externally, CSS enables the site developer to give the pages of a Web site a uniform look and alter style of presentation as desired without having to rewrite source code.

Case
In machine binding, a cover made completely before it is attached to the body of a book, consisting of two boards and a paper inlay covered in book cloth or some other protective material. The edition binder submits a *specimen case* to the publisher for approval showing the size, boards, covering, lettering, and squares. The process of attaching the case to the text block by pasting down the endpapers is called *casing-in*.

Casebook
A book containing records or descriptions of actual cases that have occurred in a professional discipline, selected to illustrate important principles and concepts, for the use of students as a textbook and practitioners for reference. Legal casebooks are typically plainly bound. Compare with case study

Case File
In archives, a folder or other file unit containing material related to a specific project, task, action, event, person, place, or other subject, or a collection of such folders or units, also known as a *project file* or *transaction file*.

Case-Sensitive
A computer system or software programme in which uppercase letters and lowercase letters are *not* interchangeable as input. On the Internet, Web addresses are case-sensitive, but e-mail addresses and filenames usually are not.

Case Study
In the social and medical sciences, analysis of the behaviour of one individual in a population, or a single event in a series, based on close observation over a period of time, often to reveal principles underlying individual behaviour or events in general. A case study may be published as an article in a journal, as an essay in a collection, or in book form. In bibliographic databases that permit the user to limit retrieval by type of publication, case studies may be one of the options. Synonymous with *case report*. Compare with casebook.

Cash Book
A blankbook used to record all money spent or received as payment, generally in a business in which it is necessary or desirable to know the amount of cash on hand at any given time, or in a partnership in which an accurate record of total assets must be maintained. Today, computer software is available for recording such transactions electronically. In libraries, a *petty cash book* may be used to record monies received and spent. Also spelled *cashbook*. Compare with account book.

Casing-in
case binding.

CASL
Canadian Association for School Libraries.

CASLIS
Canadian Association of Special Libraries and Information Services.

Cassette
A flat, completely enclosed container, usually made of metal or hard plastic, designed to hold a length of film or magnetic tape wound on two cores past an opening through which the film is viewed or the tape is read. The most common varieties used in libraries are audiocassettes, videocassettes, and cassette microfilm. The term is sometimes used interchangeably with cartridge, but some cartridges have only one hub.

Cassette Single (CS)
A commercially released audiotape recording containing two tunes, a format first released in large scale in 1987. Some cassette singles contain one song on each side, similar to 45 rpm phonograph record singles; others have the same two songs on both sides. Abbreviated *cassingle*.

Cast Paper Print
An artistic work in paper made by pouring wet pulp, coloured or uncoloured, into a mold and allowing it to dry. Produced since the 1970s, such works may be difficult to distinguish from embossed prints.

Catalogue Album
A record album owned by a recording company, which it has previously released but is no longer promoting. *Billboard* magazine defines a catalogue album as one over eighteen months old, which has fallen below position 100 on its *Billboard 200* list of highest selling music albums.

Catalogue Card
In manual cataloguing systems, a paper card used to make a handwritten, typed, or printed entry in a card catalogue, usually of standard size plain or ruled.

Catalogue Code
A detailed set of rules for preparing bibliographic records to represent items added to a library collection, established to maintain consistency within the catalogue and between the catalogs of libraries using the same code. In the United States, Great Britain, and Canada, libraries use the *Anglo-American Cataloguing Rules* developed jointly by the American Library Association, Library Association and Canadian Library Association. Synonymous with *cataloguing code.*

Cataloguer
A librarian primarily responsible for preparing bibliographic records to represent the items acquired by a library, including bibliographic description, subject analysis, and classification. Also refers to the librarian responsible for supervising a cataloguing department. British spelling is *cataloguer*. Synonymous with *catalogue librarian*.

Catalogue recordI
n the manual card catalogue, all the information given on a library catalogue card, including a description of the item, the main entry, any added entries and subject headings, notes, and the call number. In the online catalogue, the screen display that represents most fully a specific edition of a work, including elements of description and access points taken from the complete machine-readable bibliographic record, as well as information about the holdings of the local library or library system taken from the item records attached to the bibliographic record. British spelling is *catalogue record*. Compare with entry.

Cataloger's Desktop
Published on a single CD-ROM, *Cataloger's Desktop* is a product of the Library of Congress that provides basic cataloguing documentation, the *Library of Congress Subject Headings* list, Cutter Tables, *Anglo-American Cataloguing Rules* (*AACR2*), *Library of Congress Rule Interpretations* (*LCRI*), and more.

Cataloguing
The process of creating entries for a catalogue. In libraries, this usu-

ally includes bibliographic description, subject analysis, assignment of classification notation, and activities involved in physically preparing the item for the shelf, tasks usually performed under the supervision of a librarian trained as a cataloger. British spelling is *cataloguing*.

Cataloguing Agency

A library or other institution that provides authoritative cataloguing data in the form of new bibliographic records and modifications of existing records, for the use of other libraries. In the United States, the leading source of cataloguing data is the Library of Congress. In the MARC record, the identity of the cataloguing agency is indicated by its three-letter OCLC symbol in the cataloguing source field.

Cataloguing and Classification Section (CCS)

The section of the Association for Library Collections and Technical Services (ALCTS) within the American Library Association (ALA) charged with promoting the improvement of cataloguing and classification of library materials in all formats and in all types of institutions.

Cataloguing Cultural Objects (CCO)

cultural object.

Cataloguing-in-Publication (CIP)

A prepublication cataloguing programme in which participating publishers complete a standardised data sheet and submit it with the front matter or entire text of a new book to the Library of Congress for use in assigning an LCCN and preparing a bibliographic record, which is sent back to the publisher within 10 days to be printed on the verso of the title page. The Library of Congress distributes CIP records to large libraries, bibliographic utilities, and book vendors on a weekly basis to facilitate book processing. If incomplete, the initial record may be amended by the Library of Congress after the U.S., Copyright Office receives the deposit copy of the published work. The CIP Programme began at the Library of Congress in 1971 and is used throughout the world.

Catch Letters

A sequence of letters printed at the top of a page in a dictionary, gazetteer, or similar work that duplicates the first few letters of the first or last word on the page. Those printed on the verso indicate the first letters of the *first* word on the page; those on the recto, the first letters of the *last* word on the page. In some works, the letters appear in two groups separated by a hyphen, representing the first *and* last words on the page. Compare with catchword.

Catchword

A word or part of a word printed in boldface or uppercase at the top of a column or page in a dictionary or encyclopaedia that repeats the first and/or last heading appearing in the column or on the page. Synonymous with *guideword*. Compare in this sense with catch letters. In medieval manuscripts and early printed books, a word or part of a word appearing in the lower margin of the last page of a quire that duplicates the first word on the first page of the following quire, enabling the binder to assemble the gatherings in correct sequence. In hand-copied books, the sequence of catchwords is unique to a specific copy. Michelle Brown notes in *Understanding Medieval Manuscripts* that the practice was probably introduced into Europe by the Moors. Also refers to a word or phrase repeated so frequently that it has become a motto or slogan. Compare in this sense with cliché.

Catchword Title

A partial title composed of an easily remembered word or phrase likely to be used as a heading or keyword in a search of the library catalogue; sometimes the same as a subtitle or the alternative title. Synonymous with *catch title*.

Categories for the Description of Works of Art (CDWA)

A specification developed by the Art Information Task Force (AITF) defining metadata elements to be used in describing works of art and architecture and surrogates of such works from an art-historical perspective.

Cathedral Binding

A cloth or leather binding decorated with architectural motifs of the Gothic period blocked in gold, ink, or blind, sometimes including a rose window, popular in France and England from about 1815 to 1840 when interest in Gothic art underwent a revival.

Catholic Library Association (CLA)

Established in 1921, CLA has a membership of librarians, teachers, and booksellers involved with Catholic libraries and the writing, publication, and distribution of Catholic literature.

Caucus

An interest group within a political faction or party, legislative body, or organisaton formed to address an immediate need for action on a given issue or series of related issues, usually by formulating policy, supporting candidates for political office, drafting campaign strategy, lobbying, etc.. Compare with task force.

CAV

An abbreviation of *constant angular velocity*, a disc recording technology in which the disc is spun at constant speed in playback regardless of whether the heads are reading the inside or the outside. Because the tracks on the inside are shorter than those on the perimeter, the constant speed of rotation means that when the heads are reading the outside tracks, they traverse a much longer linear path than when the inside is read, so linear velocity does not remain constant. The main advantage of CAV is that it allows special playback features such as freeze frame, step frame, slow motion, and reverse not possible in CLV format; however, CAV has significantly less data storage capacity than CLV.

Caxton, William
England's first printer, Caxton learned the trade relatively late in life while living in Cologne and Bruges. He brought the first printing press to England and installed it in the Chapter House at Westminster Abbey, issuing the first dated book known to have been printed in England in 1477. By the time he died in 1491, his press had issued approximately 100 works, including folio editions of Chaucer's *The Canterbury Tales* and Mallory's *Morte D'Arthur*, which he sold to English readers in bound copies. He was an expert editor and translated into English many of the works he printed.

CBA
Canadian Booksellers Association, Centre for Book Arts, and collective bargaining agreement.

CBBAG
Canadian Bookbinders and Book Artists Guild.

CBC
Children's Book Council.

CBIP
Children's Books in Print.

CC
Closed Caption and Common Carrier.

CCA
Comics Code Authority.

CCAHA
Centre for the Conservation of Art and Historic Artifacts.

CCBC
Canadian Children's Book Centre.

CCC
Copyright Clearance Centre, Inc.

CCS
Cataloguing and Classification Section.

CCTV
Closed Circuit Television.

CDP
Collection Development Policy.

CD-R
Compact Disc-Recordable, a blank compact disc invented by Philips and Sony, on which the user can permanently record audio and other digital data, using a CD burner, and then read the content repeatedly. The entire disc does not have to be written in the same session but once recorded, the information is not erasable. Most CD-R discs have a capacity of 80-90 minutes. The format retains a high degree of compatibility with standard CD and CD-ROM readers. Synonymous with *CD-WO* and *writable CD*.

CD-ROM Changer
A computer hardware device designed to store a small number of CD-ROMs or disc modules, with carousels and robot arms to move one disc at a time to an optical or magnetic reader and back to its storage location. Colloquially known as a *jukebox*. Compare with

CD-ROM drive and CD-ROM tower.

CD-ROM Drive
A hardware component designed to read data recorded on a CD-ROM disc, originally an external device but built into most newer microcomputers. CD-ROM drives can also be used to play audio compact discs when attached to a sound card via cable. Compare with CD-ROM changer and CD-ROM tower.

CD-ROM Network
A client-server system that makes multiple CD-ROM discs stored in a CD-ROM tower accessible to users authorised to log on to a computer network. Most bibliographic databases available on CD-ROM require special licensing for network access. Synonymous with CD-ROM LAN.

CDS
Cataloguing Distribution Service.

Cel
A thin sheet of transparent material of standard size having the same proportions as a frame of motion picture film, on which is drawn or painted a single image in a sequence of animation. Original cels from early animated films may have independent value as works of art.

Celestial Atlas
A book of charts of the heavens. The 'golden age' of the celestial atlas occurred from about 1600 to 1800. The early *star atlas* was not intended to be a guide to amateur star-gasing, but rather for the use of working astronomers, as a backdrop on which to plot, as accurately as possible, the changing positions of the moon, planets, and comets. The best celestial atlases were produced by notable astronomers, based on their own observations.

Celestial Chart
A map of the heavens, showing the relative positions of known celestial bodies and systems of interest to astronomers and amateur stargazers, usually printed in light tones against a dark background to simulate the night sky.

Celestial Globe
A map of the heavens on the surface of a sphere. Celestial globes were originally used to represent the stars and constellations of the night sky, record their relative positions, and solve astronomical problems. Mounted on a stand that included a broad horizontal band representing the horizon, the globe could be adjusted to make the elevation of the pole above the horizon correspond to the user's latitude. In such a position, the globe's rotation corresponded to the apparent diurnal rotation of the stars at the given latitude.

Cellocut
An intaglio or relief print made from a plate consisting of a base covered with a layer of celluloid dissolved in acetone that is allowed to solidify before the artist begins working the design into its surface. The result often resembles a linocut.

Cellulose Diacetate

An early acetate plastic base for motion picture film, introduced in 1909.

Cellulose Nitrate

A flexible base produced by Eastman Kodak from the 1890s until the early 1950s for use in photographic negatives and motion picture film. Its combustibility made handling 35mm film a hazardous occupation until the introduction of safety film. Because nitrate film is also chemically unstable, organisatons such as the National Film Preservation Foundation provide grant assistance to film archives to facilitate the copying of moving image collections from cellulose nitrate to a more permanent base, such as cellulose acetate or polyester. Because of the potential fire hazard, the National Fire Protection Association (NFPA) issues guidelines for the construction of cabinets and vaults used to store nitrate-based motion pictures. Libraries and archives often store nitrate film off-site. Synonymous with *nitrate base*.

Cellulose Triacetate

The strongest acetate plastic base used in the manufacture of motion picture film, introduced in the 1940s.

Cellulose

A long-chain polymer commonly found in fibrous vegetable material, occurring in almost pure form in cotton fibre. When used in papermaking, it is obtained primarily from wood, but was formerly derived from cotton or linen rags. Cellulose in paper and board made from wood pulp is weakened in time by the presence of acid unless lignin is removed and an alkaline buffer added in manufacture. Also, a family of plastics that includes cellulose nitrate, cellulose acetate, and cellulose triacetate, used as the base in photographic and motion picture films.

Censorship

Prohibition of the production, distribution, circulation, or display of a work by a governing authority on grounds that it contains objectionable or dangerous material. The person who decides what is to be prohibited is called a *censor*. Commonly used methods include decree and confiscation, legislation, repressive taxation, and licensing to grant or restrict the right to publish. The *ALA Code of Ethics* places an ethical responsibility on its members to resist censorship of library materials and programmes in any form and to support librarians and other staff who put their careers at risk by defending library policies against censorship. The Electronic Privacy Information Centre maintains a Web page on *Internet Censorship*. Compare with suppressed.

Census Tract

One of many small geographic areas into which a state or country is divided for the purpose of gathering and reporting census data. In the United States, the average tract contains 4,000 residents or approximately 1,200 households. Census tract outline maps are available from the U.S., Census Bureau.

Centre Fold

The two innermost facing pages of a section in a book or other bound publication. In sewn bindings, the threads can be seen along the fold. In a saddle-stitched periodical or pamphlet, wire staples can be seen in the fold. Also spelled *centrefold.* Synonymous with *centre spread.* In magazines, a gatefolded spread, usually a portrait such as a pin-up or nude, inserted in the middle of the publication—a special feature developed by Hugh Hefner, publisher of *Playboy Magazine.* In saddle-stitched magazines, the centre fold has no blank space, allowing the illustration to be removed for display as a poster.

Centre for Book Arts (CBA)

Founded in 1974, CBA is a non-profit organisaton with head-quarters in New York City, dedicated to preserving the traditional craft of bookmaking and encouraging contemporary interpretations of the book as an art object through exhibitions, lectures, publications, and services to artists, including courses, workshops, and seminars on all aspects of the book arts.

Centre for Research Libraries (CRL)

Founded in 1949, CRL's members are large research libraries that seek to improve access to scholarly collections. CRL publishes a bi-monthly newsletter and serves as a depository for infrequently used research materials that its members may use cooperatively.

Centre for the Book

An educational outreach programme established in 1977 by the Library of Congress to stimulate public interest in and awareness of books, reading, and libraries and to encourage the study of books and the printed word, the Centre for the Book is a public-private partnership between the Library of Congress, 35 affiliated state centres, and over 50 national and civic groups. The Centre publishes *Centre for the Book News* and sponsors the annual National Book Festival.

Centerpiece

In bookbinding of the late 16th and early 17th centuries, an ornamental design such as a diamond tooled or stamped in the centre of the front and/or back cover, sometimes accompanied by matching cornerpieces.

Central library

The administrative centre of a library system where system-wide management decisions are made, centralised technical processing is conducted, and principal collections are located. Synonymous with *main library.*

Central Records

The files of more than one unit of an organisaton, consolidated and maintained in a single location to allow greater efficiency than is possible with decentralised records. Also, the records of several individuals or entities consolidated under a common filing system. In such a system, the files of each unit or individual are usually maintained separately from those of other units, but organised according to a prescribed filing plan, with each file assigned a classification code under which it is filed.

Centralised Cataloguing
The preparation of bibliographic records for books and other library materials by a central cataloguing agency that distributes them in printed and/or machine-readable form to participating libraries, usually for a modest fee. Also refers to the cataloguing of materials for an entire library system at one of its facilities, usually the central library, to achieve uniformity and economies of scale. Also spelled *centralised cataloguing*.

Centralised Processing
The practice of concentrating in a single location all the functions involved in preparing materials for library use, as opposed to technical processing carried out at multiple locations within a library or library system. Centralisaton allows processing methods to be standardised, but increased efficiency may be offset by the cost of distributing materials to the units where they will be used.

Ceramic Photograph
A photographic image made by any one of a variety of processes on a ceramic support, such as porcelain or earthenware. Ceramic photographs, often oval in shape, have been used since the mid-1800's to adorn cemetery headstones and other grave markers with a likeness of the deceased.

Certificate
A written or printed statement attesting the validity of a fact, promise, qualification, status, or accomplishment, often in the form of a document of standard format issued in the name of an authorising body.

Certificate of Issue
In a limited edition, the statement in each copy giving the total number of copies printed and the copy number. In an autographed edition, the certificate may also bear the signature of the author, editor, or illustrator.

Certified Records Manager (CRM)
An information professional who has significant experience in the management of active and inactive records systems and in related areas and who has been certified by the international Institute of Certified Records Managers (ICRM) as meeting established standards of education, training, and work experience after passing required examinations. ICRM certification must be maintained by completing a prescribed number of hours of approved educational activity during each five-year period following initial certification.

Cessation
A serial or annual for which publication has ceased. Cessations are listed alphabetically by title in a separate section of *Ulrich's Interna-*

tional Periodicals Directory published annually by Serials Solutions, a division of ProQuest. A serials vendor should notify its customers of the demise of a publication to enable libraries to adjust their records accordingly. In the library catalogue, the holdings of a serial that has ceased publication are indicated in a closed entry.

CF
Christian Fiction.

CGI
Common Gateway Interface.

CGP
Catalogue of U.S., Government Publications.

Chain Stitch
In bookbinding, a sewing stitch linked to previous sewing threads but not sewn to a support. In Islamic binding, chain stitching was in multiples of two or four chains. Jane Greenfield notes in *ABC of Bookbinding* that it was also used in Coptic binding and in France during the 16th century and that modern machine stitching is a form of chain stitch. Synonymous with *unsupported sewing.*

Chain
bookstore chain and chained book.

Champie Initial
In medieval manuscripts, a style of decorated initial letter in which the body of the letter is usually in plain gold set against a parti-coloured background, often of blue and red highlighted with delicate white lines. Common in Gothic manuscripts, champie initials sometimes have small extenders, as in these four examples in a 14th-century French *Apocalypse.*

Champlevé Binding
A style of book cover, produced in Europe from the 11th to the 13th century, consisting of a thin sheet of gold or copper in which designs were cut and the cavities filled with coloured enamel. On some bindings, the enamel is limited to border and corner decoration. According to Matt Roberts and Don Etherington, champlevé can be distinguished from cloisonné bindings by the irregular widths of the metal separating the enameled areas.

Chancery
Historically, a court of record or office of public archives. In law, a court of equity and its laws, practices, and proceedings.

Chancery Rolls
From the end of the 12th century, the Chancery of England, in its original role as the royal secretariat, began to transcribe onto parchment important documents it produced. The copies were 'enrolled' to facilitate handling. The National Archives of England, Wales, and the UK maintains a great variety of such records preserved in the original format, including charter rolls, close rolls, fine rolls, liberate rolls, parliament rolls, patent rolls, pipe rolls, scutage rolls, and more. Of great interest to historians, they are listed by series in calendars, some of which have been published.

Chancery Script

A cursive script used from the 14th to the 16th century in the offices of royal, noble, and ecclesiastical houses for writing letters and less formal documents, adapted in 1501 as the basis of a typeface commissioned by the publisher Aldus Manutius and executed by the lettercutter Francesco Griffo.

Changed Title

title change.

Channel

A pathway along which data is transmitted electronically from one computer, terminal, or device to another. The term also refers to the physical medium carrying the signal and to the properties that distinguish a specific channel from others. In data storage, a track on a specific storage medium on which electrical signals are recorded. In communications, a band of frequencies assigned by the Federal Communications Commission (FCC) to a radio or television transmitting station for its exclusive use. In a more general sense, a one-way communications link. Also refers to the blank space dividing columns of text written or printed on a page.

Channeling

In film conservation, a pattern of irregular veins formed in photographic negatives by the separation of the emulsion from the base, a sign of advanced deterioration characteristic of acetate-base films. With the passage of time, the base shrinks but the emulsion does not, producing stress that eventually breaks the bond between emulsion and base, causing the emulsion layer to buckle and separate from the base. In some cases, the emulsion tears as it buckles.

Chapbook

From the Anglo-Saxon root *ceap*. A pamphlet containing a popular legend, tale, poem, or ballad, or a collection of prose or verse, hawked for about a penny a copy in the streets of England from the late 17th through the 19th century, and in the United States, by traveling peddlers called *chapmen* or colporteurs. The content was usually sensational, educational or moral. Chapbooks were typically of small size, containing up to 24 pages illustrated with woodcuts, bound in paper or canvas, usually with a decorated cover title.

Chapter Drop

The position below the chapter heading at which the text of a chapter begins—lower than on succeeding pages of the text and, in most books, the same for all chapters.

Chapter Heading

A display heading in a book or manuscript usually consisting of a roman numeral indicating the chapter number, followed by the chapter title, written or printed on the first page of the chapter in uniform style and position above the first paragraph of the text. Set in a type size larger than the text and running heads, chapter headings are sometimes embellished with an illustration or head-piece in older editions.

Chapter Title

The title that appears at the beginning of a chapter in a book, usually bearing some relation to the content of the division of the work. Chapters may simply be numbered or given a number and a title. They are listed in order of appearance by number and/or title in the table of contents in the front matter.

Characteristic

An attribute, property, or quality that forms the basis for dividing a class into clearly differentiated subclasses, for example, the characteristic 'period' dividing the class 'European literature' into the subclasses 'classical,' 'medieval,' 'renaissance,' 'modern,' and 'contemporary,' as opposed to the characteristic 'form' dividing the same class into 'drama,' 'essay,' 'novel,' 'poetry,' 'short story,' etc.

Charter

A legal document recording the franchise or granting of specific rights to an individual or corporate body by a governmental authority such as a legislature or sovereign, for example, the Charter of the United Nations. The texts of important charters are usually available in the government documents or reference section of large libraries. The originals are preserved by the institutions and individuals that own them, usually in archives.

Chartered Institute of Library and Information Professionals (CILIP)

A new professional association formed in April 2002 by the union of the Institute of Information Scientists (IIS) and the Library Association (UK), CILIP is now is the leading professional body for librarians, information specialists, and knowledge managers in the UK, with nearly 23,000 members working in all sectors, including business and industry, science and technology, education, local and central government, health services, national and public libraries, and the voluntary sector.

Chartered Librarian

In the UK, a librarian who has obtained a qualification from the Chartered Institute of Library and Information Professionals (CILIP) in addition to a degree or diploma in librarianship, upon presentation of sufficient evidence of professional development.

Chartulary

A list or register of charters. Also, a collection or set of charters or copies of charters, especially when bound into one or more volumes for the use of the monastery, landowner, corporation, etc., to which they belong, synonymous in this sense with *cartulary*.

Chase

In letterpress, the portable rectangular metal frame in which assembled type and display matter, composed into pages, is firmly locked into position. The resulting forme is then ready to be transferred to the bed of the press for printing. The expression *in chase* means 'ready for printing.'

Chased Edges
gauffered edges.

Chat
A real time computer conferencing capability between two or more users of a network by means of a keyboard rather than voice transmission. Most Internet service providers offer a *chat room* to their subscribers.

Chat Reference
digital reference.

CHEA
Council for Higher Education Accreditation.

Check Digit
A character added to a sequence of digits, related arithmetically to the sequence in such a way that input errors can be automatically detected whenever the sequence is entered as data into a computer, for example, the last character of the ISBN. When a calculated check digit is the number 10, it is represented as the character X. Synonymous with *checksum*.

Checked Out
The circulation status of an item that has been charged to a borrower account and is not due back in the library until the end of the loan period. In the online catalogue, the due date is usually displayed as a status code in the catalogue record to indicate that the item is currently unavailable for circulation. Synonymous with *on loan*.

Check-in Record
A separate record attached to the bibliographic record for a serial title in which the receipt of individual issues or parts is entered on an ongoing basis, usually by an assistant working in the serials department. Most online catalogs allow users to view the check-in record to determine if a specific issue or part has been received. The check-in record may also indicate whether an issue is missing, claimed, or at the bindery. In most library management systems, the check-in record is separate from the holdings record.

Check-in
The ongoing process of recording the receipt of each issue of a newspaper or periodical, a routine task accomplished by the serials department of a library, manually or with the aid of an automated serials control system. Some automated systems allow the patron to view the check-in record for a given title.

Checklist
A comprehensive list of books, periodicals, or other documents that provides the minimum amount of description or annotation necessary to identify each work—briefer than a bibliography. Also, the log kept by a library to record the receipt of each number of a serial publication or part of a work in progress. Also refers to a list of items required, or procedures

to be followed, such as the steps in a library's opening or closing routine. Also spelled *check-list*.

Checkout Slip
Instead of stamping the date due slip in each item at checkout, many libraries now print a computer-generated slip listing the items a patron has checked out. A good checkout slip should facilitate return of materials by reminding the patron of the date on which the borrowed items are due back at the library. Checkout slips should also give the library's name and phone number, respect the user's privacy, include item type for clarity, and be easy to read. Some libraries also use checkout slips to facilitate renewal, promote library events, broadcast library policy changes, and alert users to special hours.

Chemise
A thin sleeve designed to wrap around the covers and spine of a book to protect the binding from abrasion as it is removed from and reinserted in its slipcase.

Chemise Binding
A slip-on cover of soft leather or cloth designed with pockets to fit over the boards of a hand-bound book, sometimes secured to the boards with bosses, used in Europe from the 12th to the 15th century as a substitute for full binding or to protect a permanent leather binding from wear.

Chiaroscuro Woodcut
A woodcut printed from two or more blocks: the *line block*, cut to print contours and crosshatching, usually in black, and one or more *tone blocks* to print neutral or background colours, creating differences in tonal value—a technique developed in Europe in the 1500s to imitate the appearance of a type of drawing on coloured paper known as *chiaroscuro*. In areas cut away on all the blocks, the unprinted surface of the paper serves as highlighting.

Chief Academic Officer (CAO)
The senior academic officer at an institution of higher learning in the United States, to whom the library director usually reports. Because a CAO's influence on the library can be decisive, particularly in matters of budget, his or her working relationship with the library director is very important. Some institutions use the title *provost, dean of faculty,* or *vice-president of academic affairs*.

Chief Information Officer (CIO)
The title of the person in a commercial company or non-profit organisaton who is responsible for managing the flow of official information, including computing and any library services—a relatively new position in companies and organisatons that recognise the need for such a management function.

Chief Officers of State Library Agencies (COSLA)
An independent organisaton of the chief officers of state and territorial agencies designated as the state library administrative agency

and responsible for statewide library development, COSLA is dedicated to identifying and addressing issues of common concern and national interest, furthering state library agency relationships with federal government and national organisatons, and initiating cooperative action for the improvement of library services to the people of the United States.

Chief Source of Information
The source of bibliographic data prescribed by *AACR2* as having precedence over all others in the preparation of the bibliographic description of an item, usually the title page or a substitute, for example, the title frame at the beginning of a filmstrip or motion picture, or the title screen of a Web page.

Chiffon Silk
A layer of extra-thin but strong silk tissue applied to mend or strengthen a leaf in a book or other document printed on paper.

Children's Book Award
A literary award or prize given to the author or illustrator of a book published specifically for children. In the United States, the two best-known awards are the Caldecott Medal and the Newbery Medal.

Children's Book Council (CBC)
Established in 1945, the CBC is a non-profit trade association dedicated to encouraging literacy and the use and enjoyment of children's books. Its membership includes publishers and packagers of children's trade books and producers of book-related multimedia for children. The CBC sponsors Children's Book Week, celebrated in schools, libraries, and bookstores throughout the United States each November, and Young People's Poetry Week, celebrated in April in conjunction with National Poetry Month.

Children's Book Week
Sponsored since 1919 by the Children's Book Council, Children's Book Week is a local and national celebration held each November in which librarians, booksellers, publishers, and educators schedule book exhibits, read-a-thons, story hours, swap sessions, contests, book raffles, and other activities to stimulate interest in books and reading among young people. Synonymous with *Book Week*.

Children's Book
A book written and illustrated specifically for children up to the age of 12-13. Included in this category are juvenile fiction and non-fiction, board books, nursery rhymes, alphabet books, counting books, picture books, easy books, beginning readers, picture storybooks, and storybooks. Children's books are shelved in the juvenile collection of most public libraries and in the curriculum room in most academic libraries. Currently available children's titles are listed in *Children's Books in Print* published by Bowker.

Children's Books in Print (CBIP)
An author, title, and illustrator index of currently available books

for children and young adults, published annually by Bowker since 1962. Each volume includes an index of major book awards for the past 10 years. The separately published *Subject Guide to Children's Books in Print* includes indexes by publisher, wholesaler, and distributor. Former title: *Children's Books for Schools and Libraries.*

Children's Collection
juvenile collection.

Children's Librarian
A librarian who specializes in services and collections for children up to the age of 12-13. Most children's librarians have extensive knowledge of children's literature and are trained in the art of storytelling.

Children's Literature Review (CLR)
An annual reference serial published since 1976 by Gale, providing excerpts from reviews, criticism, and commentary on books for children and young adults, arranged alphabetically by name of author, with cumulative author and title indexes at the end of each volume. ISSN: 0362-4145.

Children's Magazine
A periodical published specifically for young people, usually geared to a specific reading level. Some children's magazines focus on a particular subject or interest and *Ranger Rick* in natural history. A selection of magazines for children is provided in the reference serial *Magazines for Libraries. Yahoo!* also provides a list of magazines for kids.

Children's Room
The area in a public library, or one of its branches, reserved for collections and services intended specifically for children up to the age of 12-13, usually staffed by at least one children's librarian and furnished to accommodate persons of small stature. Some children's rooms include a comfortable corner or alcove designed for group storytelling, puppetry, etc.

Children's Services
Library services intended for children up to the age of 12-13, including juvenile collection development, lapsit services, storytelling, assistance with homework assignments, and summer reading programmes, usually provided by a children's librarian in the children's room of a public library. Compare with adult services and young adult services.

Chine-Collé Print
French for 'Chinese tissue paper' and 'attached'. A print made on a thin surface, such as Japanese paper or linen, cut or torn to the desired shape, and adhered permanently to a heavier backing sheet in a single run through the printing press, using either the intaglio or lithographic method, a technique first used in the 1800's for fine quality book illustration and individual works of art.

Chinese American Librarians Association (CALA)
Established in 1983, CALA seeks to promote better communication between Chinese American librar-

ians employed in the United States and serves as a forum for discussion of the problems of its members. An affiliate of the American Library Association, CALA publishes the semiannual *Journal of Library and Information Science* in English and Chinese, the *CALA Newsletter* in three issues per year, and the semiannual *CALA E-Journal*.

Chinese Style

In China and Japan, the evolution of the book proceeded as in the West, from scroll to leaves enclosed in a cover, but by a different route. Instead of binding separately cut leaves in codex form, a continuous roll of writing material was accordion-pleated, creating a series of folded leaves left uncut at the fore-edge with writing on one side only. Also known as *Japanese style*.

Chip

A shortened form of *microchip*, a high-speed miniaturized integrated circuit, etched in a semiconducting material on the surface of a tiny, wafer-thin piece of metal, for use as microprocessor and memory in computers and other electronic equipment. The design of increasingly powerful microchips has been the driving force behind the information technology revolution that began in the second half of the 20th century.

Chip Board

A thin, cheap, low-density board manufactured from recycled paper and other cellulose fibres. Although chip board is sometimes used in case binding, binder's board is preferred in hardcover trade editions. Also spelled *chipboard*.

Chipped

The condition of a book that has small pieces missing from the edges of its cover, dust jacket, or pages, not as prized in the market for antiquarian books as a copy in mint condition.

Chi-Rho

A monogram consisting of the letters XP, the first two characters of the name of Jesus Christ in Greek, often used as a symbol in early Christian art, including manuscript decoration in Gospel books, as in this example from the *Book of Kells*.

Chirograph

A handwritten document, usually a deed or other public instrument. Also, an early method of preventing counterfeiting in which a written record, usually of an agreement or transaction, was made in two copies on the same sheet, often with writing across the space separating the copies, then cut or torn down the middle in serrated fashion, each of the parties receiving one of the two pieces, which served to authenticate the other.

Chiro-Xylographic

A type of blockbook produced during the 15th and 16th centuries, combining woodcut illustrations with manuscript text, an early method of producing multiple copies of illustrated books.

Choir Book
A book containing music sung or chanted by the choir in religious services. Medieval choir books used in services of the Catholic Church were of large size in order to be visible to the entire choir, often beautifully illuminated for display on a lectern in the sanctuary. The category includes the antiphonal, gradual, and missal.

Choropleth Map
From the Greek *choros* and *plethos*. A thematic map on which colour, shading, hatching, or some other graphic technique is used to show the density or frequency of a quantifiable variable in each of several administrative or enumerative areas, based on average number of occurrences per unit of area, usually divided into classes. On these maps of the United States, colour is used to indicate the topography of poverty. This example shows transit collisions by state in the United States for the year 2000.

Chorus Score
The score of a musical work originally written for solo voice and chorus, which shows only the choral parts and any accompan-iment arranged for keyboard instrument.

Chrestomathy
A collection of choice passages from the literary works of an author, especially one compiled as a sample of literary specimens or as an aid in the study of a language.

Christian Fiction (CF)
Novels and stories in which Christian religious belief is a major element in the development of plot, theme, and character. The market for Christian fiction has expanded considerably in the United States in recent years. New titles are regularly reviewed in *Booklist* and *Library Journal*, and at the Web site *Christian Fiction Review*.

Chromolithograph
A colour lithograph produced by preparing a separate stone for each colour of ink and printing one colour in register over another, as opposed to applying tints by hand after printing to produce a *coloured lithograph*. For some prints, as many as 30 stones were used to create the desired effect. Introduced in the 1830s, the technique did not come into widespread commercial use until the 1860s and remained the most popular method of colour printing until the end of the 19th century when less expensive photographic processes were developed for reproducing colour.

Chronicle Play
A drama based on material from the chronicle histories of England, for example, those written by Hall and Holinshead. Popular during the Elizabethan period, chronicle plays were at first loosely structured but evolved into sophisticated character studies, exemplified by the history plays of William Shakespeare. A more recent example of a history play is *A Man for All Seasons* by Robert Bolt.

Chronogram

An inscription in which certain letters, made conspicuous, when read as roman numerals, indicate a specific date, for example, the motto ChrIstVs DVX; ergo trIVMphVs on a medal struck in 1632 by the Swedish King Gustavus Adolphus, the capitals of which when added produce the sum 1632. Also, the record made by a chronograph.

Chronological

The arrangement of data, records, items, headings, entries, etc., according to their relation in time, from earliest to latest. In library classification systems, the period subdivisions added to subject headings are listed in chronological order. The opposite of reverse chronological.

Chronological File

In archives, a file containing materials arranged by date or some other time sequence. When circulated for reference, such a file is called a reading file. Abbreviated *chron file* and *chrono file*. Synonymous with *continuity file* and *day file*.

Chronological Subdivision

In library cataloguing, a subdivision added to a class or subject heading to indicate the period of time covered by the work. Generally associated with historical treatment of a topic, chronological subdivisions are often used after the subdivision - History, as in the heading France - History - 1789-1815. They are also used under artistic, literary, and music form/genre headings to modify the main heading, as in American poetry—20th century. Synonymous with *period subdivision*.

Chronology

A book or section of a book that lists events and their dates in the order of their occurrence. Most chronologies are limited to a specific period, event, or theme. Book-length chronologies are usually shelved in the reference section of a library.

Chrysography

From the Greek *chrys* and *graphia*. The art and craft of writing in ink made from powdered gold, as practiced by the medieval scribes who produced illuminated manuscripts from the early Christian period through the 16th century.

Church and Synagogue Library Association (CSLA)

Founded in 1967, CSLA provides a forum for church and synagogue libraries to share practices and find solutions to common problems, inspire a sense of purpose among church and synagogue librarians, and guide the development of church and synagogue librarianship towards recognition as a formal branch of the profession. CSLA publishes the bimonthly publication *Church and Synagogue Libraries*.

CI

Competitive Intelligence.

CILIP

Chartered Institute of Library and Information Professionals.

Cinching

A condition that results when loosely wound film is rewound too tightly on a reel, causing the film to move against itself on the roll. As the film tightens, any dirt or other irregularities on its surface will cause fine scratches, called *cinch marks,* angled in the direction of movement. Also, the wrinkling or folding over of magnetic tape on itself, caused when a loose tape pack is stopped suddenly.

Ciné Mode

The arrangement of successive images on roll film with the frames oriented vertically, parallel with the edges of the film. Synonymous with *motion picture mode* and *vertical mode*. In microfiche, the arrangement of images with the frames filling the rows in a column, from top to bottom, before proceeding to the next column. Compare with comic mode.

Cinema

A broad term encompassing the motion picture industry and distribution system, the films produced, and the art form they represent. It is also used in Europe and the UK to refer to the theater in which motion pictures are publicly shown.

Cinematography

Derived from the name of the Cinematographe apparatus invented in 1895 by Auguste and Louis Lumière, the term is applied both to the art and scientific methods of motion picture photography and to the entire process of making motion pictures, including photography, processing, editing, printing, and projection. The *cinematographer* is typically in charge of the camera crew and provides advice to the film director as needed concerning the camera angles and shots that are possible in each scene and their technical requirements. Also refers to the act of making a motion picture. In the United States, an Academy Award is given each year for best cinematography.

CIO

Chief Information Officer.

CIP

Cataloguing-in-Publication.

CIP

A *Children's Internet Protection Act.*

Cipher

The initials of a personal name, written or arranged in ornamental form of such complexity and/or artistry as to form a private mark or symbol. In a more general sense, secret writing or code intended to be understood only by those who know the key to it. In data processing, an encrypted character that can only be decrypted with a key.

Ciphertext

In cryptography, encrypted information that cannot be read without knowledge of the secret 'key' or rules for converting it back into its original plaintext form, except through the process of cryptanalysis.

CIPO

Canadian Intellectual Property Office.

Circa
A Latin word meaning 'about,' used to indicate lack of certainty but reasonable probability concerning a date, for example, the approximate birth and/or death date(s) of a person for whom official records are lacking. Abbreviated *c.* or *ca. Example*: *c.* 1922

Circuit Edges
A style of flexible leather binding with projecting covers that fold over at the head, tail, and fore-edge, completely covering the edges of the sections like a box, used mainly on Bibles and prayer books carried by clergymen who traveled a regular circuit of rural parishes, presumably to protect the text from exposure to the elements. Synonymous with *divinity circuit* and *divinity edges*. Compare with Yapp binding.

Circular
A promotional piece usually in the form of a printed letter or leaflet distributed to a large circle of people at the same time via the mail, as a newspaper insert, door-to-door, or at a commercial establishment and intended to be passed on to others interested in its content. Compare with circular letter.

Circular Letter
Correspondence intended to be distributed throughout an organisaton or group to ensure that important information is disseminated systematically and consistently. In the 18th century, this form of communication was used by politicians to make their views on public issues widely known. One of the most famous examples is a letter issued in 1767 by the Massachusetts legislature to other colonial assemblies in response to the Townshend Acts, urging American colonists to unite in resisting taxation without representation in the British Parliament.

Circulating Book
A book that can be charged to a borrower account for use inside or outside the library facility, as opposed to one restricted to library use only. Compare with non-circulating.

Circulating Collection
Books and other materials that may be checked out by registered borrowers for use inside or outside the library. In most academic and public libraries in the United States, circulating materials are shelved in open stacks to facilitate browsing. Compare with non-circulating.

Circulation Analysis
Close examination of statistics compiled on the circulation of library materials, usually broken down by classification, material type, category of borrower, time of year, etc., to determine patterns of usage, an important tool in budgeting, collection development, staffing, etc.

Circulation Desk
The service point at which books and other materials are checked in and out of a library, usually a long counter located near the entrance

or exit, which may include a built-in book drop for returning borrowed materials. In small and medium-sized libraries, items on hold or reserve are usually available at the circulation desk, which is normally staffed by one or more persons trained to operate the circulation system and handle patron accounts.

Circulation Statistics

A count maintained of the number of items checked out from a library during a given period or the number of times a specific item is checked out during a given period, usually broken down by type of material and/or classification. Circulation statistics can be kept by hand, but most automated circulation systems provide detailed statistical reports by day, week, month, and year, which can be analyzed to determine usage patterns, an important aid in budgeting, collection development, staffing, etc. Compare with circulation history.

Circulation Status

The conditions under which a specific item in a library collection is available for use. An item may be on order, in process, at the bindery, for library use only, available to be checked out, on loan until a certain due date, recently returned, missing, lost, or billed. Compare with loan status.

CIS

Community Information System and Congressional Information Service, Inc.

Citation

In the literary sense, any written or spoken reference to an authority or precedent or to the verbatim words of another speaker or writer. In library usage, a written reference to a specific work or portion of a work produced by a particular author, editor, composer, etc., clearly identifying the document in which the work is to be found. The frequency with which a work is cited is sometimes considered a measure of its importance in the literature of the field. Citation format varies from one field of study to another but includes at a minimum author, title, and publication date. An *incomplete* citation can make a source difficult, if not impossible, to locate. Abbreviated *cite.*

Citation Analysis

A bibliometric technique in which works cited in publications are examined to determine patterns of scholarly communication, for example, the comparative importance of books versus journals, or of current versus retrospective sources, in one or more academic disciplines. The citations in student research papers, theses, and dissertations are also examined by librarians for purposes of collection evaluation and development. Synonymous with *citation checking*.

Citation Chasing

A legitimate research technique in which the bibliographies of works already located in a literature search are examined for additional sources containing further information on the topic. The process can be facilitated by using a citation index.

Cite

To quote or refer to an authority outside oneself, usually in support of a point or conclusion or by way of explanation or example. In scholarly publication, the source of such a reference is indicated in a footnote or endnote. Also used as a shortened form of the term citation.

City Directory

A three-way directory that lists the residents and businesses located in a specific town or city alphabetically by name, with street address and telephone number included in each entry. In a second section, name(s) and addresses are listed by phone number, and in a third section, names and phone numbers are listed by street address. Published annually and sold by subscription, current city directories often include zip code and census tract locators for use in marketing. In libraries, they are usually shelved in ready reference or in the reference stacks.

Cityscape

A general or broad view of a city or town made by photographic or artistic means, usually from a distant and/or elevated point of view, often showing the skyline; the urban equivalent of a landscape.

Civil Register

An official record of births, marriages, deaths, and other major events in the lives of the citizens of a governmental unit. Some countries have a national civil register, for example, the UK. Its General Register Office is part of the Identity and Passport Service.

CJCLS

Community and Junior College Libraries Section.

CLA Book of the Year for Children

A literary award established in 1947 and presented annually under the auspices of the Canadian Library Association to the author of the most outstanding children's book of creative writing published in Canada during the preceding year. The author must be a citizen or permanent resident of Canada.

CLA

Canadian Library Association and Catholic Library Association.

Claim

A notice from a library informing the publisher or subscription agent that a specific issue of a newspaper or periodical on subscription, or item on continuation order, has not been received within a reasonable time, with a request that a replacement copy be sent. Claimed items are noted in the check-in record attached to the bibliographic record that represents the publication in the library catalogue.

Claim Report

The publisher's or vendor's response regarding the status of a claim made by a library for material not received as expected on subscription or continuation order. Synonymous with *claim check*.

Clamshell Box
A protective container, often fitted to the dimensions of the enclosed object, hinged along one side to open like a book, allowing the contents to be inspected without removal. Libraries typically store videocassettes intended for circulation in hard plastic clamshell boxes. Those used in archival storage are usually buffered and may be designed to pass the Photographic Activity Test (PAT).

Clam Shell Case
clamshell box.

Clandestine Publication
A book, pamphlet, newspaper, broadsheet, speech, song, etc., published and distributed in secrecy, without official knowledge or sanction, usually expressing controversial views during a time of political unrest and censorship.

Clasp
A hinged fitting made of ornamented metal, ivory, or bone attached to the fore-edge of the boards of a book, used from the 14th to the early 17th century to keep the leaves pressed firmly together and to prevent the covers from warping. Prior to 1200, leather strap fastenings were used for this purpose. Greek-style bindings sometimes had a clasp at the head and tail and two on the fore-edge. Michelle Brown notes in *Understanding Illuminated Manuscripts* that in English bindings the catch or pin was attached to the lower board, and in most Continental bindings to the upper board.

Class Number
The specific notation used in Dewey Decimal Classification to designate a class, for example, 943.085 assigned to works on the history of the Weimar Republic in Germany. In Library of Congress Classification, the corresponding notation is DD237.

Classic
A widely read work recognised as outstanding in its field. Such a work remains in print long after initial publication; is translated, adapted, and issued in multiple editions; and continues to be the subject of criticism, commentary, study, and analysis. Also refers to a feature film or documentary that has withstood the test of time. Compare with classics.

Classical Border
An ornamental band around text and/or miniature in a medieval manuscript, containing motifs derived from the art of ancient Rome, a style of manuscript decoration that flourished in Italy during the Renaissance.

Classics
All the non-Christian works written in the Greek and Latin languages prior to A.D. 600. In a broader sense, outstanding books on any subject, whether fiction or non-fiction, written for adults or children. Compare with classic.

Classification

The process of dividing objects or concepts into logically hierarchical classes, subclasses, and sub-sub-classes based on the characteristics they have in common and those that distinguish them. Also used as a shortened form of the term classification system or classification scheme.

Classification Society of North America (CSNA)

A non-profit interdisciplinary organisaton devoted to promoting the scientific study of classification and clustering and to the dissemination of scientific and educational information related to its fields of interest. CSNA publishes the biannual *Journal of Classification* and the *CSNA Newsletter*.

Classification System

A list of classes arranged according to a set of pre-established principles for the purpose of organising items in a collection, or entries in an index, bibliography, or catalogue, into groups based on their similarities and differences, to facilitate access and retrieval. In the United States, most library collections are classified by subject. Classification systems can be enumerative or hierarchical, broad or close. In the United States, most public libraries use Dewey Decimal Classification, but academic and research libraries prefer Library of Congress Classification.

Classified

The status of a document to which access is restricted to a few authorised individuals within a military or government agency, research institution, private corporation, or other organisaton, usually because it contains highly sensitive information that might be misused by unauthorised persons. When secrecy is no longer required, the document may be declassified.

Classified Catalogue

A subject catalogue in which entries are filed in the notational order of a pre-established classification system, with bibliographic records under as many subject headings as apply to the content of each item. An alphabetical subject index facilitates the use of a classified catalogue, which is usually maintained alongside an author and/or title catalogue. Synonymous with *classed catalogue* and *class catalogue*. Compare with dictionary catalogue and divided catalogue.

Classified Index

An index in which entries are arranged under headings and subheadings indicating hierarchical divisions and subdivisions within classes based on the subject matter indexed, rather than in alphabetical or numerical sequence. To use such an index effectively, a subject index is required.

Classify

To arrange a collection of items according to a system of classification, based on the characteristics of each item. Also, to assign a class number to an individual item in a collection, based on its characteristics.

Classroom Collection

A small semi-permanent collection of library materials selected by a school library or academic library for the general classroom use use of an instructor and the students enrolled in a course. Compare with classroom library and classroom loan.

Classroom Loan

A small collection of library materials on temporary loan from a school library or academic library to a classroom, for the use of instructor and students, usually in support of a specific project or curriculum unit. Compare with classroom collection and classroom library.

Clay Tablet

The earliest known books were inscribed on small, thin, wet slabs of clay, using a thin, sharp instrument called a stylus to incise the wedge-shaped cuneiform characters of the written languages of ancient Mesopotamia. The finished tablets were sun-dried or kiln-fired, then enclosed in a protective outer shell of dried or fired clay inscribed with a title or abstract of the contents.

Clearinghouse

An organisaton or unit within an organisaton that functions as a central agency for collecting, organising, storing, and disseminating documents, usually within a specific academic discipline or field. A clearinghouse may also assist the research process by maintaining records of information resources for referral. Also spelled *clearing house.*

CLENE

Continuing Library Education Network and Exchange Round Table.

CLENERT

Continuing Library Education Network and Exchange Round Table.

Cliché

From the French word *clicher,* meaning 'to stereotype.' A word, phrase, or expression so overused that it has lost its impact and, to some degree, its original meaning. Considered unimaginative, clichés are avoided by serious writers and speakers, except in dialogue when the author wishes to make a point about the mentality of the speaker. Dictionaries of clichés are available in the reference section of larger libraries. In literature, an overused plot element or character type whose lack of originality detracts from the overall quality of the work.

Cliché-Verre

A photomechanical method of printmaking, popular with French painters in the 1850s, in which the image is created by exposing photographic paper to light through an image scratched with a sharp instrument in an opaque ground-coating on a smooth, transparent surface, such as glass or film, a technique permitting fluidity of line similar to that achieved with etching.

Click-and-Drag

To change the position of an icon, filename, window, or other movable element on a computer screen by clicking on it with a pointing device, such as a mouse, and then holding down the button to shift the element to another location on the screen. The technique can be used to reposition windows on a microcomputer desktop, move computer files from one directory or subdirectory to another in storage, and organise bookmarked Web sites in folders in most Web browsers.

Click-on License

Licensing terms stated in a notice appearing on the installation or opening screen of a software or electronic information product, which the manufacturer considers the user to have accepted by the act of selecting an icon or link to continue. Such agreements often include provisions and restrictions that have not been uniformly enforced in the courts, because they give software publishers more rights than are permitted under federal copyright or patent law. The controversial *Uniform Computer Information Transactions Act (UCITA)* would allow software publishers to embed non-negotiable, enforceable contract terms in this type of mass-market license. Synonymous with *click-through license* and *click-wrap license.*

Clientele

All the people who use a library's services and collections on a regular or irregular basis, usually those living in the district that fundss its operations or who are members of the institution it serves. Successful collection development depends on the librarian's knowledge of the information needs and preferences of the library's users. The *primary clientele* consists of the largest or most important category of person using a library's services and collections on a regular basis, for example, undergraduate students at a college library. The hours that a library is open may be established to accommodate the needs of its primary clientele.

Clipboard

A small amount of computer memory reserved as a temporary storage place in the exchange of data between software applications. In word processing, this is normally accomplished by selecting the option to 'cut' or 'copy' from one document and 'paste' into another. Data transferred to the clipboard is lost when another cut/copy operation commences, unless saved as a separate file. The term originally referred to a thin, rectangular piece of rigid material, a little larger than an 8 1/2 x 11-inch sheet of paper, equipped with a spring clamp at the top for holding down paper, designed as a portable writing surface.

Clipping

A page, piece of a page, or pages cut or torn from a printed publication, usually from a newspaper or magazine, by a person who wishes to save an article, editorial, letter to the editor, photograph, cartoon, etc. Large collections of clippings are usually stored in a *clipping file,* arranged by subject or some other method of classification. Compare with cutting and tear sheet.

Clipping Service

A service, usually performed in a special library, in which news announcements, articles, photographs, and other items of interest to the host organisaton are clipped from current periodicals and news services on a daily or weekly basis to be forwarded to appropriate personnel within the organisaton, based on pre-established interest profiles. Directory information for commercial clipping services is available in the reference serial *Literary Market Place.* Synonymous with *clipping bureau.*

CLMP

Council of Literary Magazines and Presses.

Cloisonné

From the French *cloison* meaning 'partition' or 'compartment.' An elegant style of book cover produced by Italian and Greek craftsmen of the 11th century in which an ornamental design in narrow metal strips was soldered onto a metal plate, and the open spaces between the strips filled with enamel in various colours, to form the outer surface of the cover. Books bound in this style are usually very valuable, especially when in good condition.

Close Classification

A classification system in which the main classes and divisions are minutely subdivided, allowing very specific characteristics of each subject to be differentiated. Also, the classification of works to the fullest extent permitted by the notation of a classification system (*DDC*). The opposite of broad classification.

Close Score

A vocal music score in which all the parts are given on a minimum number of staves, usually two, as in a hymn (*AACR2*).

Closed Caption (CC)

A continuous moving line of text along the bottom of the screen in a television broadcast giving the narration or dialogue and noting any non-speech vocalisatons or sound effects. Used mainly for the hearing-impaired and in bilingual programming, *closed captioning* is visible only with the aid of a special decoder. In library cataloguing, the phrase *closed captioned* is entered in the note area of the bibliographic description to indicate that an item includes the feature.

Closed Catalogue

A library catalogue to which new bibliographic records are no longer added or in which additions are restricted to certain categories, although existing records continue to be removed as they are revised, corrected, and/or converted to machine-readable format. After retrospective conversion is completed, a closed catalogue is usually removed from public access and eventually discarded. Compare with frozen catalogue and open catalogue.

Closed Entry
A note in the bibliographic record for a serial or continuation giving the complete information for all the parts or volumes published, or in the holdings statement in the catalogue record for such a title, indicating all the parts or volumes held by the library, as distinct from the open entry for an *ongoing* serial subscription or continuation order. For newspapers and periodicals, a closed entry usually indicates that the subscription was canceled or the publication ceased.

Closed Reserve
An item on reserve that may be checked out by a registered borrower but may not be removed from library premises. Also, a reserve collection shelved in a closed stack from which requested items must be retrieved by a member of the library staff. Compare with open reserve.

Closed Stacks
A shelving area in a library to which only members of the library staff have access, established to protect the collection or conserve space by using aisles narrower than the width that is standard in open stacks. Materials are retrieved from closed stacks by staff members upon request.

Closed-end Index
An index covering one or more documents or publications compiled all at one time. Compare with open-end index.

Closeout
A book title offered for retail sale at a significantly reduced price because the publisher is allowing it to go out of print. A rebate may be offered by the publisher to the bookseller for copies that do not sell.

Closet Drama
A play written to be read rather than performed on the stage, for example, the dramatic works of the French poet Alfred de Musset. Also refers to a drama originally intended for performance, which survives as a work of literature but is rarely if ever performed.

Cloth Book
A small, illustrated children's book printed entirely on sturdy woven fabric and given a flexible binding for toddlers who have not yet developed sufficient manual dexterity to turn paper pages without tearing them. To withstand drooling, the cloth pages may be treated with a moisture-resistant substance. In the 19th century, this type of toy book was called a *rag book*.

Cloth Map
A map made on woven material instead of parchment or paper, often designed for use in the field. Cloth maps are more durable than paper maps, especially in wet conditions, and they can be easily rolled up or folded for storage and transport. The technique of printing maps on cloth reached a peak during World War II with highly accurate registration of multiple

colours on both sides of a single piece of fabric.

Club Line
A single indented line at the beginning of a paragraph when it appears at the foot of a printed column or page of text, considered awkward by skilled typesetters and avoided whenever possible. Compare with orphan.

CMDS
Collection Management and Development Section.

Coat of Arms
A shield or its representation bearing the heraldic insignia traditionally associated with a specific person, family, institution, etc., often found in or on the bindings of books owned by royalty or members of the aristocracy.

Coaxial Cable
A high-capacity metal cable consisting of four layers: a solid or stranded wire encased in insulation, shielded by braided wire covered in plastic insulation. Various types of coaxial cable are used extensively in cable television transmission and computer networks because 'coax' can carry more data and is less susceptible to interference than the twisted pair wire used in older telephone systems. Compare with optical fibre.

Co-Citation Coupling
The idea that two scholarly papers cited in a third (C) are bibliographically related in a way that is likely to be of interest to researchers, even when they do not directly cite one another. The relationship is stronger when both A and B are also cited in other papers besides C. Compare with bibliographic coupling.

Cocked
A serious binding defect in which the spine of a book is angled or twisted in a way that prevents the boards from lining up evenly with each other.

Cockled
The condition of a book in which the leaves or boards appear puckered, wavy, wrinkled, or curled, usually due to uneven distortion produced by excessive heat and/or humidity in drying. In a book cover, the condition can result from the incorrect use of adhesive.

Coda
From the Latin word *cauda*, meaning 'tail.' An independent passage added at the end of a musical work or literary composition to bring the piece to a graceful conclusion by drawing preceding motifs and themes together in a satisfying resolution. The last chapter of a biography, the last essay in a collection of essays, or the last story in a book of short stories is sometimes written as a coda to tie the other parts together.

Codebook
The metadata that describes a social science data set. Although codebooks have been digitized since the 1970s, social scientists continue to refer to them as 'books' because they originally existed in

the form of bound manuals. A codebook contains bibliographic information about a scientific study, describes the composition and format of data files, and documents methodology and study variables.

CODES

Collection Development and Evaluation Section.

Codification

The process of creating systematic rules to govern a specific activity, such as the cataloguing of bibliographic materials. In the United States, Britain, and Canada, the joint efforts of the American Library Association, the Library Association (UK), and the Canadian Library Association have produced *Anglo-American Cataloguing Rules*, which apply to library materials in various formats.

Co-Edition

An edition for which two or more publishers share responsibility, for example, *The Great Libraries: From Antiquity to the Renaissance*, published in 2000 by Oak Knoll Press and the British Library. In most cases, the original publisher grants the exclusive right to market and distribute the publication within a specific sales territory to one or more other publishers. The title page of a co-edition may bear the imprint of the originator, of one of the companies granted distribution rights, or of all the co-publishers. Compare with export edition and joint publication.

Coextensive Entry

The principle in indexing that the subject heading or descriptor assigned to a work should encompass *all* the significant concepts covered in the item. Thus a book about painters and poets would require the heading 'Painters and poets,' rather than the separate headings 'Painters' and 'Poets.' Coextensive indexing is attempted in the PRECIS system. Also spelled *co-extensive entry*. Compare with specific entry.

Cognitive Style

The way a person habitually organises a problem-solving or learning experience, or consistently receives and responds to information, especially whether the individual prefers content already structured or is more likely to impose his/her own structure on the material. Differences in learning style have important implications for the delivery of reference services and bibliographic instruction and for the design of online tutorials and library Web pages.

Cold-Crack

The tendency of the adhesive on the spine of a perfect-bound book to split at very low temperatures, reducing the text block to a pile of loose leaves. The inability of hot-melt adhesives to withstand cold temperatures makes them unsuitable for use in bindings marketed in countries like Finland and Russia where winter temperatures can be severe. The problem is eliminated in Otabind adhesive binding, which uses slower-drying, cold-resistant polyvinyl acetate (PVA) adhesive.

Collaborator

A person who works closely with one or more associates in producing a work to which all who participate make the same kind of contribution or different contributions, for example, essays written by different authors for publication in a collection or illustrations for a children's book in which the text is written by a person other than the illustrator.

Collagraph

A print made from a rigid substrate on which the image is composed of a collage of various textured, comparatively flat materials glued to the surface, sometimes with the application of modeling media. An *intaglio* collagraph is made by rubbing ink into grooves and fissures and then wiping away the ink on the surface before the print is pulled. A *relief* collagraph is taken from ink rolled over the surface, leaving grooves and fissures untouched. The two techniques can be combined in the same print.

Collected Edition

An edition of the previously published works of an author, issued in a single volume or uniform set of volumes, usually under a collective title. Compare with author's edition.

Collectible

Any class of things, usually old or rare but lacking intrinsic value, that people accumulate as a hobby or in the expectation that the value will rise. Also used as an adjective to describe something sought by collectors, for example, first editions and incunabula. Also spelled *collectable.*

Collecting Archives

An independent organisaton, or unit within a larger organisaton or institution, responsible for building a collection of records and documents from a variety of outside sources, in keeping with the mission of the parent institution and an acquisitions policy, for example, a manuscript repository in the library of a major university. Archives of this type may provide online access to a portion of their resources, or be completely electronic.

Collection Agency

A commercial enterprise that specialises in collecting past-due bills from people who owe them, usually by informing them that their credit record will suffer unless prompt payment is received. Most public libraries enter into a contractual agreement with such an agency to handle the collection of unpaid bills for items lost, damaged, or long overdue. Academic institutions have the option of withholding grades or diploma from a student until the balance on a student's library account is paid.

Collection Assessment

The systematic evaluation of the quality of a library collection to determine the extent to which it meets the library's service goals and objectives and the information needs of its clientele. Deficiencies are addressed through collection development. Synonymous with *collection evaluation.*

Collection Development and Evluation Section (CODES)
The section of the Reference and User Services Association (RUSA) within the American Library Association (ALA) that addresses the collection development interests of reference and user services librarians in libraries of all types. CODES studies questions of reference collection development and maintenance, readers' advisory, user communities, and reference publishing.

Collection Development Policy (CDP)
A formal written statement of the principles guiding a library's selection of materials, including the criteria used in making selection and deselection decisions and policies concerning gifts and exchanges. An unambiguously worded collection development policy can be very helpful in responding to challenges from pressure groups.

Collection Level Cataloguing
The encoding level used to control separately published documents that are unrelated bibliographically and do not warrant the expense of full level or even minimal level cataloguing but have research value and can be cataloged as a single item under a collective title because they share at least one unifying characteristic. Synonymous with *collective cataloguing.*

Collection Management
The application of quantitative techniques, such as statistical and cost-benefit analysis, to the process of collection development, usually limited to large libraries and library systems. In a more general sense, the activity of planning and supervising the growth and preservation of a library's collections based on an assessment of existing strengths and weaknesses and an estimate of future needs.

Collection Management and Development Section (CMDS)
The section of the Association for Library Collections and Technical Services (ALCTS) within the American Library Association (ALA) devoted to promoting the improvement of collection management and development and to the selection and evaluation of library materials in all formats and in all types of institutions.

Collective Bargaining Agreement (CBA)
A legally binding contract signed on behalf of library staff organised in a *collective bargaining unit* by elected representatives authorised to negotiate terms of employment with management, including salaries and wages, benefits, job responsibilities, evaluation for promotion and tenure, grievance procedures, etc. Librarians employed at colleges and universities that grant librarians faculty status may

be members of the same bargaining unit as the teaching faculty. The Association of College and Research Libraries (ACRL) has expressed its policy on collective bargaining in *Guideline on Collective Bargaining*.

Collective Biography
A work in one or more volumes containing separate accounts of the lives of two or more individuals who lived within a specific time period, distinguished themselves in the same field or activity, or have some other characteristic in common. Written by one or more biographers, the essays in a collective biography are usually longer than the entries in a biographical dictionary and may include a biobibliography or list of references for further reading.

Collective Record Group
In archives, a collection of records assembled according to artificial rather than conventional criteria, usually by the archivist from a number of comparatively small, short-lived, or satellite agencies that are related in some way, often by administration or function. The purpose of the consolidation is generally to simplify records management by reducing the number of fonds. Within such a record group, the records of each agency are typically segregated as an identifiable subgroup or series.

Collective Title
In library cataloguing, the title proper of a bibliographic item containing several works by one or more authors issued in a single volume or uniform set of volumes, each with its own title distinct from that of the whole. Also refers to the title assigned by a cataloger to a group of separately published materials cataloged collectively.

Collective Work
For purposes of copyright, a work in which a number of contributions by one or more authors, each a separate and independent work, are assembled, usually by an editor, to constitute a whole. Included are individual issues of a periodical, anthologies, collections of essays, conference proceedings, etc.

Collector's Edition
A special edition of a book, videocassette, or DVD designed to be appeal to collectors who will wish to keep it permanently in a private collection. In books, a collector's edition may be printed on better quality paper and include additional illustrations, with a binding also of superior quality. In audiocassettes and DVDs, a collector's edition may be housed in a specially designed container and include printed programme notes and material not found in the standard edition. Copies are sold for a higher price, even in the secondhand market if the item is in good condition.

College Libraries Section (CLS)
Established in 1940, CLS is the section of the Association of College and Research Libraries (ACRL) within the American Library Association (ALA) devoted to ad-

vancing college librarianship and to encouraging the development of library services in baccalaureate degree-granting institutions.

College Library

A type of academic library maintained by an independent four-year college, or by one of several colleges within a larger university, for the use of students and faculty. The Association of College and Research Libraries (ACRL) has established *Standards for Libraries in Higher Education*. Compare with undergraduate library.

Collegiality

From the Latin *collegium,* meaning 'community,' 'association,' or 'fraternity.' Engagement by the members of a group in relations based on civility and an awareness of common interests, as between *colleagues*.

Colloquy

A literary work written in the form of a conversation or dialogue. Plural: *colloquies*. Also refers to a conference in the form of a seminar, with several speakers participating in a discussion that is conversational in style and tone. Synonymous in this sense with *colloquium*.

Collotype

A photomechanical reproduction process in use from about 1870 to 1920 in which one surface of a glass plate is coated with a gelatin silver emulsion and exposed, when dry, to ultraviolet light in contact with a reverse negative. The light-sensitised gelatin hardens in proportion to the amount of light striking it, leaving the unexposed areas of the plate capable of absorbing moisture. Washed in water, the unhardened gelatin dissolves, leaving a raised image that can be inked to produce continuous-tone prints on high quality paper. Because the gelatin surface is delicate, collotype print runs are limited to about 2,000 copies.

Colon Classification

A classification system in which subjects are analyzed into facets based on their uses and relations, then represented by synthetically constructed classes with the parts separated by the colon (:). Developed by S.R. Ranganathan in the 1930s, Colon Classification is used in libraries in India and in research libraries throughout the world.

Colonial Edition

An edition of a book, usually a work of fiction, produced from sheets sold by the British publisher to other publishers or separately issued by the publisher, often on paper of inferior quality and in a less expensive binding, for distribution and sale in other parts of the British Empire at a significantly lower price than the original edition. A replacement title page may indicate that the edition is intended for the colonial market.

Colophon

A Greek word meaning 'finishing touch.' A statement appearing at the end of the text of an early manuscript, usually giving details of production. The colophon may also include an expression of gratitude to the patron or client commissioning the work, a warning against unauthorised copying, or a brief comment by the scribe. Colophons occur sporadi-cally in medieval manuscripts, sometimes decorated or embelli-shed with flourishes.

Colour Balance

In the graphic arts, the range of colours in an image, especially as regards deviation from the accurate reproduction of tones in the original subject, inaccurate colour balance giving a general cast, subtle or pronounced, to the image. Colour balance can be manipulated by the artist to express mood or to create the desired impression. In video production and transmission, colour balance is tested and calibrated by means of colour bars. Also refers to the ability of photographic materials to reproduce colours accurately, which may diminish as the material ages, posing problems for preservation.

Colour Bar

A standardised electronic signal recorded at the head of a videotape for use as a benchmark to test and calibrate the colour balance of video and television monitors. Established by the Society of Motion Picture and Television Engineers (SMPTE), the standard test pattern for the NTSC analog television system used in North America appears as vertical bars of seven colours: white, yellow, cyan, green, magenta, red, and blue.

Colour Chart

A calibration target consisting of a matrix or spectrum of chromatic samples set to a known standard. In computing, colour charts provide reference points to ensure accurate colour capture and to calibrate output devices. Synonymous with *colour patch*. Compare with gray scale.

Colour Fading

The deterioration of colour photographs and film over time, caused by the chemical instability of the image-producing dyes used in the emulsion. As the dyes gradually break down, contrast is lost, giving the image a washed-out monochromatic appearance.

Colour Plate

An illustration in colour, usually printed separately from the text on a different grade of paper and bound with others in one or more sections of a book. Colour plates are often numbered and listed by number in the front matter of a book. In publishing, colour printing almost always increases cost of production.

Colour Separation Positive

One of a set of transparencies, usually three or four in number, used to make a plate for printing one colour in register with the others, to create a photomechanical print in full colour.

Colour Supplement

A magazine printed in colour to be issued with a Sunday newspaper. Also refers to a section of illustrations printed in colour for insertion in the centre of a magazine or book, whether removable or not.

Colporteur

From the French words *col* and *porter*. A peddler of newspapers and books printed in inexpensive edition who traveled about the countryside in Europe, carrying his wares in a box or basket attached to a neck strap as he hawked them in the streets and door to door. In Britain, itinerant salesmen were sometimes employed by religious societies to sell or distribute religious tracts on foot. *Colportage* flourished from the late 15th century, when printed works first became available, until the end of the 18th century despite unsuccessful efforts by the French government to suppress the trade because it helped spread the new ideas that eventually led to reformation and revolution.

Column

One of two or more vertical sections of written or printed text separated from each other by a ruled line or blank space, as in ancient scrolls, newspapers, and language dictionaries. The length of a newspaper article is expressed in column inches. Abbreviated *col.*

Column Inch

In newspaper and magazine publishing, the unit of measurement in which the length of an article or size of a paid advertisement is expressed, equivalent to the width of a column of type multiplied by one inch of depth.

Column Picture

A miniature in a medieval manuscript that fills the entire width of a column of text but not necessarily it full height, as in this example in an early 15th-century French manuscript.

Columnist

A journalist who writes regular commentary on current issues for publication in a magazine or newspaper, or in more than one newspaper, usually from a political position left or right of centre, or expressing an original point of view on a matter of interest to readers. National political columnists are often syndicated. Also refers to a specialist in a particular field or on a given subject who writes regular commentary for a magazine or trade journal.

COM

Computer Output Microform

Comb Binding

A form of mechanical binding in which a row of interconnected curved plastic teeth is inserted into slots punched along the binding edge of the leaves of a publication to hold them together, used for binding calendars, lab manuals, instruction manuals, and workbooks that must open flat to be used conveniently. If the plastic spine is wide enough, the title may be printed on it. Plastic comb bindings are easily broken.

Combination Rate

The special discounted price offered by a publisher when subscriptions to two or more serial publications are purchased by the same subscriber. The publisher normally determines the eligibility of a specific title for such a discount.

Comedy-Drama
A genre of theatre, film, and television in which humorous and serious content are equally or nearly equally balanced. Synonymous with *dramedy* and *seriocomedy*. Compare with tragicomedy.

Comes-With Title
In acquisitions, a title that is not a supplement, received by a library at no additional charge as a result of purchasing another title, for example, a newsletter or directory supplied by an academic society or professional association with a paid subscription to a journal.

Comic Book
A booklet, usually printed in colour on paper made from wood pulp, containing one or more stories told pictorially in a continuous strip of panels drawn in cartoon style, with dialogue or monologue enclosed in balloons or given in captions. An extended form of the comic strip published in daily newspapers, comic books are often issued in series and classified by genre. They are acquired by libraries for special collections on popular culture and are of considerable interest to private collectors.

Comic Card
A small paper card, issued individually or as part of a set, bearing a printed caricature or cartoon, often with a line or two of humorous text, popular from the 1850s until the early part of the 20th century. In *AACR2*, comic cards are cataloged as graphic materials.

Comic Mode
The arrangement of successive images on roll film with the frames oriented horizontally, perpendicular to the edges of the film. Synonymous with *horizontal mode*. In microfiche, the arrangement of images with the frames filling the columns in a row, from left to right, before proceeding to the next row. Compare with ciné mode.

Comic Strip
A succession of cartoon panels that tells a story graphically, with monologue or dialogue provided in balloons or captions. A comic strip may be complete in itself or part of a longer narrative published serially. The comics section of the Sunday issue of most major newspapers provides a selection of syndicated comic strips printed in colour. The most famous American comic strip was *Peanuts* created by Charles Schulz. Other classics include *Li'l Abner* by Al Capp and *Pogo* by Walt Kelly.

Comics Code Authority (CCA)
A watchdog organisaton founded in 1954 by the Comics Magazine Association of America (CMAA) in response to public concern about inappropriate content in comic books. Publishers could sub-

mit their publications to the CCA for screening and receive authorisaton to use the CCA seal of approval on the cover of comic books that conformed to its Comics Code. Although the CCA had no legal authority over publishers, magazine distributors often refused to carry comics lacking the CCA seal of approval.

Command-Driven

A computer interface in which the user must type a command statement or query to achieve the desired result, usually faster than a menu-driven interface but not as user-friendly for novices who must invest time and effort in learning the system's command language.

Commemorative Print

A print bearing an image of a significant event, such as the signing of an important document, the founding of an institution, or a decisive military battle, shown in narrative or allegorical style, often bearing text indicating commemorative intent.

Commendatory Verse

A poem in praise of an author and his work, written by another author. In the 16th century, publishers began printing such verses in the same volume as the commended work, for example, two poems by Ben Jonson were include in the First Folio of Shakespeare's plays.

Commentary

A critical or explanatory note or collection of notes on a sacred or literary work, accompanying the text or issued separately, usually written by a person or persons other than the author. In a more general sense, a series of remarks or observations made by someone with authority to speak and be heard on the subject, for example, a journalist writing a column on a political or social issue.

Commercial Journal

A scholarly journal or trade journal published by a for-profit company, as opposed to a journal published by a university press or non-profit organisaton, such as a scholarly society or professional association.

Commercial Publisher

A publisher in the business of producing and selling books and/or other publications for profit, as opposed to a university press or the publishing arm of a scholarly society, professional association, or other non-profit organisaton operating on a cost-recovery basis. The term includes trade publishers and popular presses. In commercial publishing, the decision to publish is influenced by sales potential, sometimes at the expense of originality and quality.

Commercial Television

Television broadcast stations for which profit is the prime concern. In the selection of programming, commercial stations rely heavily on ratings because their advertisers are motivated by the desire to reach the widest possible viewing audience. Compare with public television.

Committee on Accreditation (COA)
The official body within the American Library Association responsible for accrediting graduate programmes leading to the first professional degree in library and information science offered at universities in the United States, under *Standards for Accreditation of Master's Programmes in Library and Information Studies.*

Common Carrier (CC)
A telecommunication service, such as a telephone or cable company, that provides wire and/or microwave services to businesses and the general public, usually at rates regulated by federal, state, or local government.

Common Gateway Interface (CGI)
A programme interface installed on a Web server that allows Web pages to be linked to databases and other programmes in such a way that input can be entered via the Web page and sent to a database management system for searching. Results are sent back by the DBMS and presented to the user in HTML format.

Commonplace Book
A book with blank pages in which passages in prose or verse are recorded irregularly by its owner as ideas for future exploration or contemplation, sometimes arranged by subject. The writer may note only his own thoughts and ideas or excerpt those of other writers or speakers. Commonplace books kept by persons of literary or historical importance, such as Ralph Waldo Emerson and Thomas Jefferson, have been deemed worthy of publication. Although interest in this form of literary expression has waned, it is still used by poets.

Community and Junior College Libraries Section (CJCLS)
The section of the Association of College and Research Libraries (ACRL) within the American Library Association (ALA) devoted to enhancing library service and librarianship in libraries and learning resources centres that support the educational programmes of community and junior colleges and equivalent institutions.

Community Information
A format in MARC 21 designed to carry descriptions of non-bibliographic resources that fulfill the information needs of a community, including programmes, services, events, organisatons, and individuals.

Community Information System (CIS)
A centralised source providing government, business, historical, and geographic information about a local community or small group of communities, intended primarily for the use of local residents, prospective residents, and visitors.

Compact Cassette
A format for magnetic audiotape introduced by Philips in 1963,

compact cassettes quickly became the de facto standard for sound recordings on audiotape. Just under 4 - 2 1/2 inches in size, the audiocassette contains 1/8-inch wide, four-track tape wound on two hubs in a hard plastic shell. When played, the tape moves at 1 7/8 inches per second. Standard tape lengths are 60, 90, and 120 minutes. In the commercial market place, the medium has been largely superseded by compact discs.

Compact Disc (CD)

A digital audiorecording medium introduced in 1982 capable of storing up to 74 minutes of high-fidelity stereophonic sound in a single spiral track on one side of a 4.75-inch disc, similar to the track on a phonograph record. Designed to be read by a laser beam and decoded inside a device called a *CD player*, compact discs not only provide clearer sound than phonograph records and audiotape but are capable of recording a much wider range of volume.

Compact Edition

An edition in which the physical size of a long work is reduced, usually by altering the format without changing the content, for example, *The Compact Oxford English Dictionary*, reproduced micrographically and issued in a slipcase with a microprint reader. Compare with concise edition.

Compact Shelving

Library shelving designed to maximize the storage capacity of a given space by incorporating movable elements such as shelf ranges on tracks. Because it is considerably heavier than normal shelving when filled, compact shelving requires more structural support, an important design consideration in the construction and renovation of a library facilities. Compare with high-density shelving.

Compact Storage

A library shelving area, often reserved for low-use materials, in which narrow aisles, higher-than-normal shelves, and/or compact shelving is employed to maximize storage capacity. The building must be structurally capable of supporting the additional weight. Compact shelving with movable parts may be subject to electrical or mechanical failure.

Companion

A handbook intended to be used in connection with the study of a particular subject or field. This type of reference work is often an edited collection of essays. Compare with companion book.

Companion Book

A book published in conjunction with a motion picture or television programme or series, usually a work of non-fiction intended to complement documentary or instructional content, for example, *Lewis and Clark: An Illustrated History* by Dayton Duncan, based on the PBS television mini-series *Lewis and Clark: The Journey of the Corps of Discovery* by Ken Burns. In library cataloguing, the note *Com-*

panion volume to: is included in the bibliographic description, followed by the title of the work on which the book is based. Compare with tie-in.

Comparative Librarianship
The study and analysis of similarities and differences in librarianship as practiced in different countries, to identify or clarify underlying principles, expand awareness of successful practices, facilitate cooperation, etc.

Comparative Table
An alphabetical list of selected topics in a complete or extensive revision of Dewey Decimal Classification (DDC), giving the class number in the current edition and the corresponding number used in the preceding edition. In most cases, only numbers for comprehensive works are given.

Compass Rose
A circular or star-shaped device drawn or printed on the face of a map or chart, graduated from the reference direction in compass points or in degrees or both.

Compatibility
The ability of computer software to run on hardware other than that for which it was originally designed. Compatibility can be *upward* in programmes capable of running on newer, more powerful machines, or *downward* in programmes that will run on older, less powerful machines.

Compendium
A work that presents in condensed form the main points of a longer work, prepared by a person other than the original author. Also, a work that treats a broad subject or entire field of knowledge briefly and concisely, sometimes in the form of an outline. Used synonymously with digest and epitome.

Competencies
The capabilities expected of a person hired to perform a specific job or upon successful completion of a course of study or training. In librarianship, the knowledge, skills, and experience necessary to effectively handle professional responsibilities, usually within a specialisaton, expressed inclusively rather than as a set of minimum standards.

Competition
In marketing, rivalry among providers of a product or service aimed at increasing profits, market share, sales volume, etc., usually by altering the marketing mix. For libraries, the main competition is from bookstores, book clubs, video stores, Internet cafes, community events, and other agencies that receive public funds. In the United States, public libraries rarely compete with each other because their geographic service areas do not overlap, but the quality of a college or university library can be a factor in attracting enrollment in the market place for higher education.

Compilation
A work assembled from the works of various authors, or the various

works of a *single* author, into an ordered whole by a person other than the original author, without editorial alteration of the original text. Laws, rules, procedures, regulations, and technical data are particularly subject to compilation. The person who puts such a work together is a compiler. In a broader sense, any book or other written work assembled, sometimes over an extended period of time, from materials gathered from a variety of sources, for example, a bibliography or index. Compare with anthology and collection. Also refers to the activity of preparing a new or revised map or chart from existing map data, aerial photographs, field surveys, and other pertinent sources.

Compile
To gather and put together pieces of information or materials from various sources in an orderly structured whole, as in the creation of a bibliography or index. The person who assembles such a work is the compiler, and the resulting work is called a compilation.

Compiled Map
A map that incorporates information assembled from various sources having no connection with the map's creation, as opposed to one based on survey data collected specifically for the purpose of its creation.

Compiler
A person who selects and assembles written material from the works of various persons or bodies, or the various works of a *single* person or body, into a ordered whole, without editorial alteration of the original text. The resulting document or collection is called a compilation. When the compiler's name is indicated in or on the chief source of information, it is entered in the statement of responsibility area of the bibliographic record that represents the item in the library catalogue. Compare with editor.

Complete
Used in the holdings statement to describe a serial title for which the library owns 95-100 percent of the published run. Compare with incomplete.

Completeness
An indication of how much of the published run of a serial title is held by a library, usually given in the holdings statement as: *complete, incomplete,* or *scattered.*

Complex Subject
In library classification, a subject that has more than one defining characteristic, for example, the subject 'unemployed librarians,' which has the facets 'employment status' and 'occupation.'

Composer
The original creator of a musical work in any form, entered as author in the bibliographic record created to represent the edition in the library catalogue. Compare with arranger and performer.

Composite Book
A book assembled from portions

of other books. Because page size may vary slightly, the edges are apt to be irregular.

Composite Daguerreotype
A daguerreotype consisting of more than one image, usually made in a studio from a series of individual daguerreotypes

composite photograph
A photograph in which the image is produced by (1) multiple exposure of negatives, (2) sandwiching two or more negatives, or (3) some other method of combining negatives

Composite Print
A positive print of motion picture film that carries both synchronised images and sound. Synonymous with *combined print* and *married print*.

Composite Volume
A bound volume containing two or more separately published works, for example, a collection of brochures or music scores.

Composite Work
An original work produced as the result of a collaboration between two or more authors or composers in which the contribution of each is a separate and distinct part of a planned whole. Compare with joint author.

Compound Name
A name formed by joining two or more proper names with a hyphen, conjunction, or preposition.

Compound Subject Heading
A subject heading consisting of two or more words that together represent a single concept or two related concepts. In some cases, semantic factoring yields false drops.

Compound Surname
A surname composed of two or more proper names, usually joined by a hyphen, preposition or conjunction. In *AACR2*, compound surnames are entered under the element preferred by the person, with cross-references from the other elements, for example, Lloyd George, David, 1863-1945 with a reference from George, David Lloyd, his correct paternal surname. Hyphenated surnames are entered under the first element.

Comprehensive Number
In Dewey Decimal Classification, a class number covering all the components of the subject treated within the discipline, whether the components are represented by a span of consecutive class numbers or distributed throughout the schedule or table, for example, 305.2, representing the heading 'Age groups,' also used for comprehensive works on the generation gap (*DDC*).

Comprehensive Review
Periodic review of a library and information studies programme by the Committee on Accreditation (COA) of the American Library Association to determine if the programme conforms to the ALA's *Standards for Accreditation of Master's Programmes in Library and Information Studies*. The two-year

process includes submission of the Programme Presentation document and a two-day on-site review by an External Review Panel (ERP), followed by the COA's accreditation action.

Comprehensive
All-inclusive or all-encompassing. An index, bibliographic database, or other work of reference compiled with the stated goal of covering all possible aspects of a subject or all the published literature on a subject or in a given discipline or field. In bibliography, an attempt to list of *all* the works that meet the criteria for inclusion established by the bibliographer as to author, subject, publication type, currency, etc. The opposite of selective.

Compulsory Arbitration
The process in which representatives of organised labour and management, having reached an impasse in contract negotiations, submit their differences to a legally designated *arbitrator* or *arbitration board* authorised to hear arguments from both sides on unresolved issues and reach a final binding decision. Both sides are required to accept the outcome.

Compulsory Retirement
Mandatory retirement at a fixed age, usually established by the employer and stipulated in its personnel policy, a controversial legal issue in the United States. Organisatons with no mandatory retirement age may offer periodic retirement incentives to longtime employees, usually to reduce personnel costs.

Computer-Aided Retrieval (CAR)
The use of a computer to facilitate access to information stored in physical media, especially microfilm. CAR systems generally include an index, with or without a brief searchable description of the stored material. Once desired information has been identified, the system may be designed to: 1) automatically load microfilm or offline storage media containing the relevant materials, 2) locate the material within the appropriate container, and 3) display it to the user. Synonymous with *computer-assisted retrieval.*

Computer File
Data or programmes encoded in machine-readable format for processing by a computer. Data files stored on a computer are usually organised by topic or other characteristic in directories and subdirectories. Synonymous with *machine-readable data file.*

Computer-Generated Map
A map produced electronically by the manipulation of digital data files, using software that is usually part of a geographic information system (GIS), often involving the application of layers of data to a base map.

Computer Graphics
The art of creating or altering images by the use of a computer system, which may simulate drawings, paintings, photographs, etc.

Sophisticated computer graphics software is available for professionals. Computer graphics images are used in Web pages and in computer games and modeling, and to create special effects in motion pictures, video, and television.

Computer Literacy
The skills required to retrieve information efficiently and communicate effectively using computer hardware and software, based on a conceptual understanding of computer technology and how it can be used to accomplish specific tasks, including an awareness of its inherent limitations, as well as its advantages. Because hardware and software are progressively upgraded, an ongoing effort is required of the user to remain computer literate. Compare with information literacy.

Computer Output Microform (COM)
Computer output produced directly on microfiche or microfilm without ever having been printed on paper. A device called a *COM recorder* converts digital data into a form that can be read by the human eye before recording it on film.

Computer Output Microform Catalogue
A library catalogue produced directly on microfiche or microfilm from a file of machine-readable bibliographic records, using a special recording device called a *COM recorder*. *Comcatalogs* are more compact than card catalogs, but a microform reader-printer machine is required to display and print individual catalogue records. Prior to the development of online catalogs, this format was preferred for state, regional, and consortial union catalogs.

Computer Programme
A set of instructions written in a symbolic programming language, which enables a computer to process data, perform operations, and solve logical problems. Synonymous with software.

Computer-Assisted Retrieval
computer-aided retrieval.

Computus Text
A medieval manuscript or early printed book devoted to the calculation of time. The category includes calendars, Easter tables, almanacs, and various astronomical and astrological texts used in medicine and for other purposes, often illustrated with diagrams.

Concatenate
From the Latin *con* and *catenare*. To join two or more data fields within a record to create a single field. In a more general sense, to link items together in a series, for example, several related essays or long excerpts for publication in a collection.

Concept Album
An audiorecording containing a collection of musical pieces linked by a unifying theme, which can be instrumental, compositional, narrative, or lyrical.

Conte
The French term for a narrative tale or short story of the medieval period, originally dealing with events of an imaginative nature. In modern usage, the term is associated with any brief story of a few printed pages, regardless of genre.

Contemporary Binding
A binding made in the same time period as the text block, but not necessarily at the same time the text was printed or hand-copied. Older books are often rebound in the style of a later period and the original binding discarded when badly worn.

Content Designator
Characters used as tags, indicators, and subfield codes in a machine-readable bibliographic record to identify or provide additional information about the data elements of which it is composed.

Content Enrichment
Information added to the bibliographic description of an item not included in the original machine-readable record format, for example, an image of the front cover or dust jacket, table of contents, first page or first chapter, excerpts from or links to reviews, biographical information about the author and/or illustrator, etc. Synonymous with *record enrichment*.

Contents
All the divisions, chapters, articles, or individual works contained in a book, periodical, or other publication, usually listed in order of appearance with locators in the table of contents in the front matter of a book or on a page near the front of an issue of a periodical. Compare with content. Also refers to all the items physically contained in a box, binder, case, or holder designed to keep loose materials together, for example, a pamphlet file or portfolio.

Contents Note
A note in the bibliographic record for a book listing its major divisions or the works contained in it usually by title in order of appearance in the text.

Convention Discount
A discount given on orders placed at a publisher's exhibit booth during a conference or convention, usually 10 to 20 percent, with 15 percent the norm. Librarians sometimes compile lists of selected new books prior to attending a major library conference to be prepared to take advantage of the anticipated discount. At the end of the conference, display copies may be sold at an even deeper discount, especially if the dust jackets are no longer in perfect condition. Synonymous with *show discount*.

Cookbook
A type of how-to book that gives instructions for preparing food, including recipes for specific dishes, notes about tools and ingredients, weights and measures, and sometimes directory infor-mation on culinary suppliers.

Copyright Clearance Centre, Inc. (CCC)

The largest licenser of photocopy reproduction rights in the world, CCC was established in 1978 by a group of authors, publishers, and users of copyrighted material in an effort to facilitate compliance with U.S., copyright law. CCC manages the rights to over 1.75 million works and represents approximately 9,600 publishers and hundreds of thousands of individual authors and creators.

Core

The hard plastic spool around which motion picture film or raw stock is wound for storage. Film negatives are usually stored on cores rather than reels. The wider the diameter of the core, the less the film is stressed in winding. Wide hubs also reduce the tendency of film to curl.

Corner

The juncture of two edges of the cover of a book. Corners can be rounded, square, or mitered and are sometimes covered in contrasting material, such as leather or heavier cloth, for protection and decorative effect. To make *library corners,* the turn-in is folded; on *Dutch corners,* it is cut.

Corporate Author

A corporate body such as an association, company, government agency, institution, or non-profit organisaton in whose name a publication is issued. In libraries, the official name or title of such a body is used as the corporate name in cataloguing publications issued in its name. Compare with *personal author.*

Corporation Library

A type of special library established and maintained as a unit within an incorporated company or organisaton to meet the information needs of its employees and facilitate the achievement of its mission and goals. Some corporation libraries also serve as the repository for the official records of the organisaton. For internal security reasons, most corporation libraries are closed to the public except by special appointment. Synonymous with *company library.* Compare with business library.

Corrected Copy

A manuscript, typescript, or printed copy of a work bearing emendations, usually made by the author, editor, or a reader, often by hand, in the preparation of a new edition or printing.

Correctional Library

A type of special library maintained inside the walls of a prison or other correctional institution for the use of inmates and staff, usually managed by a *prison librarian.* The collection usually includes general interest titles for recreational reading, educational and vocational materials, and legal resources. Synonymous with *prison library.*

Corrupted Text

A text in which words or passages have been added, deleted, or altered to suggest a meaning other than the one intended by the original author. In medieval manuscripts, this was sometimes the result of accidental copying errors, but in modern texts tampering may be done by an individual or organisaton for other purposes, such as propaganda or public relations.

Creative Control
In artistic endeavor, especially media production, the authority to determine the appearance and/or sound of the final product. In motion pictures, the term generally refers to the authority to make the final cut, usually reserved for the director or producer. Disputes over creative control sometimes lead to an Alan Smithee credit. Synonymous with *artistic control.*

Creator
In archives, the individual or agency responsible for creating, receiving, accumulating, or otherwise producing records or documents for which some form of disposition must be made once their archival value has been appraised. Also refers to the person responsible for producing an original work of visual art.

Credential
A letter, certificate, degree, or other document certifying that a person, organisaton, or institution is qualified to fill a specific position, offer a service, or exercise authority in a given field. For librarians in the United States, the most desirable credential is the M.L.S. or M.L.I.S. degree from an ALA-accredited programme. The term is usually used in the plural: *credentials.*

Credenza
Originally, a sideboard from which a lord's food was tested for poison. In libraries, a furnishing that doubles as a bookshelf and study table, having two or three tiers of shelves under a flat surface low enough to accommodate a person standing or seated on a high stool or chair.

Cross-Index
A book index that covers the contents of more than one bibliographic item, such as a group of related reference works. The author and title indexes to the various parts of the Gale *Literary Criticism Series* are an example.

Crossover Recording
A music recording intended for a specific market segment, which achieves success in one or more additional markets, as reflected by its appearance on two or more record charts, tracking the popularity of different musical genres.

Cutaway
An illustration of a mechanical device, physical structure, or other enclosed system in which the outer covering or wall is shown removed to reveal inner details.

Cut Edges
The outer edges of the sections of a book, trimmed smooth in binding using a tool called a guillotine or its predecessor, the *plough.* Compare with deckle edges and uncut.

Cut Flush

Said of a book cover that has edges perfectly even with the edges of the leaves, the result of having been cut after attachment to the sections in binding. Most paperback books are cut flush. Synonymous with *flush boards* and *trimmed flush*. Compare with squares.

Cut-in Note

A side note printed wholly or partially inside the edge of a paragraph of text, instead of in the margin, usually in a typeface heavier and smaller in size than the text type. Synonymous with *cut-in side note, in-cut note,* and *let-in note.*

D

DAB
Digital Audio Broadcasting.

DACS
Describing Archives: A Content Standard.

Daguerrotype
Daguerreotype.

DAI
Dissertation Abstracts International.

Dailies
Rushes.

Daily
Issued on a daily basis, with the possible exception of Sundays. Also refers to a serial issued daily, especially a newspaper.

DAM
Digital asset management.

Dash on Entry
Dashed-on entry.

Data Dictionary
A set of data descriptions documenting the fields in the tables of a database system. A data dictionary may describe the *data type* and other physical characteristics of fields, enumerate allowed values, and specify appropriate usage.

Data Documentation Initiative (DDI)
A project of the social science community to develop a standardised XML markup and representation for codebooks, the primary metadata describing social science data sets.

Data Element
Element.

Data Stick
USB flash drive.

Date Line
The line printed at the beginning of a story in a newspaper or article published in a news-magazine, indicating the date and place of origin of news that is not local.

Day Book
In book-keeping, a record of the details of each day's receipts and expenditures in chronological order of occurrence, as distinct from a ledger in which financial transactions are recorded by account, as

credits and debits. ;&Also, a calendar, in print or electronic format, of forthcoming events. Also used in reference to a calendar designed as a personal organiser.

DB
Decibel.

DBMS
Database management system.

DBV
Deutscher Bibliotheksverband e.V.

DCC
Digital Compact Cassette.

DCMI
Dublin Core.

DDC
Dewey Decimal Classification.

DDI
Data Documentation Initiative.

DDS
Document Delivery Service.

De Jure Standard
A criterion or consistent manner of doing something, formally established in a deliberative process involving one or more professional organizations or industry groups, a government body, or a recognized standard-setting organization. It is not unusual for the development process to require negotiations in which a consensus is reached among parties with competing interests, especially when the financial stakes are high. Compliance is not compulsory, but may be made so by national regulations. The Z39.50 client-server protocol and Ethernet are examples of de jure standards. Compare with de facto standard.

Deaccession
The process of deleting from an accession record documents and other materials that are to be removed from a library collection. Also refers to any item so removed. The opposite of accession. ? In archives, the process of removing records or documents from official custody, undertaken after careful consideration, usually as the result of a decision to transfer the material to another custodian or because the legal owner desires its return or the material is found upon reappraisal to be of doubtful authenticity or inappropriate for the collection. Synonymous with permanent withdrawal.

Deblooping
Bloop.

Decennial
Issued every 10 years. Also refers to a serial publication issued every 10 years.

Decimal Point
The period used in the numeric portion of Library of Congress Classification notation and following the third digit of a class number in Dewey Decimal Classification to indicate that succeeding digits are to be treated as a decimal fraction.

Decorated Edges
Edge Decoration.

Decorated Spine
Spine decoration.

Dedication Miniature
Presentation miniature.

Deerskin
A soft leather made from the skin of a deer. Its use in bookbinding is rare. On medieval bindings, it was sometimes applied as an outer layer to protect the inner covering material.

Defacement
Damage to library materials by deliberate intent, rather than accident or neglect, including but not limited to cutting or tearing of pages and covers, underlining or highlighting portions of text, and writing or doodling in margins. Compare with vandalism.

Default
A value, option, or setting automatically selected in a hardware or software system in the absence of specific instructions from the user. The default setting may be displayed on the data entry screen to allow the user to see what action will be taken if no input is provided.

Dehumidify
Humidity.

Delayed Publication
A book or periodical not issued on schedule, usually due to delays in production. Also refers to new information not published in a timely manner, for whatever reason.

DEM
Digital Elevation Model.

Demand Publishing
On-demand publishing.

Demand-drive Acquisition
Patron-driven acquisition (PDA).

DEMCO
A commercial company that provides furniture, equipment, and supplies for the library, school, office, and home. DEMCO also provides periodical subscription services.

Deposit
Any addition to archival holdings, usually a transfer of materials from some other location or agency, but the term also applies to materials on loan for a period of fixed or indefinite duration. The *depositor* usually retains legal ownership and responsibility, except in the case of gifts.

Depth Curve
Isobath.

Derived Cataloguing
Copy cataloguing.

Derived Indexing
Derivative indexing.

Desktop Computer
Personal computer.

Detached Board
A condition in which the front or back board of a book has separated from the rest of the binding, usually along the joint. The remedy is rebinding. Compare with broken hinge.

Detached Pages
A condition in which one or more leaves of a bound publication have separated from the book block along the binding edge, a common problem in perfect bindings when

the adhesive has dried and cracked. A few loose pages can often be tipped in but when entire sections have detached, the remedy is re-binding.

DEU

Duplicates Exchange Union.

Deutscher Bibliogtheksverband e.V. (DBV)

Founded in 1949 with headquarters in Berlin, the DBV promotes library services and professional librarianship in Germany and publishes the journal *Bibliotheksdienst*.

Dewey Decimal Classification (DDC)

The Dewey Decimal Classification (DDC), or Dewey Decimal System, is a proprietary library classification system created by Melvil Dewey in 1876. It has been revised and expanded through 23 major editions, the latest issued in 2011. Dewey was responsible for all revisions until his death in 1931. A designation number, such as *Dewey 16* for the 16th edition, is given for each revision. A library assigns a DDC number that unambiguously locates a particular volume to within a short length of shelving, which makes it easy to find any particular book and return it to its proper place on the library shelves. The system is used in 200,000 libraries in at least 135 countries.

Diacetate

Cellulose diacetate.

Diamond

In bookbinding, an ornament in the shape of a rhombus, usually built up of small massed tools done in blind, ink, or gold. A *lozenge* is a rhombus-shaped decorative design with one axis longer than the other.

Digital Book

Electronic book.

Digital Collection

A collection of library or archival materials converted to machine readable format for preservation or to provide electronic access

Digital Library

A library in which a significant proportion of the resources are available in machine readable format, accessible by means of computers. The digital content may be locally held or accessed remotely via computer networks.

Digital Library of Information Science and Technology

DLIST.

Digital Media

Multimedia.

Digital Object

In the technical sense, a type of data structure consisting of digital content, a unique identifier for the content, and other data about the content, for example, rights metadata.

Digital Subscriber Line

DSL.

Digital Television

DTV.

Digital Video Recorder

DVR.

Digital Videodisc

DVD.

Digital Watermark

Watermark.

Ding

A nick or dent that has left a visible impression on the covers or dust jacket of a book, sometimes the result of careless handling or storage.

Directive

An order, regulation, bulletin, or similar communication of instructions issued in writing, usually by a central office, military command, or other authority, with the expectation of compliance. Military directives may be classified at time of issuance.

Director

The person who has overall responsibility for controlling and supervising the performance of a work written for stage or screen, whose name appears in the credits at the beginning or end of a motion picture, video-recording, or television programme and is indicated in the note area of the bibliographic record representing the work in the library catalogue. Compare with producer, and screenwriter.

Director's Cut

After initial shooting is completed, the film director refines the editor's cut to make the film an expression of his or her artistic vision. Under rules established by the Directors Guild of America (DGA), directors have at least ten weeks after completion of primary shooting to prepare their first cut. If additional shooting is required, the editing process may take longer.

Directory of Open Access Journals (DOAJ)

Launched in May 2003 from Lund University in Sweden, *DOAJ* lists over 1,000 fully peer reviewed open access journals reporting original research in the sciences, social sciences, and humanities in all languages, with records that can be easily downloaded by librarians and entered in an online catalogue. Approximately 25 percent of the journals are searchable at the article level.

Dirty Proof

In printing, a proof of typeset copy containing many errors or one returned to the printer heavily corrected. A *clean proof* contains no errors or corrections.

Disaster

An unexpected event that puts library or archival collections at risk of serious damage or destruction, the most catastrophic being fire, flood, and earthquake. Well prepared libraries have a disaster plan in place for handling various kinds of emergencies. disaster preparedness.

Disbound

A book or other printed publication from which a previous binding has been removed, usually in preparation for rebinding, part of the process called pulling.

Disc

A generic term used in computing to distinguish read-only digital storage media from those that are rewritable. Also, an alternate spelling of disk.

Discharge
In circulation, to cancel the record of a loan upon return of the borrowed item and payment of any overdue fine. Compare with charge.

Disclaimer
A legal notice posted on a Web page, appended to an e-mail message, given on a product, or provided with a service informing the reader or consumer that the host or producer does not guarantee and cannot be held responsible for all aspects of the content or performance.

Disclosure-free Extract
A copy of a record made available for public use from which information has been selectively removed in compliance with provisions of open records or privacy laws. In the United States, this means the exclusion of all information exempted under the *Freedom of Information Act (FOIA)* and the *Privacy Act* of 1974. Synonymous with *public use file*.

Discography
A list or catalogue of audio recordings, usually of works by a specific composer or performer, in a certain style or genre, or of a specific time period. Each entry in a discography provides some or all of the following descriptive elements: title of work, name of and performer(s), date of recording, name of manufacturer, manufacturer's catalogue number, and release date

Discontinuation
In Dewey Decimal Classification (DDC), the shifting of a topic or the entire contents of a class number to a more general number in the same hierarchy, or the complete removal of the topic or number from the schedule, usually because the current literature on the topic or concept has dwindled significantly or because the distinction represented by the number is no longer valid or recognised in the field. A note is added to explain the shift or removal, and the discontinued number is enclosed in square brackets.

Discontinued Number
In Dewey Decimal Classification (DDC), a class number from an earlier edition no longer used, indicated at the appropriate location in the schedules by a note to "class in" a more general number. A discontinued number is enclosed in square brackets.

Discontinued
A serial publication for which a library subscription or continuation order has ended. In the catalogue record for the title, the library's holdings are indicated in a closed entry.

Discovery Tool
A single interface, providing integrated access to the multiple information resources to which a library has rights. Discovery systems use consolidated subject indexing and metadata. Search results are generally deduped and relevance ranked.

Discussion List
Mailing list.

Discussion Paper
Working paper.

Disinformation
The deliberate, often covert, dissemination of erroneous information, usually with the intention of influencing by deception the actions or opinions of another, a technique used in foreign relations and armed conflict to mislead an adversary. Compare with misinformation.

Disintermediation
Elimination of the mediator or "middleman." In the delivery of information services, the need for professional assistance is minimized in user friendly systems designed to facilitate end-user searching.

Disk
A generic term used in computing for a digital storage medium that is rewritable, as opposed to read-only. Compare with disc.

Disk Drive
In computing, a generic term for the hardware component that physically manipulates a specific type of magnetic disk, allowing the user to read data from and write data to it. Disk drives can be internal or external. Also spelled *disc drive*.

Diskette
Floppy disk.

Display Matter
Any printed matter that is not part of the text of a work, including illustrations, headings, captions, printer's ornaments, etc. To distinguish it from body matter, textual display matter is set in type of a different size and/or font.

Display Panel
In medieval manuscripts, a decorative section of a page, usually rectangular in shape, containing display script, often following an ornamented initial letter.

Disposal
In U.S., government archives, the destruction of non-current records that are no longer needed. Also used synonymously with disposition.

Disposition
The manner in which the non-current records of an agency or individual are handled once their utility has been appraised, whether stored in a repository in their original format, reproduced and stored on microform, sold, donated, or destroyed. Compare with disposal.

Distance Education
Distance learning.

Distance Learning Section (DLS)
The section of the Association of College and Research Libraries (ACRL) within the American Library Association (ALA) that provides leadership, support, and new ideas for librarians involved in all aspects of distance learning.

Distinctive Title
A title that is unique to a specific work. Distinctiveness of title is important in registering copyright and makes the entry for a document easier to retrieve from a library catalogue or other finding tool in a search by title.

Distortion
Warping.

Distribution Copy
In reprography, a microform copy from which additional copies of equal legibility can be reproduced.

Distribution Imprint
The statement printed on the verso of the title page of a book giving the official name(s) of the distri- butor(s) from which copies can be obtained, as distinct from the imprint of the publisher that issued the edition or the printer responsible for printing the edition.

Distribution
The sale, lease, loan, syndication, and rental of moving image works or recordings for any purpose, including exhibition. Also, the sale of a new book or edition by a publisher other than the company that issued the title, for example, by a publisher in another country.

Dit
In old French literature, a short poem or story in verse, often treating a homely subject in a didactic or satirical manner. In medieval manuscripts, collections of dits are sometimes interspersed with lyric and musical pieces, as in this example by the 14th-century poet and composer Guillaume de Machaut.

Diversity
Inclusiveness with regard to differences in age, gender, sexual orientation, religious belief, and ethnic, racial, or cultural background within a given population. In the United States, libraries strive to achieve diversity in library school admissions, hiring, collection development, services, and programmes.

Divide-like Note
A note added to a heading in a classification schedule to inform the cataloguerr that the heading is subdivided in the same way as another heading in the same schedule.

Divinity Circuit
Circuit edges.

DLC
Depository Library Council.

DLF
Digital Library Federation.

DLG
Digital line graph.

DLI
Digital Libraries Initiative.

DMCA
Digital Millennium Copy-right Act.

DML
Digital media lab.

DNS
Domain Name System.

DOAJ
Directory of Open Access Journals.

Doctored
A book that has been altered from its original condition, usually as a consequence of mending, repairs, restoration, or the addition or removal of parts. Compare with as issued.

Document Type
Publication type.

Documentary Fiction
Faction.

Dog Tooth
Agate.

Dog-eared
The condition of a book that shows definite signs of wear on the corners, especially pages that have been folded down at a corner to mark the reader's place.

DOI
Digital Object Identifier.

Door Stop
Library slang for a piece of equipment so obsolete that it cannot be given away. Such items are usually consigned to a storage room in the basement until renovation or a move into a new facility makes disposal unavoidable.

DOP
Digital Ortho Photograph

DOQ
Digital orthophoto quadrangle.

DOQQ
An Abbreviation of *Digital Orthophoto Quarter-quadrangle.*

Dot
A full stop used to divide the elements of an Internet address.

Dotting
Rubrication.

Double Column
A book or other publication in which the text is set to half the width of a page, usually with a blank space or rule dividing the two columns, a format commonly used in bibles, dictionaries, encyclopaedias, and other large format reference works..

Double Fold
Double leaf.

Double Hemisphere Map
A map representing the entire surface of the earth or another celestial body, divided into two hemispheres, usually displaying the eastern hemisphere on the right and the western hemisphere on the left, sometimes connected down the centre.

Double Spread
Text and/or illustration printed across facing pages in a book or other publication, as if on a single page, usually for visual effect.

DPI
Dots Per Inch.

DPLA
Digital Public Library of America.

DPRA
Digital Performance Right in Sound Recordings Act of 1995

Dramatic Musical Work
A dramatic work that includes music as an integral part of the production. The category includes operas and operettas, musical plays and shows, and revues.

DRG
Digital Raster Graphic.

Drill
A strong, durable, coarse cotton fabric with a strong diagonal weave, some-times used in bookbinding. Baseball caps and khaki uniforms are often made of drill.

DRM
Digital Rights Management.

DRM-free
Computer files without digital rights management (DRM) or re-

strictions on simultaneous use, printing, or downloading of content after it is sold. Music advertised as DRM-free is generally less expensive, but may also be of lower quality.

Drop Spine Box
A made-to-measure book box, used mainly in preservation, with a spine that falls away on opening to provide access to the spine of the enclosed volume, allowing it to be removed without damage.

Drop
A telecommunication outlet in a library or other facility usually consisting of a voice jack and at least one data jack to allow users to physically connect to a computer network.

Drop-down Title
The shortened version of the title of a book, printed on the first page of the text, usually the same as the running title. Compare with caption title.

Dry Cleaning
In conservation, surface cleaning by mechanical means as opposed to the use of water or chemical agents.

DTB
Digital Talking Book

DTD
Document Type Definition.

DTP
Desktop Publishing.

Duodecimo (12mo)
A book, approximately eight inches in height, made by folding a full sheet of book paper to form signatures of 12 leaves.

Dupe Negative
Duplicate negative.

Durable Paper
Permanent paper.

Dwarf Book
Bibelot.

Dwell
In tooling, the length of time the heated finishing tool is in contact with the leather or cloth surface being decorated.

Dynamic Map
A map on which flow lines and/or arrows of variable width are used to indicate the amount and direction of movement, exchange, action, or change in conditions.

E

EAD
Encoded Archival Description.

Ear
A small decorative design printed on either side of the title in the flag at the head of the front page of a newspaper. Also refers to a small projection found on the upper-right-hand edge of the lower-case "g" in some type-faces.

Earliest Entry
A method of catalogueing serials that have under-gone title changes, in which the bibliographic description is based on the earliest issue and all subsequent titles are recorded as notes in the single bibliographic record. This convention was followed in the United States in the early part of the 20th century but eventually replaced, first by latest entry catalogueing in the *ALA Rules* and then by successive entry catalogueing in *AACR*.

Early Adopter
A person, organisation, or institution that begins using a new technology at or near the time of its introduction in the market place, rather than waiting to see if it will be successful.

Early Copy
Advance copy.

Early Journal
A journal that began publication during the 17th, 18th, or 19th century. In a library, copies of early periodicals may be stored in special collections, or accessible in digital format or on microform, to protect the originals from damage. The Bodleian Library at the University of Oxford provides online access to the *Internet Library of Early Journals*.

Easel Binding
A type of comb or spiral binding designed with rigid extended covers that can be folded back to form the base of a triangle, allowing the book or notebook to stand upright when opened, with the spine across the top. The text is printed parallel with the spine, and the pages are turned up and over, instead of from side to side.

Easel
A metal, wood, or plastic rack or stand on a tripod base designed to

allow an open book or periodical to be displayed face-out as part of an exhibit or presentation. Large models are used to display flip charts in presentations.

Easy Book
A heavily illustrated book with limited text written to appeal to the interests and reading ability of children from preschool to third grade, usually shelved in a separate section of a school library or children's room in a public library. Synonymous with *easy reader*.

Easy Reader
Easy book.

e-book
Electronic book.

e-book Reader
A lightweight, portable battery-operated electronic device, similar in form to a tablet computer, designed primarily for reading books and periodicals downloaded in digitalformat (*example*: Kindle from Amazon.com). Although tablet computer screens are generally faster, e-book readers have superior text readability, achieved by the use of electronic paper display technology. Some e-book readers come with an internal dictionary, built-in Wi-Fi, text-to-speech capability, and a Web browser. Price depends on storage capacity and special features. Library compatible e-book readers, which can be used to borrow e-books from public libraries, typically support EPUB and/orPDF formats with digital rights management (DRM) protection. Abbreviated *e-reader*. Also spelled *ebook reader*.

EBSCO
A commercial company that provides subscription management services, electronic journal access, online bibliographic and full-text databases, and an online book ordering service to libraries and related institutions. EBSCO is currently one of the three leading aggregators of journals available in electronic full-text.

EBSS
Education and Behavioural Sciences Section.

E-CD
Enhanced CD.

e-collection
Digital collection.

e-conference
Mailing list.

Ecrasé Leather
Leather used in book-binding that has been mechanically crushed or flattened to give its surface a particular grain and then highly polished.

Edgar Allan Poe Awards
A series of literary awards given annually by Mystery Writers of America in the mystery fiction genre. Separate awards are given for best novel, best first novel by an American author, best paperback original, best critical/biographical work, best fact crime story, best short story, best work for young adults, best work for juveniles, best television episode teleplay, and best motion picture screenplay.

Edge Decoration
Ornamentation applied to one or more of the trimmed edges of the sections of a book, a general term term that includes gilding, gauffering, edge painting, marbling, sprinkling, staining, daubing, etc.

Edge Painting
A picture drawn or painted on the edges of the sections of a book with its leaves closed, a common form of decoration in the Middle Ages. On some books, painting was done on all three edges but on most only on the fore-edge.

Edge Title
A title written in ink on one or more edges of the sections of a book, not by the binder but by the owner. This method of marking the outside of a volume was used until the 16th century when books began to be shelved upright with the spine out, instead of flat with one of the edges facing out.

Edge
The outermost limit of the cover or sections of a book, or of one of its leaves, or of an unbound sheet. The fore-edge is opposite the binding edge of the text block. The other two edges are the head and tail.

Edge-worn
A condition in which the covering material along one or more edges of a bound volume appears roughened or has been completely worn away by abrasion, exposing the edges of the boards, more common on the tail edge than the fore-edge, and rare on the top edge.

EDI
Electronic Data Interchange.

Edible Book
An object made of ingredients that can be consumed and digested as food, which has the appearance of a book or makes reference to a book title, format, or structure, for example, a "rare book" made of thin slices of roast beef bound together by a scallion.

Editio Princeps
Latin for "original edition." Usually reserved for the first printed edition of a work previously available only in manuscript form. For other works, the term *first edition* is preferred in analytical bibliography and the antiquarian book trade.

Edition Area
In library catalogueing, the area of bibliographic description in which information pertaining to the edition is entered, usually by ordinal number and/or description, including the edition statement and statements of responsibility relating to the edition. In the MARC record, these data elements are given in field 250.

Edition Binding
Publisher's binding.

Editorial Content
The portions of a newspaper or periodical containing content controlled by the editor or editorial board, as opposed to the space devoted to advertisements, notices and announcements, etc.

Editorial Control
The assurance of quality provided

in publishing by the process of manuscript selection and editing. In scholarly publishing, control of editorial content is usually maintained through peer review. Editorial control is largely absent on the Internet where selfpublishing is the norm.

Editorialise
To put forth an opinion or position on a subject, usually with intent to persuade the listener or reader to adopt or at least consider the point of view of the speaker or writer. Also, to inject personal opinions or comments into an otherwise objective discussion or account, a technique used in essays, editorials, columns, letters to the editor, and other forms of persuasive writing but considered inappropriate in scholarly publication and in works of fiction.

Editorial Page
Editorial.

Editor's Cut
The first of several stages in the editing of a film, usually commenced while shooting is still underway, based on discussions between editor and director at the screening of "dailies", and generally longer than the final cut.

Education and Behavioural Sciences Section (EBSS)
The section of the Association of College and Research Libraries (ACRL) within the American Library Association (ALA) devoted to serving the interests of education and behavioural sciences librarians. Formed in 1968, EBSS currently has about 1,000 members concerned with issues related to bibliographic instruction, collection development, the applications of technology, library administration, and communication of research findings in education and behavioural sciences librarianship.

Educational Film
A motion picture of any length made for instructional or training purposes, usually to teach the viewer about a given subject or skill, especially one made to be viewed in the classroom. Synonymous with *instructional film.*

Educational Videotape
A videotape designed and marketed to schools and libraries as a teaching tool, sometimes for use in conjunction with a specific curriculum unit. Educational videos tend to be priced higher than feature films and mass market non-fiction videos.

EFF
Electronic Frontier Foundation.

Eggshell
A smooth, slightly pitted finish given to uncoated paper or board that produces a soft, non-glossy surface resembling the shell of a bird's egg. Most antique papers have this type of finish.

Eighteenth Century Short-Title Catalogueue
English Short-Title Catalogueue.

e-journal
Electronic journal.

Election Ticket
A slip of paper, usually long and

narrow, on which are printed the names of all the candidates officially endorsed as representing a particular political party in a specific election, along with the titles of the offices sought. As documentary evidence, election tickets are of considerable interest to historians. The term is also used collectively in reference to the candidates themselves.

Electronic Book
A digital version of a traditional print book designed to be read on a personal computer or e-book reader. Although the first hypertext novel was published in 1987 (*Afternoon, A Story* by Michael Joyce), electronic books did not capture public attention until the online publication of Stephen King's novella *Riding the Bullet* in March 2000. Within 24 hours, the text had been downloaded by 400,000 computer users. Some libraries offer access to electronic books through the online catalog. A universally accepted format and simple delivery system are needed. Click here to browse the *Yahoo!* list of electronic book sites or try *Digital Book Index*. Synonymous with *digital book, e-book, ebook*, and *online book*.

Electronic Collection
Digital collection.

Electronic Conference
Mailing list.

Electronic Discussion List
Mailing list.

Electronic Document Delivery
The transfer of information traditionally recorded in a physical medium to the user electronically, usually via e-mail or the World Wide Web. Libraries employ digital technology to deliver the information contained in documents and files placed on reserve and requested via interlibrary loan.

Electronic Frontier Foundation (EFF)
A group of people who share a passionate commitment to defending digital information, innovation, and technology from attempts by government and business to restrict freedom of expression. Current key issues include censorship, copyright law, digital rights management, *DMCA*, evoting, file sharing, privacy, RFID, spam, and the *USA Patriot Act*.

Electronic Mail
e-mail.

Electronic Newsletter
A newsletter published online, usually via the Internet, with or without a print counterpart, for example, *ALSConnect*, the newsletter of the Association for Library Service to Children, and *Children's Bookshelf* from *Publishers Weekly*.

Electronic Preservation
Digital preservation.

Electronic Records
Bibliographic or archival records stored on a medium, such as magnetic tape/disk or optical disk, that requires computer equipment for retrieval and processing. Compare with machinereadable records.

Electronic Reference
Digital reference.

Elegy

In classical literature, a lyric poem composed in couplets of alternating hexameter and pentameter lines, a form known as *elegiac meter*. In English literature through the 17th century, a song or poem of melancholy or solemn contemplation. In contemporary usage, a formal poem lamenting the death of a person or the phenomenon of mortality in general. Compare with eulogy.

Elephant Folio

In non-specialty publishing, a large folio, usually about 23 × 14 inches in size. The term *double elephant folio* refers to the very large paper size used in printing works such as *Birds of America* by John James Audubon. Compare with atlas folio.

Elhi Book

A term used in the educational book trade in the United States to refer to a textbook published specifically for elementary and high school students, usually revised and updated regularly by publishers anxious to retain market share. In a more general sense, *any* book published for elementary and/or high school age readers. Also spelled*el-hi*.

El-hi Book

Elhi book.

El-Hi Textbooks and Serials in Print

A reference serial published by Bowker since, 1985, indexing elementary and high school textbooks currently in print, by author, title, and a classified list of subjects. Textbooks published in series are indexed separately. Elhi serials are indexed by subject and title. ISSN: 0000-0825. Former titles: *Textbooks in Print* and *El-Hi Textbooks in Print*.

Elision

From the Latin *elisio*, meaning "a striking out." The omission of a vowel or silent consonant at the beginning or in the middle of a word or the omission of a vowel, consonant, or syllable in the pronunciation of a word or phrase. In orthography, the omission is indicated by an apostrophe. Compare with contraction.

Ellipsis

The use of square brackets ([]) or three full points (. . .) or a series of asterisks (****) in handwritten or printed text to indicate the omission or suppression of a word or words. Often used to reduce the length of a quotation without altering its meaning or significance. Compare with elision.

e-magazine

Electronic magazine.

e-mail Address

A string of characters used to route messages from one computer to another over a network governed by the Internet protocol for electronic mail.

Embargo

The period during which the articles published in a periodical are not available in online full-text from a journal aggregator, usually the most recent one to three years. Journal publishers have established such periods to prevent libraries from canceling print subscriptions. In most periodical databases, this restriction applies only to a small proportion of the titles indexed, but in *JSTOR* nearly all the journals are embargoed. Not to be confused with an exclusive agreement between a journal publisher and an aggregator.

Emblem
A moral fable, allegory, or abstract quality expressed pictorially, sometimes with an accompanying motto or verse. Also, a figure of an object representing symbolically a person, family, people, or nation, as on a heraldic device or image of a saint or hero.

Emblematic Decoration
Pictorial motifs used in the manner of a badge in bookbinding and manuscripts to indicate the name or identity of the author, the owner of the volume, its country of origin or ownership, or its subject content.

Embossed Print
A raised graphic image made by forcing paper into low relief by pressing it into the hollows in a printing plate or block, often with the use of little or no ink. Compare with cast paper print.

Embossed
A decorative design or lettering raised in bas-relief above the surface of a sheet or page, or the cover of a book, an effect produced by the use of printing or stamping dies. Employed throughout the history of binding and printing, embossing is a mechanical technique now used mainly in the production of art books, elegant greeting cards, and other decorative items.

Embrittled
Brittle.

Emendation
Correction or improve-ment, especially of a literary or artistic work or written document, by alteration of the text, whether done by the author or another person, such as an editor. Also, a specific instance of such an alteration.

Emergency Plan
A set of guidelines or steps prepared in advance to help the staff of a library deal with unusual occurr-ences that may tempo-rarily disrupt normal operations but are not usually disastrous. Com-pare with contingency plan and disaster plan.

e-metrics
The systematic definition, collection, and analysis of statistical data about networked environments and the use of electronic resources, particularly useful in e-commerce. The Association of Research Libraries (ARL) has undertaken an E-Metrics Project for academic libraries.

EMIERT
Ethnic and Multicultural Information Exchange Round Table.

Emmy Award
One of several awards given annually in the United States by the Academy of Television Arts and

Sciences for outstanding programming in news and documen-taries, sports, and daytime television.

Emoticon

An abbreviation of the term *emotional icon*.

Encaustum

From the Latin *encausticus*, meaning "burnt in." A purplish-black, highly durable ink made from a mixture of iron salts and gallic acid, preferred by Irish and Anglo-Saxon scribes during the early Middle Ages because it bonded well with the surface of parchment or vellum and was not grainy, compared to ink made from lampblack. Also spelled *incaustum*.

Enchiridion

From the Greek word for "handbook," a volume of a size that can be easily carried in a person's hand. In the Christian religious tradition, a manual of devotions.

Encoded Archival Description (EAD)

The EAD Document Type Definition (DTD) is a non-proprietary standard for encoding in Standard Generalised Markup Language (SGML) or Extensible Markup Language (XML) the finding aids used in archives, libraries, museums, and other repositories of manuscripts and primary sources to facilitate use of their materials. EAD was developed in 1993 on the initiative of the UC Berkeley Library and is maintained by the Library of Congress, in partnership with the Society of American Archivists.

Encoding Level

One of several modes of library catalogueing recognised by the Library of Congress as appropriate, depending on a library's resources and needs and the amount of descriptive detail available to the cataloguer. The levels are: full level, core level, minimal level, collection level, and copy catalogueing.

Encoding

In information retrieval, the process of converting a message or data into electronic signals that can be processed by a computer or transmitted over a communications channel. The opposite of *decoding*. Compare with encryption.

Encryption

The process of converting data contained in a message into a secret code prior to transmission via public telecommunication channels to make the content incomprehensible to all but authorised recipient. In computing, the modification is often done by means of a transformation algorithm. Encryption is a security measure taken to protect confi-dential information, such as credit card numbers used in online business transactions and to ensure that only those who have paid for a fee-based service can obtain it.

Encumbrance

In library acquisitions, an amount charged against a budgetary fund to cover a prior commitment to purchase materials, equipment, services, or supplies, removed once full payment is made or the order is canceled.

Encumbrances are tracked by the library to prevent over expenditure.

End Matter

Back matter.

End Support

Bookend.

Endangered

In libraries and archives, a category of item, or group of items, whose continued existence is threatened, usually by deterioration or the obsolescence of equipment required to read the format. Preservation may require conversion to a format of greater permanence. Synonymous with *at risk*.

Endbands

A collective term for the protective headband and tailband attached to the top and bottom of the spine of a book with a sewn binding. Originally hand worked, they consisted of a core of leather, parchment, cord, rolled paper, or cane covered in decorative linen or silk embroidery and sewn to the quires, with the ends laced into the boards. In modern binding, they are machine made and simply glued on.

Endnote

A statement printed at the end of a chapter or book to explain a point in the text, indicate the basis of an assertion, or cite the source of a concept, idea, quotation, or piece of factual information. Like footnotes, endnotes are numbered, usually in superscript, and listed in the sequence in which they appear in the text. Compare with in text citation.

Endowment

A permanent fund accumulated by an institution over an extended period consisting of gifts and bequests invested to provide an ongoing return, all or a portion of which is expended, sometimes for purposes specified by the donor, leaving the principal intact to generate further income. A library may be separately endowed or share in the endowment of its parent institution.

Endpaper

In bookbinding, a sheet of thick, strong paper folded down the center, one-half of which is pasted to the inside of the front or back board, the other half forming the first or last leaf, to protect the text from the boards and counteract the pull of the cover on the boards. The fold in each endpaper functions as a hinge, joining the text block to the cover and allowing the attached board to swing open and closed. For extra strength, some books have *double endpapers*.

In early printed books, binding waste was sometimes used for endpapers, as in this example. From the 17th century on, decorated endpapers were used in hand-binding.

End-user Search

In information retrieval, a literature search conducted by the person who actually intends to use the results, as opposed to a mediated search conducted by a trained specialist on behalf of the user.

End-user

In information retrieval, the person

or persons for whom a mediated literature search is conducted and to whom the results are delivered. In a more general sense, the person for whom *any* search requiring the use of library resources or other information services is performed.

e-newsletter
Electronic newsletter.

Engraved Edition
An edition of a book or other publication printed from engraved plates, rather than by the setting of movable type, a process generally reserved for limited editions due to the additional expense. From the late 16th to the early 20th century, engraving was also one of the methods used to print music scores. Engraving services are still available to composers and song-writers.

Engraving
An illustration or print made from a design incised with a sharp, pointed tool called a *burin* or *graver* on the surface of a metal plate or hardwood block. The lines are inked and an impression made by pressing a sheet of paper or some other printing surface against the plate, in a process known as intaglio. *Views in Glasgow* is a set of twenty metal engravings published in 1843 by Allan and Ferguson.

Enhanced CD (E-CD)
A certification mark of the Recording Industry Association of America (RIAA) for various technologies that combine audio-recording with other digital information for use in compact disc and CD-ROM players. Also known as *CD Extra* and *CD Plus*.

Enlarged Edition
Expanded edition.

Enlargement
A reproduction or copy produced on a larger scale than the original. Some photocopiers have the capacity to enlarge an original. The opposite of reduction. Synonymous, in photography, with blowup.

Enlargement Print
Blowup.

Ensemble Work
A musical work composed for more than one voice and/or instrument singing or playing together, for example, soprano and piano, or a string quartet.

Entry Level
Employment at the lowest grade in a system of classified positions, suitable for candidates who are beginning their careers and lack experience. Promotion usually depends on a vacancy occurring at a higher grade or classification, rather than on the development of the initial position into one requiring greater skill or responsibility. Synonymous with *entrance level*.

Entrance Level
Entry level.

Entry
A single record in the library catalogue representing an item contained in one of its collections.

Entry Word
The word under which a record in

a catalogue, index, or bibliography is filed and searched, usually the first word of the heading, initial articles excluded. In retrieving information from an online catalogue or bibliographic database, the order of terms typed as input may determine the success or failure of a search by author, title, subject heading, or descriptor, but in a keywords search, word order should not affect results if Boolean logic is correctly used. Synonymous with *filing word.*

Enumeration

A naming or counting of items, one by one, as in a list, in any amount of detail but without systematic arrangement. Also, the volume numbering of a serial issue.

Enumerative Classification

A classification system in which each subject is developed to the point of indivisibility and a notation assigned for every subdivision. Compare with synthetic classification.

Environmental Control

In the preservation of library and archival collections, creating and maintaining hospitable storage conditions is the most effective strategy for promoting the longevity of materials. Deterioration of paper, leather, cloth, plastic, etc., can be dramatically reduced by controlling temperature, relative humidity, light, and air quality in storage. Monitoring devices should be installed to ensure that materials remain cool and dry. Low illumination, ventilation that removes atmospheric pollutants, and effective pest management are also essential.

EP

Extended Play.

Ephemera Society of America

Established in 1980, The Ephemera Society of America is an association of individuals and collectors who have an interest in the printed materials of everyday life, which are ordinarily short-lived, having little or no permanent value when issued, but which may be worth preserving as examples of cultural history. The Society has published *Ephemera Journal* since, 1987 and also issues the quarterly *Ephemera Newsletter.*

Epigram

In the classical period, an inscription or epitaph, but in modern usage a tersely witty, often antithetical saying, ingeniously composed in prose or verse, delivered with aplomb to make a point in a manner calculated to enhance one's reputation in the company of people who value feats of intellectual and literary virtuosity. The satirical form, established in ancient Rome by Martial was cultivated in England from the late 16th to the early 20th century.

Epigraph

A brief quotation or motto included in the front matter of a book, usually following the dedication, or at the beginning of each chapter, suggesting an idea or theme that the author intends to develop more fully in the following text.

Epilogue

A part added as a conclusion at the close of a literary work, for example, the statement of the moral at the end of a fable. Compare with afterword.

The term also refers to the final section of a speech, also called the *peroration*, and to a brief speech delivered at the end of a dramatic performance, requesting the approval of audience and critics.

Episode

A single segment of a television series or miniseries, sometimes released on VHS or DVD in a collection with others originally broadcast during the same season, for example, "The Doorbell Rang" in the Nero Wolfe series, originally seen on the A&E network, with Timothy Hutton and Maury Chaykin in the lead roles.

Episodic

A literary work consisting of a number of more or less self-contained but loosely connected incidents strung together by the author to form a narrative.

Epistemology

From the Greek *episteme* and *logos*, the branch of philosophy devoted to the theoretical study of the nature, methods, and validity of human knowledge, including the relationship between the knower, the known, and the process of knowing.

Epistle

A composition in poetry or prose written in the form of a letter so elegant in style that it is considered a literary work worthy of publication, for example, the epistles of Cicero, Horace, Ovid, and Pliny.

Epistolary

A liturgical book containing readings for the Mass from the *Epistles* of the New Testament and sometimes from other books of the Bible, arranged according to the liturgical year.

Epistolary Novel

A form of novel that reached its greatest popularity during the 18th century, in which the narrative is developed by the author in a series of letters. Sometimes a novelist begins a work in epistolary style, then switches to conventional narrative.

Epistolary Work

A work of fiction or non-fiction based, in whole or in part, on real or imaginary letters and/or diary entries.

Epitaph

From the Greek *epi* and *taphos*, a brief valedictory verse on the life and death of a person, composed as an inscription on a grave marker, sometimes by the deceased before death. Epitaphs are usually complimentary but may be humorous or ironic. One of the most famous was written by Simonides of Ceos commemorating the 300 warriors who died at Thermopylae:

- Go, tell the Lacedai-monians, passer-by,
- That here obedient to their laws we lie.

Epithalamium

From the Greek *epi* and *thalamos*. A celebratory song or poem, often in sonnet form, in honour of a bride or groom or both, usually praising their virtues, describing the events of the wedding day, and wishing them good fortune in married life.

Epitome

A statement of the essence of a subject in the briefest possible form. Also refers to a very brief but accurate written statement of the main points of a work, usually prepared by a person other than the author.

Eponym

A single name under which several authors are published. Also, the name of a person or character so closely associated with a quality, process, or activity that the name is used in signifying it.

e-preservation

A shortened form of *electronic preservation.*

e-print

A preprint in digital format, distributed electronically. The use of e-print servers to provide access to collections of preprints is a comparatively new mode of scholarly communication, developed in the physical sciences to circumvent the delays and high cost of commercial publishing. One of the earliest and best-known e-print repositories was created at the Los Alamos National Laboratory in New Mexico. The Open Archives Initiative (OAI) aims to facilitate the retrieval of scholarly papers from disparate digital archives. Also spelled *eprint*.

EPUB

An abbreviation of electronic publication. A free and open standard e-book file format, adopted by the International Digital Publishing Forum (IDPF) in September 2007 to supersede the Open eBook Standard, EPUB enables text to be optimised for a particular display device or reading system by allowing word wrap and resizing. It also features embedded metadata, DRM support, and CSS styling. File extension is*.epub*. Also spelled *epub, ePub, EPub,* or *ePUB.*

e-publication

Electronic publication.

e-publishing

Electronic publishing.

Equal Area Projection

In cartography, a systematic representation of the graticule on which the area of any feature on the map or chart is related to the area of the corresponding feature on a globe or on the surface of the earth by a constant scaling factor. The Lambert Azimuthal Equal Area and Albers Equal Area Conic are examples of equal area projections.

Equidistant Projection

In cartography, a systematic representation of the graticule on which the distances between one or two points and every other point on the map or chart differ from the corresponding distances on the globe or on the surface of the earth by only a constant scaling factor. The Azimuthal Equidistant and the Cylindrical Equidistant are examples of equidistant projections.

Equivalence Table
A list in numerical order of the classes altered in a complete or extensive revision of Dewey Decimal Classification (DDC), giving the class number in the current edition and its equivalent in the preceding edition.

Erasure
Names or words written, stamped, or printed in a book and subsequently removed, usually with a gum eraser if in pencil or by some other abrasive means if in ink. Erasures almost always decrease the value of an item in the used book market. John Carter warns in *ABC for Book Collectors* that era-sures near the center of the title page, or in the upper half of the verso of the title page, should be regarded with suspicion because the intent may have been to remove the words *Second Edition* from the imprint.

e-reference
Digital reference.

ERes
Electronic reserves.

e-reserves
Electronic reserves.

e-resource
Electronic resource.

Ergonomics
The systematic study of the relationship between people and the environment in which they work, serving as the basis for the design and arrangement of equipment, furnishings, and workspaces with the aim of increasing productivity and avoiding negative effects on safety, health, comfort, and efficiency. Synonymous with *human engineering*.

ERM
Electronic resources management.

Erotica
Works containing sexual content calculated to stimulate the passions of the reader but that also have some artistic value and integrity. Examples are usually found in private collections and in the special collections of libraries that specialise in the history of books and publishing.

ERP
External Review Panel.

Errata Leaf
A leaf bound into a book or other printed publication indicating printing errors. Unlike an *errata slip*, which is usually tipped in, an errata leaf is included in the statement of extent of item. The presence of an errata leaf or slip may also be mentioned in a note in the bibliographic record.

Errata
The plural of *erratum*. Errors discovered after a book or periodical has gone to press but before it is distributed, brought to the reader's attention by the insertion of a list of corrections, separately printed on a small piece of paper known as an *errata slip*, usually tipped in at the beginning of the text or in the front matter. Synonymous with *corrigenda*. Compare with pastein.

ERT
Exhibits Round Table.

ES
Expert system.

Escape Key
A key located in the upper-left-hand corner of a standard computer keyboard, usually labelled Esc, that allows the user to go backward one step in a sequence of operations, terminating the current operation.

Escapist Literature
Fiction written as light entertainment, intended mainly to divert the mind of the reader into a world of imagination and fantasy. Popular genres include romance, science fiction, thrillers, etc.

e-selection
Electronic selection.

ESL
An initialism for *English as a Second Language*, a branch of English-language study and teaching.

Esparto
A type of paper named after a coarse, short-fibreed grass grown in the Mediterranean region that, when mixed with chemical wood pulp, produces the bulk and smooth finish suitable for printing fine-quality books and plates.

Estray
In archives, the legal term for a record or document no longer in the possession of its original creator or legitimate custodian.

et al.
An abbreviation of the Latin phrase *et alii*, meaning "and other people," used in bibliographic citations after the first of more than three collaborators, instead of listing all the names. Also an abbreviation of *et alibi* and *et alia*.

et seq.
An abbreviation of the Latin phrase *et sequens*, meaning "and the following one." Plural: *et seqq.*.

etc.
An abbreviation of the Latin phrase *et cetera*, meaning "and the rest" or "and so forth," used to shorten a list. Also abbreviated *andc*.

Etching
An illustration or print made from a metal or glass plate on which a design is made with a needle or other pointed tool through a layer of wax, varnish, or other resistant material. When subjected to an acid bath, areas of the surface exposed by the action of the needle are eaten away, becoming design elements that can be inked to produce an impression on paper in intaglio printing.

ETD
Electronic Theses and Dissertations.

e-text
Electronic text.

Ethernet
Conceived at Xerox PARC in 1976 and developed in cooperation with Intel and DEC, Ethernet has become the industry standard for network architecture. It is the most widely installed local area network (LAN) technology in the world, connecting nodes over twisted pair, coaxial, or fibre optic cable.

Ethics
Code of ethics.

Evangeliary
Evangelary.

Evidential Value
Archival value.

Example
In printing and the book trade, a specific copy of a given edition, no different in any respect from other copies of the same edition.

Exegesis
Scholarly explanation or interpretation of a word, phrase, sentence, or passage in a written work, based on close study and critical analysis of the text, especially to clarify an obscure point in the Bible or some other sacred work.

Exhibit Case
Display case.

Exhibition Print
A positive print of a motion picture made for film screenings rather than for release.

Exhibits Round Table (ERT)
A permanent round table of the American Library Association (ALA), ERT provides a venue for cooperation between the Association and exhibitors, with the aim of making exhibits an effective part of state, regional, and national library conferences.

Exotic Work
Novelty work.

Exotics
In the printing trade, a general term for non-Latin alphabets.

Expanded Edition
A previously published work enlarged by the addition of a significant amount of new material, sometimes in the form of at least one supplement or appendix, with little or no revision of the existing text. Compare with revised edition.

Expanded
A typeface wider in proportion to its height than the normal version of the same style. The opposite of condensed. Synonymous with *extended.* Compare with full face.

Expert User
A person with sufficient knowledge and experience to be able to use a library or computer system effectively and efficiently, with only occasional assistance. The opposite of novice.

Explanatory Reference
A cross reference provided in a library catalogue or index when more information is required than is normally given in a *see* or *see also* reference, usually an explanation of the conditions under which the heading(s) is applied.

Explication
A form of critical analysis requiring close examination of the language, style, symbolism, and structure of a literary text, intended to provide a clear and detailed exposition of its meaning and significance. Examples can be found in the literary quarterly titled *The Explicator*.

Exploded Drawing
A graphic representation in which

the individual components of an object or structure are shown disassembled, but in correct relationship to each other with respect to their positions in the assembled whole.

Exploit
In the publishing industry, to promote, advertise, publicise, or advance by other means an author and his/her works for the purpose of profit.

Export Edition
An edition of a publication prepared by the publisher specifically for distribution or sale in another country. Compare with co-edition.

Expunction
An unobtrusive method of correction used in medieval manuscripts in which a dot was written beneath one or more letters or words to indicate deletion.

Expurgated
A text or edition from which portions have been deleted usually to satisfy moral or political objections, an alternative to banning the work completely from publication or distribution. The opposite of unexpurgated.

Extended
Expanded.

Extended Binding
A binding in which the front and back covers extend beyond the trimmed edges of the leaves it encloses. Compare with flush binding.

Extended Cover
Extended binding.

Extended Offer
In publishing, an introductory offer or prepublication price continued beyond the originally announced expiration date, usually in response to strong demand. Sometimes a publisher reissues an entire sale catalogue with an extended expiration date.

Extended Subscription
Instead of resupplying claimed issues or parts, or issuing a credit, the publisher of a periodical may compensate the subscriber by lengthening the period of the current subscription.

Extender
A decorative addition to an initial letter in a medieval manuscript continuing the letterform into the margin of the page.

e-zine
Electronic magazine.

F

Fable
A fictitious story that uses animal characters to express or teach a moral lesson.

Face Up
In printing, the position of a full-page illustration printed on the recto of a leaf so that it appears on the right-hand side of the opening in a book or other publication.

Facet Analysis
Examination of the various aspects of a subject to identify the basic characteristics by which it can be divided into subclasses, the first step in developing a faceted classification system.

Facet Indicator
In Dewey Decimal Classification, a digit used to introduce notation representing a characteristic of the subject, for example, the "0" often used to introduce concepts represented by standard subdivisions.

Faceted Notation
A notation in which the facets of the classification system are indicated by symbols, for example, the colon in S.R. Ranganathan's *Colon Classification*.

Facetiae
Witty sayings or writings, sometimes of a coarse, indecent, or blasphemous nature. In bookselling, the term is sometimes used as a euphemism for erotica and pornography.

Facsimile
A facsimile (from Latin *fac simile* ('make alike'), a spelling that remained in currency until the late 19th century) is a copy or reproduction of an old book, manuscript, map, art print, or other item of historical value that is as true to the original source as possible. It differs from other forms of reproduction by attempting to replicate the source as accurately as possible in terms of scale, color, condition, and other material qualities. For books and manuscripts, this also entails a complete copy of all pages; hence an incomplete copy is a "partial facsimile". Facsimiles

are used, for example, by scholars to research a source that they do not have access to otherwise, and by museums and archives for media preservation and conservation.

Facsimile Atlas
A bound collection of facsimile maps or a printed reproduction of an older atlas made to duplicate as closely as possible the physical appearance of the original.

Facsimile Binding
A binding intended to duplicate as closely as possible the binding on a previously published edition of the same work or an earlier style of binding typical of the period in which the work was first published.

Facsimile Catalogue
A catalogue that includes in each entry a small reproduction of the picture, slide, map, or other item it represents, usually affixed to or printed on cards larger than standard size or on sheets of heavy paper filed in a loose-leaf or other type of binder.

Facsimile Edition
Facsimile.

Facsimile Reprint
Type facsimile.

Facsimile Transmission
Fax.

Fact Sheet
A brief printed handout or publication, sometimes available online, giving basic information about a subject, organisation, programme, etc. Currency is essential.

Factotum
A printer's ornament in wood or metal, designed with a space in the center, into which a unit of type bearing any letter of the alphabet can be inserted to print a large capital letter at the beginning of a chapter. In early printing, *factotum initials* were usually decorated.

Faculty Library Advisory Committee
Library advisory committee.

Faded
The condition of a dust jacket or a cloth or paper binding on which the colours have lightened as a result of prolonged exposure to the sun or to some other strong light source. The spine often fades relative to the sides of the cover on books stored upright on the shelf.

FAFLRT
Federal and Armed Forces Libraries Round Table.

Fair
A description of condition used in the book trade to indicate that a copy shows definite signs of age and/or wear, such as a torn dust jacket, foxing, a loose binding, slightly dogeared corners, etc., but retains all the text pages, although endpapers, half title, etc., may be lacking. Defects must be noted by the book-seller.

Fair Copy
In publishing, the final version of the manuscript or typescript of an original work, containing few mistakes and no corrections, having been carefully prepared from the

final draft by the author, or by a copy editor, for the use of the printer.

Fair Use
Conditions under which copying a work, or a portion of it, does *not* constitute infringement of copyright, including copying for purposes of criticism, comment, news reporting, teaching, scholarship, and research.

Fake Book
A collection of musical lead sheets, often un-bound, each containing the melody line, basic chords, and lyrics of a song, intended to help the performer learn the piece quickly and to facilitate improvisation.

Fake
Something that is not genuine, having been counterfeited, usually with intent to deceive or defraud, for example, *The Poems of Ossian*, which the 18th-century Scottish poet James Macpherson claimed were translations of ancient Gaelic manuscripts but whose authenticity was eventually disproved.

Fallen In
The condition of the spine of a book that has become concave with use, usually the result of faulty binding or improper handling by the owner. Thick volumes are especially prone to this problem, which may be due in part to the force of gravity acting on the sections as the book sits upright on the shelf.

False Imprint
Fictitious imprint.

Family
Type family.

Family Name
Surname.

Family Tree
A diagram, chart, or other graphic representation of the genealogy of a family, often a branched figure showing the descendants of a given pair of progenitors.

Fan
A book bound at only one point, usually one of the four corners.

Fan Binding
A style of leather binding developed in France and Italy during the second half of the 17th century in which the center of the boards is embellished with a design in the shape of a fan open 360 degrees, composed of small handtooled motifs repeated to resemble lacework. The four corners were often tooled in matching quarterfans. Geoffrey Glaister notes in *Encyclopaedia of the Book* that the style was adopted by Scottish binders of the 18th century.

Fan Fold
Accordion fold.

Fancy Type
In printing, a general term for decorative type in any size, used mainly for display purposes.

Fanzine
A contraction of "fan magazine." A serial publication in electronic or print format containing news and information of interest to enthusiasts of a particular pastime, phe-

nomenon, or notable person or group, which may also serve as a forum for readers to share their common interest. When published on the Web, such a publication may be called a *fansite*.

FAQ

Frequently Asked Questions, a text file available online or in print, containing answers to commonly asked questions about a specific topic, that may serve as a minihelp file for inexperienced users of a computer system or software programme. Usually maintained by one or more persons who have an active interest in the subject.

Fax

Fax (short for facsimile), sometimes called telecopying, is the telephonic transmission of scanned printed material (both text and images), normally to a telephone number connected to a printer or other output device. The original document is scanned with a fax machine (or a telecopier), which processes the contents (text or images) as a single fixed graphic image, converting it into a bitmap, and then transmitting it through the telephone system. The receiving fax machine reconverts the coded image, printing a paper copy. Before digital technology became widespread, for many decades, the scanned data was transmitted as analog.

Farce

A light, boisterous form of comedy in which the characters are exaggerated stereotypes, the action improbable to the point of being ludicrous, and the verbal and visual humor lacking in subtlety. Farce bears the same relationship to "high" comedy as melodrama to tragedy.

Farrago

In literature, an unorganised mixture of humorous prose and light verse. Also used in the context of vaudeville and musical theater to indicate a disjointed medley of tunes, dramatic skits, and comedy routines.

Fashion Plate

An illustration printed in a periodical to advertise a current fashion design. Fashion plates first appeared in the late 18th century and were very popular from the 1830s onward, particularly in women's magazines.

Fast Back

Tight back.

Fat Face

A novelty typeface in which the degree of contrast between the thick and thin strokes of each character is highly exaggerated.

Fat Matter

A printer's term for copy that does not take long to set because it contains a high proportion of white space, for example, extended passages of dialogue in a work of fiction. The opposite of lean matter.

Faux Book Box

A storage container, often decorative, designed to look like a book or set of books.

FCC
Federal Communications Commission.

FDLP
Federal Depository Library Programme.

FDsys
In 2009, the U.S., Government Printing Office launched its new *Federal Digital System*, replacing *GPO Access* which had been the central online storage, preservation, and retrieval point for the Federal Depository Library Programme since, the 1990s. *FDsys* provides free online access to official publications from all three branches of the U.S., Federal Government.

Feasibility Study
A preliminary investigation and report on a proposed policy, project, or plan to ascertain if it can be successfully carried out, for example, to determine if a new library building can be constructed on a particular site.

Feature Film
A motion picture released theatrically or direct to video in which the dialogue and characters are largely fictional, although the plot may be derived from a true story. Variable in length, feature films are at least 40 minutes long, with 90 minutes the norm. Libraries that circulate feature films usually make them available on videocassette or DVD. Compare with documentary and short film.

Federal Digital System
FDsys.

FEDLINK
Federal Library and Information Center Committee.

Feedback
In computing, output put back into the same system as input to achieve a degree of self-regulation. In library operations, the views of the users of a resource or service concerning its quality and/or usefulness, whether positive or negative. Libraries rely on user surveys and the suggestion box to obtain feed-back from patrons.

Fee-based Service
An information service provided by a library or information broker in exchange for monetary payment. In most academic and public libraries in the United States, fee-based services, provided on a cost-recovery basis, are limited to document delivery and rental collections. Synonymous with *fee-for-service.*

Fee-or-free
The ongoing debate in libraries over the ideal of providing unlimited free access to information versus charging, usually on a cost-recovery basis, for certain services. In the United States, most libraries limit fee-for-service to document delivery, interlibrary loan when the lender charges, and rental collections. Libraries may also charge users to print from computer workstations, and in most libraries, photocopiers and reader printer machines are coin-operated.

Feint
Parallel horizontal lines drawn lightly with a ruler or printed in

light-coloured ink across a sheet or page, as in an account book to keep entries separate or in a medieval manuscript to guide the hand of the scribe, as in this example on a leaf of the *Burnet Psalter*.

Feltboard
Flannel board.

Feminist Task Force (FTF)
Founded in 1970 as a task force of the Social Responsibilities Round Table of the American Libraries Association (ALA), FTF focuses on women's issues, including sexism in libraries and librarianship. FTF hosts an electronic mailing list and publishes the quarterly newsletter *Women in Libraries*.

Ferrotype
Tintype.

FIAF
International Federation of Film Archives.

Fibreboard
A very rigid form of paperboard made from heavily pressed sheets of pulped vegetable fibre, laminated together.

Fiche
Microfiche.

Figure of Speech
A form of expression employed mainly in rhetoric and literary writing in which words or entire sentences are used in a way that deviates from conventional order or literal meaning to achieve an unusual or unexpected poetic or aesthetic effect, for example, the phrase 'a flood of tears.'

File Break
Cutoff.

File Copy
A copy of a document, report, periodical article, etc., kept on file, usually with related items, for reference or future use.

File Name
Filename.

File Server
Server

File Sharing
Also spelled *file-sharing*.

File Type
In electronic data processing, the type of code in which a data file is written, indicated by a three-or four-letter extension at the end of the filename.

Filigree
An elegant style of decoration used in manuscripts and fine printing in which an initial letter or border is edged with a delicate tracery of curved lines resembling lacework. In medieval manuscripts and early printed books, this type of decoration is usually done in pen using coloured ink.

Filigree Letter
An initial letter in a manuscript or printed book given a decorative outline or background of delicately interlaced lines resembling lacework.

Filing Title
Uniform title.

Filing Word
Entry word.

Filler
Blank unnumbered leaves added at the end of a publication to increase its bulk when bound, known in the book trade as *padding*.

Fillet
In bookbinding, one or more thin decorative bands or lines impressed in gilt or blind on the boards and/or spine of a book, usually around the circumference of the cover. Also refers to the rolling tool used, when heated, to apply such lines. A *French fillet* consists of three unevenly spaced gilt lines.

Film Loop
A work composed of a length of motion picture film with the ends spliced together to allow it to run through a film projector or other viewing device continuously until the equipment is turned off. The actualities shown in the last years of the 19th century up to about 1910 were often of this form.

Film Negative
A photographic negative on a flexible base, such as celluloid, introduced commercially in the 1880s, or polyester, used commercially since, the 1980s.

Filmslip
A very short filmstrip mounted like a slide in a rigid holder instead of stored in a short flexible roll.

Filmstrip Projector
Filmstrip.

Finding List
A list of a library's holdings in which each item is represented by a very brief entry containing incomplete bibliographic information. Compare with catalogue.

Finding Tool
A general term for a resource designed to be used in a library to locate sources of information, usually in a search by author, title, subject, or keywords. The category includes catalogues, bibliographies, indexes, abstracting services, bibliographic databases, etc. The corresponding term in archives is *finding aid*.

Findings
Information or evidence uncovered as a result of systematic research or investigation. Also, the conclusions of an official enquiry or hearing on a particular topic or issue, usually presented in the form of a report that may be preserved as a legal document.

Fine Binding
Hand-binding that adheres to a very high standard of workmanship, usually in leather of excellent quality with some degree of ornamentation, but not necessarily luxurious in appearance.

Fine Book
A book of exceptional quality with respect to its design, printing, illustration, and binding, often a copy of a deluxe edition. Very fine books are usually sold by antiquarian booksellers and at book auctions. Libraries preserve them in special collections. Compare with rare book.

Fine Copy
In the used book trade, a copy in clean, crisp condition that sur-

passes good but, due to the merest trace of use, falls short of mint. Compare with very good.

Fine Edition
Deluxe edition.

Fine Paper Copy
A book printed on paper superior in quality to that of the rest of the edition, normally printed on ordinary book paper. When the paper is also of larger size, the copy is known as a large paper copy.

Fine Press
A publisher/printer that specializes in the production of books of exceptional quality, designed to meet the highest aesthetic standards and serve as an inspiration to the book arts. Fine presses are often private.

Fine Printing
The art and craft of producing beautifully designed and executed books

Fine-free Period
Grace period.

Finis
A French word printed at the end of an old book, or appearing at the end of an early motion picture, meaning "the end" or "conclusion". Compare with explicit.

Finish
A general term for the texture of the surface of a grade of paper, determined by the materials and techniques used in manufacture. The terms used to describe finish are descriptive: antique, cockle, eggshell, glossy, matte, stipple, etc. In binding, to apply lettering and/or ornamentation to the cover of a book in a process known as finishing.

Finite Resource
Seriality.

First American Edition
The first edition published in the United States of a work previously published in another country.

First Appearance
A term used in the book trade to mean:

- An author's initial appearance in print;
- The first time a given work by an author appears in print, especially a short work; or
- The first treatment of a subject to be published in book form.

First Book
In publishing, the first appearance in print of a book-length work written entirely by the author. The initial books of many well known writers remain comparatively obscure.

First Issue
The first installment of a newly published periodical. Also refers to the first installment received by a library in response to a new periodical subscription, not necessarily the first issue published.

First Name
The first of one or more given names or Christian names, as distinct from the surname identifying members of the same family. In *AACR2*, personal name headings for persons known by their initials begin with the surname, followed by a comma, then the initials, followed by the full given names.

First Published Edition

An edition issued for sale to the general public after the work has been distributed to a restricted audience, for example, a motion picture released for public viewing after it has been previewed by a limited audience, usually persons invited by the producer.

First Thus

In bookselling, a descriptive term indicating that although earlier editions of the work exist, this is the first to contain a notable feature, such as a desirable set of illustrations, a special appendix, large print, etc.

First Trade Edition

The first edition of a book to be published for sale to the general public, as distinct from a previously issued limited edition.

Firsts

First edition.

First Search (FS)

A service of OCLC that provides access to over 40 online bibliographic data-bases in a wide range of disciplines via a proprietary interface, on a per search or subscription basis, by licensing agreement. Some of the databases in *FirstSearch* include full-text. *WorldCat,* the largest union catalogue in the world, is available in *FS.*

First-to-file

In trademark law, many countries grant owner-ship of a trademark to the first person who registers it, but not the United States. Compare with first-to-use.

First-to-use

In the United States, but not in most other countries, ownership of a trademark commences from its first use; how-ever, registration still guarantees maximum legal protection. Compare with first-to-file.

Fiscal Value

Archival value.

Fisheye View

Fisheye photograph.

Fittings

Furniture.

Five Laws of Library Science

Ranganathan, S.R.

Five Laws of Library Science

The Five laws of library science is a theory proposed by S. R. Ranganathan in 1931, detailing the principles of operating a library system. Many librarians worldwide accept them as the oundations of their philosophy. These laws are:

1. Books are for use
2. Every reader his book
3. Every book its reader
4. Save the time of the reader
5. The library is a growing organism.

Fixed Rate

A stipulation in a contract or other agreement that the rate of payment agreed upon in advance will not change over time.

Flag

The title of a newspaper exactly as printed across the top of the front page, including any design elements on either side, called ears. A gothic typeface is often used. Synonymous with *nameplate*. In data processing, a special character used to mark the occurrence of a condition specified in advance.

Flame
To communicate via e-mail in an angry, sarcastic, or critical tone. A protracted dispute in a newsgroup or mailing list discussion is known as a *flame war*. Such disputes are usually mediated or terminated by the other participants or by the moderator.

Flannel Board
A large square or rectangular board covered in felt, used in storytelling and instruction to display letters, symbols, and shapes cut from fabric or some other textured material that sticks to the felt surface when the board is held in an upright position. Synonymous with *feltboard* and *cloth board*.

Flap Binding
A style of binding in which the back cover of a book extends beyond the sections in a wide flap that folds over the fore-edge and is usually fastened to the front cover in some fashion. In Islamic binding, an envelope flap often fits inside the upper board. The category includes wallet bindings.

Flap
One of the two ends of the paper dust jacket wrapped around the cover of a book bound in hardcover. The list price and the publisher's promotional blurb are usually printed on the front flap. The back flap provides brief biographical information about the author and/or illustrator, usually with a small portrait photograph of each person.

Flash Drive
USB flash drive.

Flat Back
A type of binding in which the back of a book is not rounded or backed after gluing, leaving the front and back covers to meet the spine at a right angle. Synonymous with *square back*.

Flat Panel
A computer peripheral device in the form of a thin, flat screen that uses LCD or plasma technology, rather than a cathode ray tube, to display output. In laptops, the flat panel folds down to cover the keyboard.

Flex-cover
Flexible binding.

FLICC
Federal Library and Information Center Committee.

Flick
A slang term for motion picture.

Flier
An inexpensive, widely distributed handbill or circular of small size used flat or folded for advertising and announcements. Also spelled *flyer*. Synonymous in the UK with *leaflet*.

Flock Paper
A type of specialty cover paper,

originally intended to simulate tapestry or velvet brocade, produced by coating the sheet with size applying specially dyed flock powder and removing any excess that does not adhere to the surface.

Floppy
Floppy disk.

Floret
Printer's flower.

FFlow Map
Dynamic map.

Flush Cover
Flush binding.

Flush
Said of a line of type aligned along a right or left margin without indention.

Flyer
Flier.

FOIA
Freedom of Information Act.

FOL
Friends of the Library.

Fold Test
Two-double fold test.

Fold-out
Also spelled *foldout.*

Foliated Initial
Foliate initial.

Folio Number
Foliation.

Follow Through
Letter-by-letter.

FOLUSA
Friends of Libraries USA.

Foot
The bottom edge of a book or page in a bound publication. The opposite of *head*. Synonymous with *tail.*

Footline
Running foot.

Fore-edge Painting
Edge painting.

Fore-edge Title
A title hand-lettered on the fore-edge of a volume to facilitate identification when it was standard practice to shelve books fore-edge out

Foreign Language Dictionary
Language dictionary.

Forename
A name preceding a person's surname given at birth to distinguish him or her from others of the same family or clan. Synonymous with *given name.*

Format
A general indication of the size of a book, based on the number of times the printed sheets are folded in binding to make the leaves.

Formation Photograph
A group photograph taken from an elevated point of view, showing a number of people, specially assembled to form numerals, letters of the alphabet, or a symbol or pictorial design.

Four-colour Process
Process colour.

FPBA
Fine Press Book Association.

FPF
Frames per foot.

FPS
An abbreviation of *frames per second.*

Fractional Scale
Representative fraction.

FRBR
Pronounced "furbur."

Freeware
A term coined in the 1980s to refer to software available at no cost, usually distributed over the Internet by the developer who retains copyright. Compare with shareware.

Freeze Drying
Vacuum freeze drying.

French Dash
In printing and book-binding, a ruled line with a swell, usually at its center. Synonymous with *french rule* and *swelled rule.*

Freshman Experience
First-year experience.

Fretwork
Ornament used in bookbinding and manuscript decoration, consisting of a closely repeated, open rectilinear geometric pattern.

FRFDS
Fund Raising and Financial Development Section Benefits.

Front Page
The first page of the first section of a newspaper, bearing the flag and headlines of the major news stories of the day. Also, the first page of a newsletter, magazine, or journal. Compare with title page.

Frontis
Frontispiece.

FTE
Full-time equivalent.

Full Face
A typeface that has not been condensed and is therefore more readable than a version of the same style in which the characters are narrower than normal.

Fulfilment Year
The period of time for which a subscriber who has paid for an annual periodical subscription is entitled to receive issues. Compare with subscription period.

Full-colour Printing
Process colour.

Full-duplex
Duplex.

Full Measure
Measure.

Full Point
A printer's term for the punctuation mark used to indicate the end of an ordinary sentence and as a mark of abbreviation. Synonymous with period and full stop.

Full-page Border
Full border.

FVR
Free voluntary reading.

FYE
First-year experience.

G

Galleys
Galley proof.

Garland
A type of anthology containing a collection of prose extracts or short literary compositions, usually ballads or poems.

Garter Book
A pictorial book of arms of the Order of the Garter, the highest order of chivalry in England.

Gauffering
Gauffered edges.

Gauffered Edges

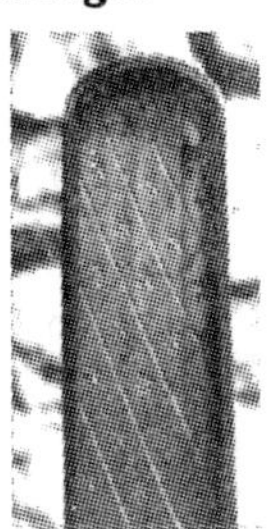

Gauffering describes the act of applying a patterned decoration to the text block edges of a book. This type of ornamentation is used most often on books with gold or *gilded* edges. The example shown is a copy of The Poetical Works of John Dryden, which has been gauffered with a rope and star pattern using heated metal stamps and rollers.

Gauze
Crash.

Gaylord
A library supplier that provides office and library supplies, furniture, security systems, and automation software to libraries, schools, and other educational institutions largely through its trade catalogue.

Gazette
A news sheet in which current events, legal notices, public appointments, etc., are recorded on a regular basis. Formerly, a journal devoted to current news. Also, a journal officially issued by a government, particularly in Great Britain. The word is derived from the name of an Italian coin that was equivalent at one point in time to the price of a news sheet.

Gazetteer

A separately published dictionary of geographic names that gives the location of each entry. Also, an index of the names of the places and geographic features shown on the maps contained in an atlas, usually printed in a separate section following the maps, with locations indicated by page number and grid coordinates. Some gazetteers include information about major geographic features such as rivers, lakes, mountains, cities, etc.

GBW

Guild of Book Workers.

Gelatin Print

Gelatin silver print.

Gem Photograph

A very small tintype, usually a portrait, about 1/2 × 1 inch in size for mounting in jewelry or in a carte-de-visite size cardboard holder designed to be inserted into a Victorian carte-de-visite photograph album, popular from the mid-1860s until about 1880.

Genealogical Table

A diagram, usually in the form of an inverted tree, with branches showing the lineage of a person or group of persons who share a common ancestor, sometimes printed on the endpapers of biographical or historical works, particularly those concerning the reigns of sovereigns or the lives of titled nobility.

Genealogy

The study of the descent from a common ancestor of a specific individual, family, or group of persons. Genealogical research often requires the use of archival materials. Genealogical resources are increasingly available in digital form.

General Encyclopaedia

An encyclopaedia that provides basic information on a broad range of subjects but treats no single subject in depth as distinct from a subject encyclopaedia that provides greater depth of coverage within a more limited scope.

General Interest Magazine

A magazine of interest to a wide audience. Most public libraries make an effort to subscribe to the most popular general interest magazines but are more selective in subscribing to special interest magazines. Compare with newsmagazine.

Generic Relation

Semantic relation.

Geographic Name Index

Place name index.

Geographic Name

The name most commonly used to identify a specific geographic location, feature, or area, preferred by cataloguers in establishing the correct form of entry, not necessarily the same as the political name.

Geographic Index

An index in which the entries are listed by their geographic location

Geologic Time Scale

A chronological arrangement of events in geologic history, usually presented in the form of a vertical chart with the event earliest in time at the bottom and the latest at the top

German Library Association
Deutscher Bibliotheksver-band e.V.

Giant Bible
Atlantic bible.

Gift Binding
A leather binding produced for presentation by someone other than the author

Gift Book
An elaborately printed, expensively illustrated, ornately bound book of poetry or prose, usually published annually, popular as a gift item during the early part of the 19th century. Also known as a *keepsake*.

Gigabyte (GB)
Byte.

Gigabyte
The gigabyte is a multiple of the unit byte for digital information storage. The prefix *giga* means 10^9 in the International System of Units (SI), therefore 1 *gigabyte* is 1000000000 bytes. The unit symbol for the gigabyte is GB or Gbyte, but not *Gb* (lower case *b*) which is typically used for the gigabit.

GIGO
In computing, an initialism that stands for "garbage in, garbage out," a slang expression for the axiom that the quality of output a user receives from a computer is directly proportional to the quality of the input submitted.

GILS
Government Information Locator Service.

Girdle Book
A book with an outer wrapper made of cloth or soft, flexible leather extending beyond the edges of the inner cover far enough to be knotted, allowing the volume to hang upside down when the knot was slipped under a belt or girdle tied round the waist.

GIS
Geographic information system.

Given Name
One or more names chosen for a person, usually by the parents at birth or christening sometimes the same as that of a living relative or deceased ancestor but distinct from the surname identifying members of the same family. Given names can be compound. Compare with first name.

Glaire
Glair.

Glamour Photograph
A photograph made primarily to display a person's physical attractiveness. The subject may be scantily clad, but for the purpose of conveying unusual beauty or desirability rather than erotic appeal. Compare with fashion photograph and publicity photograph.

Glass Print
Cliché-verre.

GLBTRT
Gay, Lesbian, Bisexual, and Transgendered Round Table.

Glitch
A malfunction in the hardware of a computer system, usually temporary or random, sometimes difficult to distinguish from a bug in the software. In a more general sense, any unanticipated problem that brings a process to a halt. Also spelled *glytch.*

Gloss Ink
Printing ink that appears shiny even when dry because it contains a higher than normal proportion of varnish, used mainly in display work.

Glossarial Concordance
Concordance.

Glossarial Index
An index at the end of a book that includes in each entry a definition or description of the term indexed, as well as the page number referenced.

Glossary
An alphabetically arranged list of the specialised vocabulary of a given subject or field of study, with brief definitions, often appearing at the end of a book or at the beginning of a long entry in a technical reference work. Long glossaries may be separately published.

Glossy
A finish in which the surface of paper or board is given a smooth, shiny coat of varnish to enhance the appearance of visual material. Most magazines are printed on glossy paper to attract readership, as are dust jackets to heighten the sales appeal of new books. In publishing, the term also refers to a photograph printed on smooth, shiny paper, the format preferred by printers in reproduction work.

Glue
A type of adhesive made from protein derived from the collagen in animal by products boiled to form a brownish gelatin that can be thinned with water. Most glues are not suitable for use in binding because they become brittle with age. Glue also attracts insects that damage books.

Gluing Off
In bookbinding, the application of adhesive to the binding edge of a book after the sections are sewn and before rounding and backing. The adhesive is forced between the sections to help hold them together. In adhesive binding, gluing replaces sewing.

Glyph
A visual representation of a textual element made by any means: handwritten, inscribed, printed, electronically displayed, etc. In computing, the standard code for a character set does not define the appearance of the individual characters. Image is rendered by the software or hardware using the code. Also used as a shortened form of *hieroglyph.*

Glyphic
In printing, a typeface derived from a carved or chiseled form, rather than from a calligraphic hand.

GMD
General material designation.

Gnawed
A book that shows signs of having been chewed by an animal on at least one edge or corner, a condition that reduces its value considerably in the used book market and makes it a candidate for weeding in libraries.

GODORT
Government Documents Round Table.

Gold Foil
An inexpensive substitute for gold leaf, made by spraying a thin deposit of gold or a look-alike substitute onto an adhesive backing, used extensively to decorate edition bindings and library bindings and also in hand-binding when economy is desired. Synonymous with *blocking foil*.

Goodread
A slang term for a book recommended by a friend or acquaintance as worth reading.

Google Books
Google Books (previously known as Google Book Search and Google Print) is a service from Google Inc. that searches the full text of books and magazines that Google has scanned, converted to text using optical character recognition, and stored in its digital database. The service was formerly known as Google Print when it was introduced at the Frankfurt Book Fair in October 2004. Google's Library Project, also now known as Google Book Search, was announced in December 2004.

Google Print for Libraries
Google Books.

Gouge
A visible nick or hole made accidentally in the cover or spine of a book. Also refers to a finishing tool used in bookbinding to make curved lines on a book cover.

Govdocs
Government documents.

GPO
The U.S., Government Printing Office, the government agency responsible for collecting, publishing, and distributing federal government information. The GPO publishes a printed index to government documents under the title *Monthly Catalogue of U.S., Government Publications*. Its online equivalent is *FDsys*.

GPS
Global Positioning System.

Gracing Policy
The number of issues the publisher of a magazine or journal will allow a subscriber to receive following the expiration date of a subscription that has not been renewed.

Gradient Tint
Hypsometric tint.

Grained
Leather used in book-binding that has been processed to accentuate the natural grain or give the surface an artificial texture, either as decoration or to enhance durability. Pebble-grained goatskin is an example. *Graining* is accomplished by

working a cork-covered board across the tanned skin or by using engraved metal plates or rollers to impress the desired pattern.

Graininess

The perceptible granular appearance of the image on a photographic negative, print, or slide, caused by the clumping together of particles of silver halide in the emulsion that bears the image, an effect that becomes more pronounced with the use of faster film and with degree of enlargement. Filmmakers sometimes use graininess to imitate old films or to give their work a documentary look.

Grammage

Mass per unit area expressed in grams per square meter (g/m^2), a unit of measurement used in comparing grades of paper. *Basis Weight and Grammage Conversion Tables of Use in the Publishing Industry* are provided online, courtesy of EDS Inc. Compare with basis weight.

Grammar

A book written to instruct students in the formal rules of speaking and writing a language, based on scholarly study of its morphology and syntax. During the Middle Ages, the term referred to the study of classical Latin, the language in which most books were written.

Gramophone Record

Phonograph record.

Gramophone Record

A gramophone record, commonly known as a phonograph record (in American English), vinyl record (in reference to vinyl, the material most commonly used after about 1950), or colloquially, "a record", is an analog sound storage medium consisting of a flat disc with an inscribed, modulated spiral groove. The groove usually starts near the periphery and ends near the center of the disc. Phonograph records are generally described by their diameter in inches (12-inch, 10-inch, 7-inch, etc.), the rotational speed at which they are played ("33^1D_3 rpm", "78", "45", etc.), their time capacity ("long playing"), their reproductive accuracy, or "fidelity" ("high fidelity", "Orthophonic", "full-range", etc.), and the number of channels of audio provided ("mono", "stereo", "quadraphonic", etc.).

Gramophone

The British term for phonograph.

Grangerised

An edition into which illustrations, letters, and/or other matter is inserted after publication, sometimes taken from other books. The practice began in 1769 when James Granger published *A Biographical History of England* containing blank leaves for the insertion of portrait engravings after printing. Synonymous with *privately illustrated.*

Graphic Narrative

A work that tells a story in the pictorial panel-to-panel format of comic books. The category includes graphic novels, manga, bandes dessinées, fotonovelas, and sequential art.

Graphic Scale
Bar scale.

Gravure
Photogravure.

Green Library
Sustainable library.

Green Paper
A printed document issued in green paper covers by a ministry or department of the British government to elicit public comment and debate on a proposed new policy or change in an existing one. The practice began in 1967. Compare with white paper.

Grey Literature
Gray literature.

Guestbook
A blankbook used to record the names of persons attending a ceremony or event, such as a wedding or exhibition, or visitors to a facility, such as a museum, gallery, club, etc. The date and street address or place of origin of each guest may also be recorded.

GUI
Graphical user interface.

Guideword
Catchword.

Gum Arabic
Binding medium.

Gutter
The blank space formed by the inner margins of facing pages in an open book, from the binding edge to the area bearing printed matter. The width of the *gutter margin* is an important factor in determining whether a book can be rebound.

Gutter Press
Tabloid newspapers and magazines that publish salacious gossip, usually of a personal nature concerning the lives of prominent people. Synonymous with yellow press.

H

HABS/HAER
Historic American Buildings Survey/Historic American Engineering Record.

Hachure
One of a series of short lines drawn or printed on a land map to indicate gradient—short, thick, closely spaced lines for steep grade and longer, thin, widely spaced lines for moderate grade, with direction of slope indicated by direction of line.

Hack
From the English word *hackney,* meaning "a horse let out for hire." A writer engaged in churning out fiction or non-fiction for the market place, originally at a bookseller's request, with little regard for literary quality. The term is still used in journalism. Synonymous with *hired pen.* In a more general sense, a drudge in any occupation.

Hacker
A slang term for a person with extensive knowledge of computers and computing who uses his skills to access supposedly secure computer systems for the intellectual challenge such activities provide. The best hackers take pride in leaving no "tracks" to reveal their presence.

Half Binding
A style of bookbinding in which the spine and corners are covered in a different material than the sides, usually selected for greater durability.

Half Cloth
A book bound in a cloth spine and paper-covered boards.

Half Leather
A book with spine and corners covered in leather and the rest of the binding in paper or cloth.

Half Yearly
Semiannual.

Half-duplex
Duplex.

Half-time
A part-time employee scheduled to work one-half of the hours worked by a full-time employee. If

the normal work week is 40 hours long, a half-time employee works 20 hours per week. Benefits for half-time employees may be prorated. In some libraries, part-time employees who work less than half-time are not eligible for benefits.

Hand
The way a script is actually written on the page, as opposed to the model a particular scribe has in mind when engaged in writing.

Handbill
A small notice or advertisement printed on a single unfolded sheet intended for distribution by hand but also used as a poster.

Hand-binding
The art and craft of binding books by hand without the aid of mechanisation. Medieval manuscripts and early printed books were hand-bound in wooden boards covered in leather. Today, trade editions are case bound, and hand-binding is limited to fine books. Synonymous with *craft binding*.

Handbook
A single-volume reference book of compact size that provides concise factual information on a specific subject, organised systematically for quick and easy access. Statistical information is often published in handbook form. Some handbooks are published serially. Synonymous with vade mecum.

Hand-coloured
A print, illustration, map, or photograph to which tint is added manually, rather than applied during printing or by some other mechanical process, a practice now limited to deluxe collector's editions.

Handheld Computer
Personal digital assistant.

Handmade Paper
Paper made without the aid of mechanisation, usually from pulp made from various vegetable fibres and/or cotton or linen rags. Handmade papers often bear a watermark identifying the papermaker.

Handout
A printed sheet or group of sheets, usually stapled together at one corner, intended for distribution during an oral presentation or instruction session to give the attendees a record of content covered or to provide supplementary or complementary information.

Hands-on
A library instruction session or one-on-one reference transaction in which the student or patron has the opportunity to practice, usually at a computer work-station, research techniques demonstrated by the instructor or reference librarian, often more effective than lecture style instruction.

Hang
Having a computer freeze during a session so that it does not respond to user input, usually with no indication of the probable cause. Downloading a very large

data file can create the appearance of a *hang-up*. Closing the application or rebooting will usually get the system unstuck, but unsaved data may be lost in the process.

Hanging Caption
A heading in a book, printed adjacent to the text to which it refers, as a vertical column in the margin rather than horizontally across the page.

Hanging-in
Case binding.

Hanging Indention
A form of indention in which the opening line is flush with the left-hand margin and subsequent lines are indented one or more spaces. Used in typed and printed catalogue cards and in some styles of bibliographic entry. Hanging indention is used for the terms and definitions in this online dictionary.

HAPLR
Library rating.

Hard Copy
A human readable copy on card or paper of a document or record in machine readable format or in a form not easily readable. Also used in a more general sense to refer to printed matter, as opposed to its non-print equivalent. Compare with printout.

Hardwired
A term that originally referred to a computer device containing unalterable circuitry designed to perform a specific task, as opposed to circuits that are programmable or controlled by a switch. However, the meaning has broadened to include constants built into computer software. Synonymous in this sense with *hardcoded*. In a more general sense, hardware or software that cannot be modified.

Harmony
An arrangement of biblical passages on the same topic in parallel columns to facilitate comparison. Also, an interweaving of such passages into a continuous text (*AACR2*).

Hash
Hashmark.

Hashmark
The symbol '#' used to represent the word "number" in lists and street addresses, in touchtone telephone systems that allow the caller to key input, in Web addresses (URLs) to create a link to another location in the same document, etc. Abbreviated *hash*.

HD-DVD
Blu-ray.

Headcap
The thickened edge at the upper end of the spine of a leather bound book, created by inserting a piece of cord inside the turned-in end of the covering material after the text block has been attached to the cover

Header
The lines at the beginning of an e-mail message that display the e-mail address and the name of the sender and recipient, any delivery options, and the subject of commu-

nication, as opposed to the footer at the end of the message and the body containing the text.

Headline
A few words printed in large display type across the top of the front page of a newspaper to give prominence to the most important news story of the day, or above the text of one of the other articles in the newspaper to give the reader a sense of its content. Headlines are worded to capture the reader's interest.

Headnote
A brief explanatory note printed at the beginning of a chapter, short story, poem, or other work to serve as a preface.

Headword
A word or phrase used as a main entry in a dictionary or encyclopaedia, usually printed in boldface or some other distinctive type at the beginning of a definition or other entry. In most dictionaries, headwords are arranged in a single alphabetic sequence. In classified reference works, headwords may be listed alphabetically within each section, usually with a subject or keyword index to the entire work at the end of the last volume.

Health Science Library
Medical library.

HEGIS
Higher Education General Information Survey.

Help Line
A telephone number that a person may call to receive assistance of a certain kind, for example, instructions or advice on how to use a specific type of computer hardware or software. Some help lines are more helpful than others.

Help Screen
The screen or sequence of screens in an online catalogue, bibliographic database, or other application programme providing instructions to users who need assistance in learning how to use the system. In well designed software, the help screens are context sensitive. In Windows, the help menu can be accessed by pressing the F1 key or Alt+H.

Herbal
A systematically arranged text containing practical information about herbs and other plants, especially their properties and medicinal uses, usually providing both common and scientific names and a physical description, with illustrations drawn or painted from actual specimens to aid identification. Botanical texts survive from Antiquity and were produced throughout the Middle Ages, often containing picture cycles based on classical models.

Herbarium
Herbal.

Herringbone
In bookbinding, a design resembling the skeleton of a fish, consisting of a vertical line up the center with horizontal elements arranged like ribs. Built up of small tools, herringbone was

used on the spine in Byzantine binding and on the covers of late-17th- and 18th-century Scottish bindings.

Hexateuch
The first six books of the Old Testament of the Bible sometimes produced as a separate manuscript by medieval scribes.

HHC
Homework help center.

Hickie
Printer's slang for an unintended spot or defect on a printed page, usually caused by a speck of dust, lint, or dried ink on the printing plate or negative. Also spelled *hickey*.

Hidden Agenda
Agenda.

Hidden Image Work
A work in which text or image remains hidden from view until revealed by purposeful action of the viewer, such as holding the item to a light source, exposing it to heat, or rubbing away a surface covering. The category does not include *picture puzzles* in which some of the objects or figures depicted are not easily perceived, for example, because they appear at first glance to be part of the background.

Hierarchic Relation
A semantic relation between two terms in which the concept represented by one is a subclass of the concept represented by the other.

Hierarchical Classification
A classification system in which the classes are subdivided on the principle of logical subordination, from the most general subjects to the most specific. Hierarchical classification can be broad or close.

Hierarchical Force
In classification systems based on logical subordination, the principle that the attributes of a class identified in the heading assigned to represent it, and in certain explanatory notes, apply to all its subdivisions and to all other classes to which reference is made in the notes.

Hieroglyphics
From the Greek *hieros* and *glyphikos*. A writing system in which pictures or symbols, rather than letters of a phonetic alphabet, are used to represent words, syllables, and sounds. The ancient Egyptians wrote in *hieroglyphs* that were not deciphered until after the discovery in 1799 of the Rosetta Stone, which bears the same inscription in three different scripts: *hieratic* Egyptian, *demotic* Egyptian, and ancient Greek. In a more general sense, any form of written expression that is difficult to read or understand.

Hieronym
A surname based on a sacred name.

Hi-fi
An abbreviation of high fidelity.

High-definition
In electronics, an audio/visual display device capable of reproducing sound and/or image with a

high degree of resolution or fidelity to the original. In digital television, high-definition receivers have higher resolution than standard definition TV.

High-definition Television
HDTV.

High-demand
Demand.

High Fidelity (hi-fi)
Any method of sound recording that minimizes distortion by reproducing such a wide range of audible frequencies that the result is very faithful to the original. Compare with lo-fi.

High-level Domain
Top level domain.

Highlight
To use a broad-tipped pen to mark in light-coloured ink a section of text in a book or document, usually for future reference. College textbooks donated to libraries are often heavily highlighted. In a similar fashion, the "edit" option in some computer applications allows the user to mark in shaded or contrasting background portions of electronic text to be cut or copied. In a more general sense, to give prominence to the part of a whole that is the most outstanding, interesting, pertinent, useful, etc.

High-risk Collection
An archival or library collection for which the likelihood of vandalism or theft is higher than normal due to its exceptional value or unusual content. Tighter security precautions are taken, especially when such items are placed on exhibit.

Highsmith
A commercial company in the business of providing equipment, supplies, and furnishings to libraries and schools, marketed through its trade catalogue.

High-speed
In computing, equipment that functions at a higher-than-normal speed, usually purchased at a premium. Also refers to a fast Internet connection.

Hill Shading
A method of creating the impression of three-dimensional relief on a map by depicting, in light to dark tones, shadows cast by high ground as if illuminated obliquely from a constant direction, usually northwest. Often combined with contours and/or hypsometric tint on relief maps hill shading can be done by hand or by computer.

Hinge
A narrow strip of muslin or paper attached with adhesive along the line dividing the two halves of an endpaper to reinforce the flexible joint along which the body of a book is attached to the cover. In volumes lacking this reinforcement, the hinge is formed by adhering the covering material directly to the fold in the endpaper. A *loose hinge* is one that allows the book block to shift inside the binding, usually because the hinge material has pulled away from the boards.

Hirsch Index
H-index.

Hirsch Index
The Hirsch Index (*h*-index) is an index that attempts to measure both the productivity and impact of the published work of a scientist or scholar. The index is based on the set of the scientist's most cited papers and the number of citations that they have received in other publications. The index can also be applied to the productivity and impact of a group of scientists, such as a department or university or country, as well as a scholarly journal. The index was suggested by Jorge E. Hirsch, a physicist at UCSD, as a tool for determining theoretical physicists' relative quality and is sometimes called the *Hirsch index* or *Hirsch number*.

Hiss
A high-frequency noise inherent in analog tape recordings, which can be reduced, without discer-nible side effects on the content being recorded, by the use of a Dolby noise reduction system.

Histogram
A graph representing quantitative data in a series of vertical or horizontal bars or lines drawn from a base line. The position of each bar along the base indicates the class or value of one variable, with the length of the bar indicating the corresponding value of a second variable. A third variable can be added if the bars are displayed in groups and distinguished graphically, by colour, shading, etc.

Historiated Border
An ornamental band around a miniature and/or portion of text on the page of an illuminated manuscript or early printed book, decorated with figures of animals and/or humans in a scene that illustrates the accompanying text or tells an unrelated story.

Historiated Initial
An initial letter in an illuminated manuscript or early printed book containing an identifiable figure or group of figures in a narrative scene that may or may not be related to the text.

Historic American Buildings Survey/Historic American Engineering Record (HABS/HAER)
A collection of prints and photographs owned by the Library of Congress, documenting achievements in architecture, engineering, and design in the United States and its territories, including a comprehensive range of building types and engineering technologies. Since, 2000, documents from the Historic American Land-scapes Survey (HALS) have been added to the collection.

Historical Atlas
A book of maps showing the progressive changes that have occurred over a given period of time in a geographic area or in the development of a spatial phenomenon or event. Historical atlases typically contain more text than a standard atlas, with maps often placed adjacent to the passages they are intended to elucidate. A

historical atlas may also include a chronology or timeline and biographical notes on persons whose names appear in the text.

Historical Bible

Bible historiale.

Historical Bible

The Bible from a historical perspective, includes numerous fields of study, ranging from archeology and astronomy to linguistics and methods of comparative literature. Studying the Bible may provide insight into ancient and modern culture, mythology, and morality. Scholars also examine the historical context of Bible passages, the importance ascribed to events by the authors, and the contrast between the descriptions of these events and historical evidence of their occurrence to learn information beyond the literal information presented in the Bible. Historical analysis of the Bible includes questioning the *historicity of the Bible,* whether the Bible is an accurate history of ancient Israel.

Historical Bibliography

The branch of bibliography devoted to the study of the history and methods of book production, including handcopying, illustration, publishing, printing, papermaking, binding, and preservation. Historical bibliography has merged with the field of book history.

Historical Fiction

A narrative in the form of a novel set in a specific place and period in history, or based on an event or sequence of events that actually happened. The characters may be completely fictional, but if they are known to have existed, their feelings, words, and actions are reconstructed and to some degree imagined by the author. The presence of dialogue in a historical work is usually a clue that the account is fictionalised. Sir Walter Scott established the genre in 1814 with the publication of *Waverly*, a novel of life in the Scottish borderlands, followed by several more historical romances, including *Guy Mannering* and *Ivanhoe.*

Historical Map

A map representing features, phenomena, or conditions that existed, or are assumed or inferred to have existed, during some period of time in the past, for example, a map showing the distribution of native American cultures prior to the arrival of Europeans in North America. Examples can be seen in the Perry-Castañeda Library collection of *Historical Maps of the United States*, or try the *Yahoo!* list of historical map sites.

Historical Society

A non-profit organisation devoted to preserving the historical record of a state or municipality, place, institution, art form, people, activity, achievement, event, or artifact. Well-established historical societies often support a public museum, maintain an archive or library for the use of members, and may publish books and other materials related to their sphere of interest.

Historical Value
Archival value.

History
History (from Greek *historia*, meaning "inquiry, knowledge acquired by investigation") is an umbrella term that relates to past events as well as the discovery, collection, organization, and presentation of information about these events. The term includes cosmic, geologic, and organic history, but is often generically implied to mean human history. Scholars who write about history are called historians. History can also refer to the academic discipline which uses a narrative to examine and analyse a sequence of past events, and objectively determine the patterns of cause and effect that determine them.

History Note
A brief note in an entry in a thesaurus of indexing terms giving the date the descriptor was added to the list of preferred terms and indicating any changes that have occurred in its meaning, scope, relationships to other terms, etc.

History of the Book
Book history.

History Play
Chronicle play.

History Section (HS)
The section of the Reference and User Services Association (RUSA) within the American Library Association (ALA) representing the subject interests of reference librarians, archivists, bibliographers, genealogists, historians, and others engaged in historical reference or research. The first section established within RUSA, HS brings together representatives of history collections in all formats in all types of libraries, archives, and historical societies. Through its programmes, projects, and committees, HS seeks to improve the materials and methods of historical research and reference services.

Hit
In information retrieval, a record retrieved from a database that matches the information need expressed in the query. The term is sometimes used loosely to refer to a record that satisfies the syntactic requirements of the query without necessarily meeting its semantic requirements but this is an imprecise use of the term. *Hit rate* is the percentage of all the records retrieved in a search that are relevant to the query.

Also, a popular song, recording, motion picture, play, musical, or book that achieves widespread popularity and sales, often for an extended period of time.

Hold
When a book or other item is currently on loan, most libraries permit another borrower to place a 'hold' on it by contacting the circulation desk. The patron who has the item checked out will not be permitted to renew it, and the person placing the 'hold' will be entitled to check it out after it has been returned. Some online catalogues include a feature that allows the user to place an item on hold without staff assistance.

Holding Area

In archives, a location specifically designated for the temporary storage of semicurrent records and materials, usually less accessible than the space allocated for current records.

Holdings Display

In a union catalogue, a list of all the libraries and other participating institutions that own a specific item, for example, in the OCLC *WorldCat* database, the list of OCLC symbols attached to the bibliographic record for an item, representing institutions that own at least one copy, used in interlibrary loan to generate lender strings.

Holdings Rate

The percentage of items requested by the users of a library that are in its collections. In most libraries, items not held locally may be borrowed on interlibrary loan (ILL) or obtained via document delivery service (DDS).

Holdings Record

In catalogueing, a separate record attached to the bibliographic record for a serial title or multivolume item to track issues, parts, volumes, etc., as they are acquired by the library. A format for holdings is defined in MARC 21. In most libraries, the holdings record is separate from the check-in record used for current receipts of serials. As successive issues or parts are received and volumes are completed, the record of receipt is moved from the check-in record to the holdings record.

Holdings Statement

A note added to the catalogue record for an item in a library collection indicating, in an open or closed entry, all the copies, volumes, issues, or parts held by the library or library system, usually with information concerning the location of the item. For serials, separate notes may be provided for print and microform holdings. ANSI/NISO standard Z39.71-1999 *Holdings Statements for Bibliographic Items* specifies rules for the construction and display of holdings statements for all non-unitary publications.

Holdings

The total stock of materials, print and non-print, owned by a library or library system, usually listed in its catalogue. Synonymous in this sense with library collection.

In a narrower sense, all the copies, volumes, issues, or parts of an item owned by a library, especially a serial publication, indicated in a holdings statement in the record representing the item in the catalogue. Holdings can be recorded in the MARC 21 Format for Holdings Information.

Hold-to-light Work

A graphic work, usually printed on a card or sheet of paper, with portions cut out and backed with tissue paper or some other transparent material which, when held to a strong light source, appears brightly illuminated, sometimes revealing a hidden picture.

Hollow Back
A type of binding in which the cover is not adhered to the back of a book, leaving an open space that allows the binding to flex easily when the volume is opened, without cracking the spine. A paper tube may be added between the back of the sections and the covering material, running the length of the spine, to allow the cover to move easily away from the spine upon opening. Most hardcover trade editions are bound with a hollow back.

Hollow
The open space between the cover and the back of a book in which the sections are not glued directly to the cover. A hollow back allows a book to open flat and stay open without damaging the spine.

Hologram
From the Greek *holos* and *gramma*. A photograph in which the subject is presented as a three-dimensional image that changes as the angle of viewing shifts. Produced with laser technology developed in the 1960s, holography does not require special equipment for viewing.

Holograph Manuscript
The text of an original work written entirely in the hand of the author.

Holograph
A document written entirely in the hand-writing of the person to whom it is attributed. A holographic reprint is a reproduction of such a document, made by mechanical means.

Home Movie
Amateur.

Homebound
A person unable to leave home to come to the library, usually for reasons of disability or ill health. To reach home-bound patrons, public libraries have developed extension services such as books-by-mail, bookmobiles, and direct delivery. Synonymous with *shut in*.

Homework Help Center (HHC)
Space set aside for study in a public library, usually with established hours and assigned staff trained to provide clearly defined services to students in need of assistance with their homework assignments. Volunteer tutors are used in some HHCs.

Homework Help
Services provided by a public library or library system that are specifically designed to assist public, private, and home-schooled students, usually in grades 4-12, with their take-home assignments.

Homilary
A book containing a collection of homilies to be read on Sundays and feast days, arranged according to the ecclesiastical year.

Homily
A sermon explaining or discussing a point in the Christian Bible, usually accompanied by instructions for the congregation hearing it. In a more general sense, any tendentious, moralizing speech or lecture.

Homograph
A word spelled the same as one or

more other words but different in meaning and sometimes in origin, for example, *current* and *current* but not *currant*. Every effort is made to avoid homographs in indexing, but when necessary, a parenthetical qualifier is added to the heading, as in the Library of Congress subject heading Mice (Computers).

Homonym
A word pronounced the same as one or more other words but different in meaning and origin, for example, *plate* and *plait*. The word "plate" is also a homograph: *plate*. Synonymous with homophone.

Homophone
A word pronounced the same as one or more others but which has a different spelling, meaning, and derivation.

Honourific Title
A formal title conferred on a person by a recognised authority as a mark of honour, rank, nobility, or royalty. In *AACR2*, an honourific title is included in a personal name heading only when commonly used in referring to the person. In such cases, the title follows the personal name and precedes the birth and death dates.

Horae
Book of Hours.

Horn Book Magazine, The
Published since, 1924, *Horn Book Magazine* provides articles, author interviews, editorials, columns, and lengthy reviews of children's books in each bimonthly issue. The title is derived from the name of an educational toy, called a horn book, used by young children from about the 15th to the 18th century. ISSN: 0018-5078.

Hornbook
Horn book.

Horror Vacui
A style of medieval manuscript decoration in which the artist fills all the available space on the page with illuminations, decorated initial letters, line fillers, elaborate borders, and bas-de-page scenes, often creating a dense carpet of ornamentation that may appear overcrowded or visually distracting.

Hors Commerce
A French term used in the book trade to indicate a portion of an edition that is not offered for sale in the market place, as distinct from the copies that are offered for sale.

Hors Texte
A French phrase meaning "outside the text," referring to illustrations not printed with the text, such as plates. They are usually numbered in roman numerals to distinguish them from illustrations printed with the text, which are numbered in arabic numerals or referenced by page number. The phrase *hors texte, versos blank* is used in the book trade to refer to plates without printing on the reverse side, sometimes tipped in to paper of different stock than that used for the text.

Hospital Library
A medical library maintained within

the walls of a hospital, containing a collection of print and online resources on medicine and allied health to serve the information and research needs of doctors, nurses, patients, and staff, usually managed by a medical librarian. Hospital librarians are organised in the Hospital Libraries Section of the Medical Library Association.

Hospitality
In classification, the property that allows new classes to be added to a system of notation as needed, without requiring the alteration of previously established schedules. In an *inhospitable* classification system, additions generally require changes in existing schedules.

Host Organisation
The organisation in which a special library functions as an administrative unit, for example, a museum that maintains a library on its premises for the use of curators, researchers, and members or a corporation that maintains a library for the use of employees in their work.

Host
A computer that serves as a source of data for other terminals or computers, for example, a central computer providing files to terminals connected directly to it, or a network server accessed by client machines. Also refers to the organisation or institution that provides the server on which a Web site is installed, usually indicated in its Internet address.

Hours
Library hours.

House Organ
A periodical issued by a commercial or industrial organisation for distribution internally to its employees and/or externally to its customers, not intended for wider publication. Synonymous with *house journal*.

House Style
The uniform standards of a publisher, printer, company, or organisation with reference to writing style and presentation to be followed, in the absence of contrary instructions, in publications issued in its name, usually explained in a style sheet.

Housekeeping Records
In archives, the records of an organisation that are related to its budgetary, fiscal, personnel, supply, maintenance, and other administrative operations, as distinct from the programme records related to the agency's primary functions.

Housekeeping
Routine chores that must be performed methodically in a library to maintain manual or automated systems in good order, usually delegated to a trained assistant, for example, the task of checking in serial parts in a timely manner to make them available to users and to identify missing issues that need to to be claimed.

How-to Publication
A book, pamphlet, or videocas-

sette that provides practical information and advice about how to accomplish a task, acquire a skill, or achieve a desired result, a type of publication often written in the form of step-by-step instructions accom-panied by diagrams and/or illustrations, for example, manuals on home improvement and auto repair. How-to titles are available in public libraries, shelved by call number in the non-fiction section.

HRDR
Office for Human Resources Development and Recruitment.

HRS
Human Resources Section.

HS
History Section.

HTML
Hypertext Markup Language.

HTML Editor
Computer software designed to facilitate the creation of Web pages by relieving the designer of the necessity of typing the required HTML code from scratch.

HTTP
Hypertext Transfer Protocol.

Hufnagel
A form of musical notation used mainly in German choir books of the late Middle Ages, named for its resemblance to the horseshoe-nail. David Hiley notes in *The New Grove Dictionary of Music and Musicians* that it was written in right-angle strokes without curves and used as late as the 18th century.

Human-readable
A document or code that can be read by a human being, with or without the aid of magnification, as opposed to one in a format that can be read only by a computer, for example, a printout of a text document, as opposed to its digital equivalent stored on a floppy or hard disk. Not synonymous with eye-readable, a term that excludes microforms readable by the human eye only with magnification and documents in formats specifically designed to be "read" by the visually impaired, such as Braille.

Humidify
Humidity.

Humor
A literary genre in which the author presents a story, poem, joke, etc., for the amusement of the reader. Works of literary wit are often published in anthologies.

Humor
Humour or humor is the tendency of particular cognitive experiences to provoke laughter and provide amusement. The term derives from the humoral medicine of the ancient Greeks, which taught that the balance of fluids in the human body, known as humors (Latin: *humor*, "body fluid"), control human health and emotion.

Hybrid Collection
A library collection consisting of materials in more than one format, often print and electronic books or serials. Hybrid collections limited

to a specific field or subject area may include media and multimedia, as well as items in print and other formats.

Hybrid Journal

A periodical that func-tions as both a magazine and a journal by including features typical of both. A prime example is *Analytical Chemistry* published by the American Chemical Society, which includes a magazine section in the front of each issue, followed by a longer section of research articles with its own table of contents and separate pagination.

Hydrographic Chart

Nautical chart.

Hydrologic Map

A map showing the drain-age of surface waters and other features related to hydrology for a geographic area.

Hygrometer

Any one of several meteorological instru-ments designed to measure atmospheric humidity, giving an on-the-spot reading. Hygrometers are used to monitor conditions in facilities such as libraries and museums that house materials easily damaged by water vapor. A hygrometer that displays output data in the form of a graph is called a *hygrograph*. A *thermohygrometer* measures temperature *and* relative humidity. A thermohygrometer that displays output in the form of a graph is called a *thermohygrograph*.

Hygroscopic

A material that readily absorbs and retains moisture from the air, often changing in form or consistency, for example, vellum used as a writing surface in manuscript books and in early bookbinding, which cockles with changes in relative humidity.

Hymnal

A separate collection of the metrical hymns sung in the Divine Office of the Catholic Church, arranged according to the liturgical calendar. Incorporated into Church liturgy in the 5th century, hymns were also contained in antiphonals and psalters. The contents of the hymnal were even-tually incorporated into the breviary.

Hype

An abbreviation of *hyperbole*. Publisher's slang for advertising copy written in an exaggerated style to attract attention to a new publication, not intended to be taken literally by prospective customers. Objective reviews are the best antidote. Compare with puff.

Hyperlink

Link.

Hypermedia

A hypertext document in which text is combined with graphics, audio, animation, and/or full-motion video.

Hypermodern

A term used in the book trade for collected first editions published within the last decade, or so recently that the author or title does not have a well-established reputation.

Hyperonym
Broader term.

Hypertext Markup Language (HTML)
Used to create the hyper-text documents accessible via the World Wide Web and intranets, HTML script is a cross-platform presentation markup language that allows the author to incorporate into a Web page text, frames, graphics, audio, video, and links to other documents and applications. Formatting is controlled by "tags" embedded in the text.

Hypertext Transfer Protocol (HTTP)
The communications protocol used in Web browser software to establish the connection between a client computer and a remote Web server, making it possible for data files in HTML format to be transmitted over the Internet from the server to the client machine on which the browser is installed. Most Web browsers are designed to default to http://whenever a user enters a Web address (URL) without the protocol.

Hyphen
In printing, the shortest rule used as punctuation. Also used to join the parts of a compound name or compound word and to divide a long word at the end of a line of written or printed text.

Hyphenation
Use of the hyphen to divide a word (*co-opt*), to compound two or more words (*son-in-law*), to give the impression of stuttering or faltering speech (*n-n-no*), or to indicate that a word is to be spelled out (*h-y-p-h-e-n-a-t-e*). In computerised typesetting, word division is done automatically by a system that applies a set of rules, with an exception dictionary of words that do not follow the rules.

Hyponym
A word or phrase that can be replaced without exception by another, without changing the meaning of a sentence, but not *vice versa,* for example, *azure* by *blue* or *sparrow* by *bird.*

I

i.e.
An abbreviation of the Latin phrase *id est,* meaning "that is".

I2
Internet2.

IA
Information audit.

IAA
Information Access Alliance.

IAALD
International Association of Agricultural Information Specialists.

IAML
International Association of Music Libraries, Archives and Documentation Centres.

IASA
International Association of Sound and Audio-visual Archives.

IASL
International Association of School Librarianship.

IASSIST
International Association of Social Science Information Service and Technology.

IATUL
International Association of Scientific and Technological University Libraries.

IBBY
International Board on Books for Young People.

ibid.
An abbreviation of the Latin *ibidem,* meaning "in the same place," used with a page number (or numbers) in footnotes, endnotes, and bibliographies to indicate a source that has been cited fully in a preceding note or entry.

IC
Information commons.

ICA
International Council on Archives.

ICAN
Interlibrary Cooperation and Networking Section.

ICIC
International Copyright Information Centre.

ICOLC
International Coalition of Library Consortia.

Iconic Document
A publication or other document in which the content is presented in predominantly graphic or pictorial form. Examples include atlases, children's picture books, exhibition catalogues, visual dictionaries, posters, postcards, etc.

ICRM
Institute of Certified Records Managers.

ICT
Information and Communication technology.

Identification Photograph
A photograph made to document the identity of a specific individual (person, animal, or plant), usually for legal, government, or commercial purposes. Most ID photographs are head shots taken from the front, but profiles may also be taken. Abbreviated *ID photo*.

Ideogram
A picture or symbol that represents an object or concept without expressing phonetically the sounds of its name, for example, the characters used in Chinese and Japanese writing systems. Also refers to a symbol that represents an idea, for example, the equal sign = or the plus sign +.

Idyl
From the Greek word meaning "little picture" - a short poem describing the simplicity and innocence of rural, pastoral, or domestic life. The origin of this literary form can be traced to Theocritus, who described pastoral life in Sicily for readers in Alexandria during the 3rd century B.C. An eclogue is a type of idyl. Compare with idyll.

Idyll
A narrative poem based on a romantic, epic, or tragic theme, for example, *Idylls of the King* (1859) by Alfred, Lord Tennyson, an episodic retelling of the fables of the Holy Grail, Camelot, Round Table, and Morte d'Arthur. Compare with idyl.

IETF
Internet Engineering Task Force.

IFCS
International Federation of Classification Societies.

IFLA
International Federation of Library Associations and Institutions.

IFRT
Intellectual Freedom Round Table.

IGO
An initialism for inter-national intergovernmental organisation.

IIL
Institute for Information Literacy.

IL
Information literacy.

ILAB
International League of Antiquarian Booksellers.

ILEX
Independent Librarian's Exchange.

ILL
Interlibrary loan.

Illuminated Initial
An initial letter in a medieval illuminated manuscript or early printed book painted in bright colours and embellished in gold or silver.

Illumination
The art or act of decorating a text, page, or initial letter with ornamental designs, miniatures, or lettering.

Illuminated Manuscript
An illuminated manuscript is a manuscript in which the text is supplemented by the addition of decoration, such as decorated initials, borders (marginalia) and miniature illustrations. In the most strict definition of the term, an illuminated manuscript only refers to manuscripts decorated with gold or silver, but in both common usage and modern scholarship, the term is now used to refer to any decorated or illustrated manuscript from the Western traditions. Comparable Far Eastern works are always described as painted, as are Mesoamerican works. Islamic manuscripts may be referred to as illuminated, illustrated or painted, though using essentially the same techniques as Western works.

Illusionism
A style of late medieval manuscript illumination in which the artist consciously creates the impression of a three-dimensional space on the two-dimensional surface of the page. The 16th-century Master of James IV of Scotland, identified by some as the Flemish painter and illuminator Gerard Horenbout, is considered an adept in the style

Illustrated Map
A map that includes pictures (drawings, photographs, etc.) of selected features located within the geographic area mapped, usually to aid identification, as distinct from a decorated map on which pictorial embellishment is mainly ornamental or a pictorial map on which small images are used to represent information about geographic features.

ILMP
International Literary Market Place.

IM
Instant messaging.

Image Card
Aperture card.

Image Search Engine
Image searching.

IMAP
Independent Media Arts Preservation.

Imbrication
In the book arts, a decorative pattern designed to give the impression of overlapping scales, tiles, shingles, leaves, etc.

Imitation Binding
A contemporary binding executed in a style intended to closely resemble that of an earlier period.

Imitation Leather
A synthetic or partly synthetic binding mate-rial manufactured to

resemble leather, for example, a fabric base given a textured coating, usually more washable than real leather. Synonymous with *artificial leather*.

IMLS
Institute of Museum and Library Services.

Impensis
Latin for "at the expense of," a word appearing in an imprint or colophon at the end of a work printed prior to the end of the 17th century, followed by the name of the person or entity responsible for financing the publication, usually the publisher or a bookseller or patron.

Imperfect
Said of a book discovered upon examination to have pages or sections missing, duplicated, or bound out of order or upside-down. The publisher will usually exchange or perfect copies containing binding errors and reimburse the purchaser for shipping costs.

Imperfections
Printed sheets rejected in the binding process because they contain defects or errors that require replacement sheets.

Imperial Print
A still photograph or motion picture print that is

- Unique,
- Of a significant subject,
- Made from original printing materials,
- The only print of the image known to exist,
- Made from a negative that no longer exists, and
- Printed about the time the negative was originally made (vintage). Because of their rarity, imperial prints are highly collectible.

Imposition
The arrangement of a set of pages of type for printing on a large sheet, so that the pages appear in consecutive order and correct alignment when the sheet is folded to form a signature. The purpose of imposition is to make the most efficient use of paper and to minimize printing time.

Impression
All the copies of a book or other publication printed in the same press run from the same setting of type or plates. An edition may comprise several impressions in which the typesetting remains unchanged.

Imprint Date
Publication date.

Improvisation
The practice of acting, reciting, singing, playing, composing, or creating a work of art extempor-aneously, in response to the immediate environment or the performer's inner feelings.

IMRAD
An acronym for *introduction, materials and methods, results, and discussion*.

In Loco Parentis
Latin for "in place of a parent," usually a person who temporarily assumes parental authority.

In Press
A book or other publication in the process of being printed, usually listed in *Forthcoming Books*.

In Print
A book currently available from the publisher, either as a frontlist or backlist title, as opposed to a title no longer available. Books currently in print in the United States are listed annually in *Books in Print, Children's Books in Print,* and *El-Hi Textbooks and Serials in Print*. The opposite of out of print.

In Progress
A term used by library cataloguers to indicate that a serial publication or set is as yet incomplete, usually because parts or volumes remain to be issued by the publisher.

In Quaternis
A Latin phrase used in catalogues compiled in medieval monastic libraries to refer to unbound books that may have been stitched into some kind of flexible wrappers made of parchment or vellum, rather than left loose in quires (Christopher de Hamel, *Scribes and Illuminators,* University of Toronto Press, 1992).

In Sheets
A book in flat or folded unbound sheets, before the sections have been gathered. Synonymous with *in quires.*

In Stock
An item for which the publisher or a dealer, jobber, distributor, or bookseller has a sufficient number of copies in inventory to fill an order at the time it is placed. Compare with out of stock and temporarily out of stock.

In the Can
In film production, a work not yet released or distributed, for which production has been completed.

In the Pipeline
Material in the process of development or production, which may soon be completed. Also refers to funding authorised and expected but not yet received.

Incipit Page
The beginning of a major section of text in a medieval manuscript or early printed book, embellished with a particularly large initial letter, often followed by display script in diminuendo to emphasise the importance of the division. In Gospel books, the incipit page sometimes begins with a monogram or initial capital representing the evangelist's name.

Inclusive Dates
The dates of the oldest and most recent items in an archival collection, not necessarily indicative of its chronological or period strength. Synonymous with *span dates.* Compare with bulk dates.

Incunable
Books, pamphlets, calendars, and indulgences printed, not handwritten, before 1501 in Europe. The date 1501 holds not distinct significance other than being a convenient round figure directly after Johannes Gutenberg's development of the printing press in

mid 15th century, as such works printed shortly after the 1501 cut-off are often described as "post-incunable".

In-cut Note
Cut-in note.

Independent Publisher (IP)
A trade publication, formerly titled *Small Press*, that provides articles, announcements of new books, excerpts, and over 100 reviews of small press publications in each bimonthly issue. *Independent Publisher* is known for reviewing works not reviewed elsewhere. ISSN: 1098-5735.

Independent Schools Section (ISS)
The section of the Amer-ican Association of School Librarians (AASL) within the American Library Association (ALA) that provides a forum for the discussion of and action on issues concerning librarianship in non-public schools of all types.

Index
An alphabetical listing of names or topics mentioned in the book, with their page numbers. For serials and journals, the index is usually published after the volume is completed and is found in the last issue.

Index Expurgatorius
Index Librorum Prohibitorum.

Index Map
An outline map showing the complete extent of the geographic coverage and the numbering system of a set or series of more detailed sheet maps, with or without segmentation.

Index of Prohibited Books
Index Librorum Prohibitorum.

Indexable Matter
The parts of a book or other publication included when the document is analysed for indexing, not necessarily limited to the text. Notes, appendices, and other complementary or supplementary material may or may not be indexed, depending on its potential usefulness to readers and the policy of the publisher. Bibliographies and glossaries are rarely indexed.

Indexing Language
An artificial language consisting of subject headings or content descriptors selected to facilitate information retrieval by serving as access points in a catalogue or index, including any lead-in vocabulary and rules governing form of entry, syntax, etc.

India Paper
An exceptionally thin, strong, opaque, uncoated paper made from vegetable fibre, used for printing fine books. Originally manufactured in Asia, India paper has a smooth but not glossy white surface.

Indie
Independent film and independent label.

Inedita
The plural of the Latin word *ineditum*, meaning "not made known," literary works not published, for example, the personal papers of a writer or well-known person. Works of this kind are

usually available in the special collections of the library that purchased them or received them as a gift.

Inedited
A work published as submitted by the author, without editorial changes. Such works may include passages objectionable to some readers or contain errors of fact that an editor might have corrected or omitted.

Infometrics
Informetrics.

Information and Referral (I&R)
A service available at no charge, usually from a public library or other public service agency, providing contact information about *other* organisations, agencies, and individuals qualified to offer specific information and services, both free and fee-based, usually within the local community.

Information Ethics
The branch of ethics that focuses on the relationship between the creation, organisation, dissemination, and use of information, and the ethical standards and moral codes governing human conduct in society. In the United States, the *ALA Code of Ethics* is the leading statement of ethical standards for the library profession.

Information Gap
Digital divide.

Information Law
The regulation and control of information by the state, including laws governing censorship, copyright and intellectual property, forgery, freedom of information, intellectual freedom, privacy, computer crime, and public funding of information providers, such as libraries and museums. Also refers to the specialised branch of legal studies dealing with the regulation of information.

Information Overload
A condition in which too much information is available on a topic, a common occurrence in online searching, particularly when the query is expressed in terms that are too general. Systems that facilitate the retrieval of relevant resources, sifting out the chaff, are badly needed. In the meantime, consumers of information must develop their own analytical and critical skills.

Information Science
The systematic study and analysis of the sources, development, collection, organisation, dissemi-nation, evaluation, use, and management of information in all its forms, including the channels (formal and informal) and technology used in its communi-cation. Compare with informatics and library science.

Informetrics
Informetrics is the study of quantitative aspects of information. This includes the production, dissemination and use of all forms of information, regardless of its form or origin. As such, informetrics encompasses the fields of

- scientometrics, which studies quantitative aspects of science;

- webometrics, which studies quantitative aspects of the World Wide Web;
- cybermetrics, which is similar to webometrics, but broadens its definition to include electronic resources;
- bibliometrics, which studies quantitative aspects of *recorded* information.

The term informetrics (*Informetrie*) was coined by Nacke in 1979

Information Storage and Retrieval (ISAR)

Operations performed by the hard-ware and soft-ware used in indexing and storing a file of machine-readable records whenever a user queries the system for infor-mation relevant to a specific topic. For records to be retrieved, the search statement must be expre-ssed in syntax executable by the computer.

Information Superhighway

Internet.

Information Superhighway

The information superhighway or infobahn was a popular term used through the 1990s to refer to digital communication systems and the Internet telecommunications network. It is associated with United States Senator and later Vice-President Al Gore.

Information Technology (IT)

A very broad term encompassing all aspects of the management and processing of infor-mation by computer, including the hardware and software required to access it. The Library and Information Technology Association (LITA) publishes the quarterly journal *Infor-mation Technology and Libraries (ITAL).*

Information Theory

The systematic statement of principles concerning the phenomenon of information and its trans-mission, based on the collection and analysis of quantitative and qualitative data as a means of testing hypotheses about its nature and properties. Compare with informatics.

Interleaved

When blank leaves alternate with the printed leaves a book is said to be interleaved.

International Digital Publishing Forum

The International Digital Publishing Forum (IDPF) is a trade and standards association for the digital publishing industry, that has been set up in order to establish a reliable and complete standard for ebook publishing. This is the organization responsible for the EPUB standard currently used by most e-readers.

Starting from the Open eBook Publication Structure or "OEB" (1999), which was created loosely around HTML, it then defined the OPS (Open Publication Structure), the OPF (Open Packaging Format) and the OCF (Open Container Format). These formats are the basis for the common EPUB and Mobipocket ebook file formats (Comparison of e-book formats).

While the basic standards are now established (pages,

hyperlinks, definition of table of contents, authors, etc.) some other standards intersect the hardware field, such as those for power and for features of the hardware reader devices, and are still undergoing change and evolution. Other standards for ecommerce (including Digital Rights Management protections), are tied to the way the ebook is sold or delivered, and are therefore controlled by the respective vendors.

International Edition
A textbook that has been published outside of the USA. The publishers of international editions generally do not authorize the sale and distribution of international editions in the United States and Canada and such sale or distribution may violate the copyrights and trademarks of the publishers of such works.

Internet
The Internet is a global system of interconnected computer networks that use the standard Internet protocol suite (*TCP/IP*) to serve billions of users worldwide. It is a *network of networks* that consists of millions of private, public, academic, business, and government networks, of local to global scope, that are linked by a broad array of electronic, wireless and optical networking technologies. The Internet carries an extensive range of information resources and services, such as the inter-linked hypertext documents of the World Wide Web (WWW) and the infrastructure to support email.

Issue
Synonymous with State, referring to the priority of copies within the first edition.

Issue points
Noted changes between various copies of the same book. Since collectors generally prefer the earliest issue they often use small changes (such as a spelling correction) to determine priority, any such difference is described as an issue point.

Integral
A leaf or page is said to be integral when it is one that was sewn and bound into a book during its manufacture.

Isopleth
A line on a map connecting places registering the same amount or ratio of some geographical or meteorological phenomenon or phenomena Also calledisogram isoline

Informational Value
Archival value.

Informetrics
The use of mathematical and statistical methods in research related to libraries, documentation, and information. Synonymous with *infometrics*.

Ingram
A wholesaler of trade books, audiobooks, and periodicals to libraries, booksellers, and specialty retailers, Ingram passes on economies of scale to its customers in the form of a substantial discount off the list price of items in its inventories.

Inhabited Initial

An initial letter in an illu-minated manuscript or early printed book containing within its contours one or more decorative animal, human, or imaginary figures, not necessarily related to the text, often depicted fancifully.

In-house Archives

The unit within a company, agency, or institution responsible for retaining the non-current records of the parent organisation and sometimes those of other corporate bodies and individuals with which it is closely associated, as opposed to an outside repository.

In-house

Refers to something accomplished on the premises, usually by library staff, rather than outside the library by an independent contractor, for example, binding done in the library, rather than sent offsite to a commercial bindery. in-house use.

Initial Article

An article appearing in first-word position in a title or corporate name, usually *a, an*, or *the* (or the equivalent in another language), ignored in indexing and filing under most filing rules.

Initial Letter

A large capital letter at the beginning of the first word of a paragraph, chapter, or other division of a text. In medieval manuscripts and early printed books, initial letters were often decorated or illuminated, for example, the 'B' at the beginning of the text of a psalter (the first letter of *Beatus*, the first word of the first Psalm).

Initial Title Element

The word or words selected by the cataloguer from the title of a musical work to be placed first in the uniform title for the work, for example, the word *Nocturne* from the title *Troisième nocturne*. If no additions are required by the rules, the element becomes the uniform title for the work (*AACR2*).

Initialism

A shortened form of a phrase or compound term composed of the initial letters of its words or parts spoken *letter-by-letter*, rather than pronounced as a word (*example*: IPO for initial public offering or *ADA* for *Americans with Disabilities Act*). Compare with abbreviation and acronym.

Initialise

To start a computer system, programme, or disk anew, an operation that usually requires erasing all or part of the data stored in memory. In Apple Macintosh computers, initializing a disk formats it. In computer programming, a variable is *initialised* when it is given its first value.

Ink Ball

A large, round pad made of buckskin or sheepskin firmly stuffed with a wad of cotton or wool and fastened to a short wooden handle, used by the pressman in hand printing to apply ink to type set in wooden formes. Most pressmen worked two-handed with an ink ball in each hand.

Inkhorn
A small receptacle made from the inverted horn of an animal, used to hold ink in the medieval scriptorium. Because manuscripts were written in both black and red ink, and sometimes in other colours, a scribe needed more than one ink pot. Inkhorns were usually inserted into metal hoops attached to the edge of a writing desk, into holes cut through its surface, or into free-standing holders to prevent them from overturning.

Inlay
A picture or decorative element of contrasting colour set into the cover of a book, usually in leather with or without tooling.

In case binding, the strip of heavy paper or card added as a lining between the inner edges of the boards to stiffen the spine when the case is covered in cloth, paper, or some other protective material.

Inline
An elegant display type-face in which each broad stroke has a white line down its center. Compare with outline letter.

Innocent Infringement
The U.S., *Copyright Act of 1976* includes a provision allowing the court to reduce damages below the statutory minimum in a finding of copyright infringement, if the defendant can establish that the infringement was unintentional. Burden of proof is on the defendant.

INPL
Public Libraries International Network.

Input
Data transferred to or entered into a computer system for processing, as opposed to the *results* of processing, known as output. The most commonly used *input devices* in personal computing are the keyboard and mouse. Scanners are also becoming more widespread, and significant advances are being made in voice recognition technology.

Inscribed Copy
A copy of a book that bears, as a presentation inscription, the name of the recipient and sometimes an appropriate comment or remark, followed by the signature of the donor, who may or may not be the author. The inscription is usually written on the flyleaf or title page, as in these examples. Abbreviated *insc.*

Inscription
A brief, informal dedica-tion written inside a book, usually on the flyleaf. Also, words engraved in stone or on some other hard surface, usually as a greeting or to commemorate an important event or person.

Insert
Any printed material, such as map, illustration, subscription blank, advertising supplement, etc., slipped loose (un-bound) into a book or periodical, which is not an integral part of the publication.

Inset Map
A small map drawn or printed inside the neat line of a larger map, usually showing at smaller scale the vicinity of the area covered by the

larger map or (more often) a specific detail or feature of the main map at larger scale, for example, a major metropolitan area within the borders of a state or provincial road map.

Inspection Copy
Examination copy.

Instalment Sale
A sale in which the pur-chaser pays for an item in two or more payments, usually at regular intervals of a month or more. Under this arrangement, the item is shipped when the order is received, without waiting for final payment. In the book trade, this practice is usually limited to very expensive multi-volume reference works.

Instalment
One portion of a literary work divided into parts for publication in consecutive issues of a periodical or one part or fascicle of such a work published separately, usually at regular intervals. During the 19th century, novels were often published in this fashion.

Instant Book
A book written, produced, and marketed within weeks of an important event to capitalise on current interest in the subject. Because careful research requires an investment of time and effort, works prepared in haste may contain errors of fact or lack depth of treatment. A perceptive reviewer will note such deficiencies.

Instant Photograph
A photograph made from a self-developing film packet containing its own developing chemicals, by a process introduced by Edwin Land's Polaroid Corporation in 1947 (this example). The company abandoned instant photography in 2008 to focus on digital cameras and printing.

Instruction lab
A library instruction classroom equipped with computer workstations (PCs or laptops) for the hands-on use of students, usually with an instructor station connected to an LCD projector for the demonstration of online search techniques. Wireless technology is used in newer labs. In public libraries, this type of facility is often called a *computer training room*.

Instructional Film
Educational film.

Instructional Style
Teaching style.

Instructions
Brief notes made in a medieval manuscript by a stationer, scribe, or illuminator to indicate the form, content, or colour of what was to be copied or painted, or giving details of binding and assembly, usually rendered unobtru-sively in hard point, metal point, or plummet.

Integral
Said of a leaf or page sewn or bound into a book or pamphlet when the publication was first printed.

Integrated Learning Center
Information commons.

Integrated Library System (ILS)
Library management system.

Integrating Resource
As defined in *AACR2 2002*, a category of continuing resource added to or changed over time by means of updates incorporated into the whole without remaining discrete. Examples include updating looseleaf services, databases, Web sites, etc.

Intellectual Freedom
The right under the First Amendment to the U.S., Constitution of any person to read or express views that may be unpopular or offensive to some people, within certain limitations (libel, slander, etc.). Legal cases concerning free speech issues are heard by the U.S., Supreme Court.

Intellectual Property
Tangible products of the human mind and intelligence entitled to the legal status of personal property, especially works protected by copyright, inventions that have been patented, and registered trademarks. An idea is considered the intellectual property of its creator only after it has been recorded or made manifest in specific form. Abbreviated *IP*.

Intelligence
Information about events, or concerning the activities of a government or political group, gathered systematically and often covertly, especially for its value in strategic military planning. When recorded, military intelligence usually remains classified until it becomes publicly known.

Intent-to-use
An application filed with the U.S., Patent and Trademark Office to place an unused and unregistered trademark or service mark on temporary "hold" for a specified period of time, based on the applicant's good faith intention to use it in commerce after the application has been filed.

Interactive Map
A map in digital format designed to allow the user to view a portion of its surface on a different scale or gain access to additional information, usually by selecting a hot spot on its surface with a pointing device such as a mouse (*examples*: *Mapquest* and the National Geographic Society's *Maps* site).

Interactive
A computer interface designed to respond to input from a human being, usually in the form of commands and/or data. A back-and-forth dialogue between a computer programme and its human user is an *interactive session*. Highly interactive systems, such as computer games, are designed to anticipate the user's needs, instead of responding in a prescribed way. Once started, a programme that is *not* interactive proceeds without further human input.

Intercolumn
The blank space between columns of text on a page in a printed book or in a manuscript written in the form of a roll or codex. In medieval manuscripts, the intercolumn is sometimes decorated, as in this 13th-century psalter.

Interdisciplinary Journal
A scholarly periodical that pub-

lishes articles of primary interest to researchers in two or more specific academic disciplines or fields (*examples*: *Language and Cognitive Processes* and *Medical Engineering and Physics*). Compare with multidisciplinary journal.

Interface
The point or process that joins two components of a data processing system, for example, the screen display that functions as intermediary between a software programme and its human users. Some interfaces are more user-friendly than others.

Interlace
A decorative design in a medieval manuscript or early printed book composed of an intricate pattern of intertwined vines, snakes, animal or human limbs, or purely abstract lines, sometimes in the form of a complex knot.

Interlinear
A form of gloss in which translation, commentary, or explanatory notes are handwritten or printed above the lines of text to which they refer, usually in a different script or typeface or in letters of smaller size.

Intermediate Records
Records used so infrequently by an agency or individual in the conduct of business or affairs that normal operations are not hampered by their transfer to a storage area less accessible than the location where active records are housed.

Intermediate Storage
In archives, a separate area where inactive or intermediate records are stored temporarily prior to final disposition, often less accessible than the location where active records are housed. Synonymous with *secondary storage*.

Intermediate
In motion picture production, any film material, negative or positive, created in the process of making duplicate copies from an original source, for example, a *master positive,* a high-quality positive print made from the original negative for use in making duplicate negatives from which release prints are made.

Intermediate-scale Map
A systematic representation on a two-dimensional surface of a land area of medium extent, at a representative fraction of 1:50,000 to 1:100,000, showing a moderate amount of detail.

Intern
Internship.

Internal Document
A document, such as a memorandum or report, intended for distribution *within* an organisation, rather than for wider publication. Sensitive internal documents may be classified to restrict access to authorised personnel, and shredded when no longer needed.

International Coalition of Library Consortia (ICOLC)
Formed in 1997, ICOLC is an informal, self-organised group of over two hundred library consortia from around the world, dedi-

cated to facilitating discussion of issues of common interest.

International Copyright Information Centre (ICIC)
A clearinghouse with headquarters in Paris, established by UNESCO in 1971 to offer assistance to publishers from developing countries in securing rights to books and other publications protected by copyright in other countries.

International Copyright
Copyright protection extended to works published outside a country's borders, currently governed by national copyright law and international agreements, such as the *Berne Convention* and the *Universal Copyright Convention.*

International Federation of Classification Societies (IFCS)
Founded in 1985, IFCS is a federation of national, regional, and linguistically based classification societies devoted to promoting research in classification. The IFCS publishes the *IFCS Newsletter* and supports the *Journal of Classification* published by the Classification Society of North America.

International Intergovernmental Organisation (IGO)
An international corporate body created by cooperative action between governments of sovereign states (*AACR2*). Examples include the United Nations (UN), the International Monetary Fund (IMF), and the World Health Organisation (WHO).

International League of Antiquarian Booksellers (ILAB)
An organisation encompassing 20 national associations representing antiquarian booksellers in 30 countries, ILAB was founded in Amsterdam in 1947 to uphold and improve professional standards in the antiquarian book trade, promote honourable conduct in business, and contribute to a broader appreciation of the art and history of the book.

Internet Explorer
Web browser.

Internet Protocol
IP address.

Internet Use Policy
Acceptable use policy.

Intrinsic Value
Archival value.

Introductory Title
Leadin title.

Inverted Heading
In indexing, a multiword heading in which conventional word order is transposed to bring the most significant word into firstword position (*example*: the Library of Congress subject heading Combustion, Spontaneous human).

Inverted Title
A title divided by a bibliographer or indexer into two parts and transposed to bring a significant word into firstword position, for use as an entry in a bibliography or as a heading in an index (*example*: *Language and Linguistics, Dictionary of*).

Invisible Web
Deep web.

Invoice Symbol
Invoice.

IP
Intellectual property *and* IP address.

IPEDS
Integrated Postsecondary Education Data System.

IPI
Image Permanence Institute.

IPM
An abbreviation of *integrated pest management.*

IPS
An abbreviation of *inches per second.*

IR
Information retrieval and institutional repository.

IRA
International Reading Association.

IRO
International Relations Office.

IRRT
International Relations Round Table.

IS
Information system and Instruction Section.

ISA
Information Science and Technology Abstracts.

ISAR
Information Storage and Retrieval.

ISBD
International Standard Bibliographic Description.

ISBN
International Standard Book Number.

ISDS
International Serials Data System.

ISI
Institute for Scientific Information.

ISMN
International Standard Music Number.

ISO
International Organisation for Standardisation.

Isopleth
Isogram.

Isorithm
Isogram.

ISP
Internet service provider.

ISRC
International Standard Recording Code.

ISRN
International Standard Report Number.

ISS
Independent Schools Section.

ISSN
International Standard Serial Number.

ISTC
International Standard Text Code.

IT

Information technology.

Item

Bibliographic item and record item.

Iteration

A single instance of an integrating resource, either as first published or as subsequently updated (*AACR2*).

Iterative Search

A search for information in which the researcher or investigator repeatedly poses questions until an answer or solution is found.

ITSO

Integrated Tool for Selection and Ordering.

J

Jacket
Dust jacket and sleeve.

Jacket
The jacket /dust jacket (sometimes book jacket, dust wrapper or dust cover) of a book is the detachable outer cover, usually made of paper and printed with text and illustrations. This outer cover has folded flaps that hold it to the front and back book covers. Often the back panel or flaps are printed with biographical information about the author, a summary of the book from the publisher (known as a blurb), critical praise from celebrities or authorities in the book's subject area. In addition to its promotional role, the dust jacket protects the book covers from damage. However, since it is itself relatively fragile, and since dust jackets have practical, aesthetic, and sometimes financial value, the jacket may in turn be wrapped in another jacket, usually transparent, especially if the book is a library volume.

Jade Book
A book consisting of text inscribed on thin jade tablets bound along one edge or strung together on one or more cords, a luxury format reserved in traditional Chinese society for the most highly esteemed texts.

Jansenist Binding
A bookbinding with an austere exterior, lacking ornamentation, except perhaps a small amount of gold tooling above and below the bands on the spine, but in some cases luxuriously decorated on the interior.

Japanese Style
Chinese style.

Japon
Japanese vellum.

Jargon
The specialised vocabulary and idioms of a group of people engaged in the same activity or line of work, for example, the MARCese used by library cataloguers in reference to the bibliographic record and its component fields. In a more general sense, speech that is unintelligible or incoherent.

Java
A high-level programming language widely used for writing application software for the World Wide Web. Introduced in 1995 by Sun Microsystems, Java allows programmes to run on a Java enabled Web browser regardless of platform, eliminating the need to write plat-form-specific versions of the same programme. Netscape developed the JavaScript language to make programming in Java easier, especially in the design of interactive Web pages, but it is less powerful and limits the designer to the HTML interface.

Jeremiad
A fierce denunciation of a particular evil, or the evils of society in general, in which current misfortunes are considered a just penalty for past misdeeds and repentance extolled as the only road to a happier, more secure future. The term is derived from the *Lamentations of Jeremiah* in the Old Testament. The sermons of Puritan preachers in colonial New England provide abundant examples of this literary form.

Jestbook
A collection of jokes, witty anecdotes, epigrams, exempla, and ribald tales, usually with didactic endings. Introduced into Europe from the Muslim world during the 8th century, jestbooks enjoyed greatest popularity during the 16th and 17th centuries. Because of their ephemeral nature, few early examples survive. Also spelled *jest book*. Synonymous with *facetiae*.

Jewel Case
A hinged hard plastic container of standard size with transparent front and back, designed to hold one or more compact discs (CDs) and a small printed booklet or paper inserts front and back describing the product. The disc(s) snap into interior tray(s) made of clear or opaque plastic.

Job Description
A detailed description of the duties and responsibilities associated with a specific position in an organisation, used in training, performance evaluation, and the allocation of workload. Compare with position description.

Job Lot
Copies of a book or other publication offered by the publisher at lower than list price to a wholesale bookseller known as a jobber, usually to reduce or close out stock of the title. Compare with remainders.

Job Performance
The skill and competence with which an employee executes the duties and responsibilities associated with the position filled, usually assessed periodically in a formal evaluation process. In academic libraries, peer evaluation is commonly used to assess the performance of librarians.

John Cotton Dana Award
Inaugurated in 1946 at the annual conference of the American Library Association, the John Cotton Dana Award is given annually to several libraries for their achieve-

ments in public education and public relations. Each winner receives a cash development grant of $3,000 from the award's sponsor, the H.W. Wilson Foundation. The award is named after John Cotton Dana, a librarian who began his career in Denver in 1889 and closed it in 1929 in Newark, N.J., having become a key figure in innovative librarianship during the progressive era. Selections are made by the Library Leadership and Management Association (LLAMA), a division of the ALA.

Joint

In bookbinding, the exterior junction of the covers and spine of a book, formed by the narrow portion of covering material affixed directly to the endpaper in case binding, along the groove separating the board from the inlay over the spine. On the inside, the hinge is formed by the fold in the endpaper, reinforced in some editions with a paper or cloth strip. Together, hinge and joint allow the cover to open and close like a door. A bound volume has a *front joint* connecting the front board to the spine and a *back joint* connecting the back board to the spine.

Joint Author

In *AACR2*, a person who collaborates with one or more others to produce a work in which all who contribute perform the same function. The contributions of the individual collaborators may not be indicated and are usually not separable. In catalogueing, main entry is made under the name of the author listed first on the chief source of information, with added entries for the other authors, unless primary responsibility clearly rests with one author. Bibliographic style manuals differ in the maximum number of joint authors included in a citation.

Joint Committee on Printing (JCP)

The congressional committee responsible under *Title 44 U.S.,C.* for overseeing the functions of the U.S., Government Printing Office (GPO) and general printing procedures of the federal government. The Committee includes members of the Senate and House of Representatives from both political parties.

Joint Imprint

The imprint of two or more publishers appearing on the title page of the same edition of a work. In most instances, the co-publishers market and distribute the work in different countries or regions of the world.

Joint Publication

Publication of the same work by two different publishers in separate editions, often in hard-cover by a university press and in paperback by a trade publisher.

Joint Steering Committee for Development of RDA (JSC)

The committee respon-sible for developing and maintaining *Anglo-American Cataloguing Rules* for the construction of catalogues and other lists in general libraries of all sizes, covering the description of, and provision of access points for, all library materials commonly collected. Its members are the American Library Association (ALA), the Australian Committee on Cataloguing (ACOC), the British Library, the Canadian Committee on Cataloguing (CCC), the Chartered Institute of Library and Information Professionals (CILIP), and the Library of Congress. In 2004, the JSC began working on a new code, *RDA: Resource Description and Access*, to replace the *Anglo-American Cataloguing Rules* first published in 1978. A full draft of *RDA* was issued in November 2008. JSC discussed the responses to the full draft at its meeting in April 2009, and the revised text was delivered to the publishers in June 2009. *RDA* was published in the *RDA Toolkit* in June 2010.

Joint Use

A cooperative arrangement between a library and another institution, such as a school, community college, or university, in which both institutions share the same facility and/or collections for example, the Dr. Martin Luther King, Jr. Library in San Jose, California, a partnership between the City of San Jose and San Jose State University in which the San Jose Public Library and the University library share the same building and collections.

Journal

A periodical devoted to disseminating original research and commentary on current developments in a specific discipline, subdiscipline, or field of study usually published in quarterly, bimonthly, or monthly issues sold by subscription. Journal articles are usually written by the person who conducted the research. Longer than most magazine articles, they almost always include a bibliography or list of works cited at the end. In journals in the sciences and social sciences, an abstract usually precedes the text of the article, summarizing its content. Most scholarly journals are peer-reviewed. Scholars often use a current contents service to keep abreast of the journal literature in their fields of interest and specialisation.

A library usually binds the all the issues for a given publication year in one or more annual volumes or converts its print issues to microform. Articles from some journals are available in digital format in full-text bibliographic databases, usually by licensing agreement. Some journal publishers also provide an electronic version accessible via the World Wide Web. Abbreviated *jour*. Compare with magazine and journal of commentary.

Journal Boycott

On January 31, 2012, *The Chronicle of Higher Education* reported a protest against high journal subscription prices by more than 2400 scholars who signed an online Cost of Knowledge pledge not to publish in or contribute editorial services to journals published by Elsevier, a leading publisher of scientific journals worldwide. The protest began with a blog post on January

21, 2012 in which award winning mathematician Timothy Gowers of the University of Cambridge suggested boycotting Elsevier for restricting access to scholarly information by charging exorbitant subscription prices. Libraries have long complained about prohibitively high journal prices. This is the first sign of rebellion among researchers who produce the information.

Journal Club

A formal or informal group that meets professionally to discuss recently published scholarly journal articles on topics in an academic discipline or profession. Often moderated, journal clubs are common in the sciences and medicine, serving as vehicle for continuing education.

Journal of Commentary

A periodical that specialises in the publication of news analysis and discussion of political, social, and cultural issues, usually from an editorial position somewhere on the political spectrum, for example, the *National Review* on the Right and *The Progressive* on the Left. Journals of commentary are usually issued monthly and sold at news stands, in book-stores, and by subscription. Compare with journal and magazine.

Journal Pagination

In journal publishing, page numbers often begin with the first page of the first issue in a volume and continue in a single numeric sequence through the last page of the last issue in the volume. This means that the pagination in each issue begins where the previous issue ended. Since, most journals are published quarterly and bound into annual volumes, continuous pagination makes it easier for the user to find a specific article by page number in the appropriate volume. Compare with magazine pagination.

Journalese

The rather trite style of writing used by some newspaper and broadcast journalists who rely on clichés and hackneyed expressions to pitch a story to the widest possible audience avoided in serious journalism.

Journalism

The art of gathering news, writing and editing copy, or directing the publication of a newspaper, magazine, or journal. A person who turns news into copy is a *journalist*. A photographer who specialises in capturing news on camera is a *photojournalist*. In the United States, Pulitzer Prises are awarded annually for distinguished public service in journalism and for reporting in a variety of categories.

Journals Consortium

An organisation that handles the production and distribution of a number of journals but does not necessarily exercise editorial control over them if they are owned by other organisations. In the United States, one of the best-known examples is the journals publishing division of the Johns Hopkins University Press (JHUP), which provides online access through *Project MUSE* to the full-text of its own journals, plus many titles from other scholarly journal publishers.

JPEG

An acronym for Joint Photographic Experts Group, a standard for compressing still images in digital format at ratios of 100:1 and higher. Data compression is accomplished by dividing the image into small blocks of pixels, halved again and again until the desired ratio is reached. Data is lost each time the compression ratio increases. Pronounced "jay-peg."

JSTOR

A non-profit organisation that began as a digital text initiative of the Andrew W. Mellon Foundation aimed at easing the space problems faced by libraries that own long runs of journal back files, *JSTOR* provides searchable bibliographic data-bases containing the complete full-text of core scholarly journals in a wide range of disciplines, current to within 2-5 years. In 2009, *JSTOR* merged with ITHAKA.

Jukebox

Originally, a phonograph record player with an automatic record changer and speaker, designed to allow the user to select and play music from a self-contained collection of recordings. First introduced in 1928 by Justus P. Seeburg, coin-operated jukeboxes played 78 rpm shellac discs until the 1950s when the Seeburg Corporation introduced a model that played only 45 rpm vinyl singles. Jukebox design became more elaborate as their popularity increased, reaching its peak in the 1960s. Compact discs replaced phonograph records in jukeboxes in the 1980s, and by the end of the 20th century, several companies introduced digital jukeboxes that play recorded music stored on a dedicated proprietary server. Also used as a synonym for CD-ROM changer.

Jumbo File

A collection of prints, pictures, and/or documents of unusually large size, organised for ease of access in a folder, port-folio, or other container of a size sufficient to accommodate them.

Jump Page

The page of a newspaper, magazine, or journal on which a story or article that begins on the first page is continued, usually indicated by the references "Continued on page..." and "Continued from page..." at the break in the text.

Junk Mail

Unwanted postal mail and e-mail messages, usually advertising not solicited by the recipient.

Juried

Peer-reviewed.

Justification

In typesetting, the equal and exact spacing of words and letters in a line of type to make the text block appear vertically even at the right and/or left-hand margins. Type aligned with the left margin is said to be *left-justified*. Aligned with the right-hand margin, it is said to be *right-justified*. Type can also be *centered* on a page, as in headings. Compare with alignment.

Justified
Justification.

Juvenile Collection
A library collection of books and other materials intended specifically for children under 12-13 years of age, shelved separately from the adult and young adult collections, sometimes in a children's room with separate sections for juvenile fiction and nonfiction, beginning readers and easy books, picture books, and books for very young children. Juvenile collections are usually managed by a librarian with specialised training in children's services.

Juvenile Literature
Children's literature.

Juveniles
A term used by publishers and serious collectors to refer to children's books as a type of publication. Compare with juvenilia.

Juvenilia
Works produced during the childhood or youth of an artist or writer, which may reveal literary or artistic immaturity but often compensate with an abundance of youthful enthusiasm and a style or approach that is highly innovative.

K

Kanji

A subset of approximately 5000 Chinese ideograms borrowed or adapted by the Japanese for use in their own written language. In 1946, the Japanese government selected a smaller subset of 1850 for use in official publications and in newspaper/magazine publishing.

Keep Down

In typesetting, an instruction to the typesetter to use capital letters sparingly in the titles of works mentioned in the text. The opposite of keep up.

Keep Up

In typesetting, an instruction to the typesetter to use capital letters at the beginning of each word of the title of any work mentioned in the text. Prepositions, conjunctions, and initial articles are usually kept down, making 'The Adventures of Huckleberry Finn' an *all up* setting. In modern British practice, only the first word and proper names are capitalised. In French, only the first word following the initial article and proper names are capitalised. In Italian, only the initial article is capitalised. In German, all nouns are capitalised.

Keepsake

An item given or kept as a memento, especially something printed for distribution by a club or organisation on a special occasion.

Kelmscott Press

A private press founded in 1891 by the architect, designer, writer, calligrapher, and typographer William Morris, who sought to revive, in modern book production, the aesthetic of the medieval period and early printing. Although the Press survived only until 1894, the 53 books it issued set a very high standard of beauty and craftsmanship.

Kerf

A shallow groove cut into the binding edge of the sections of a book, perpendicular to the spine near the head and tail of the text block, to allow the kettle stitching to be recessed.

Kern

The portion of the face of a unit of type that extends beyond the edge of its body to overlap an adjacent character, for example, the lowercase italic *f* in many typefaces.

Kettle Stitch

In hand-binding, a special end stitch taken near the head and foot of each section to lock the sewing thread after it passes down the fold, linking adjacent sections through their folds and producing two rows of kettle stitches perpendicular to the binding edge, one near the top and the other at the bottom of the spine. In some editions, a shallow groove called a kerf is cut into the binding edge at each end of the spine to recess the kettle stitching.

Key

Text or a diagram identifying specific items, features, or people shown in a print, photograph, or picture, or on a map, either located on the same sheet or on a separate sheet.

Keyboard

A thin, flat peripheral device that allows a computer user to enter input by manually depressing keys marked with letters, numerals, and special characters. The keys can be arranged in a single set of parallel rows or split into two sets of rows to make them more ergonomic. A computer keyboard can be built in, as in a laptop, or a separate piece of equipment, as in most desktop personal computers.

Key Control

The process of establishing and maintaining the list of persons authorised to access keys to the door locks and lockable equipment in a library, as a means of securing the facility's locking system. A full survey of all locks and lock locations must first be conducted and an inventory made of all existing keys. Then key distribution is carefully recorded, including keys retrieved from employees who leave library employment. Access to master keys is limited to essential personnel, using a two-key system in areas where security is especially important. When not in use, keys are stored in a secure cabinet, with a log for recording name of borrower, date of issue, and date of return.

Key Map

A map showing the coverage of a set or series of more detailed maps, usually distinguished on the larger map by number, letter, or some other system of symbols. The keyed maps may or may not be overlapping

Key Title

The unique name assigned to a serial publication by the centers of the ISSN Network under the International Serials Data System (ISDS), usually the same as the title proper. In library catalogueing, the key title is entered immediately following the ISSN in the bibliographic record. If there is no ISSN, the key title is not added.

Keynote Address

A formal speech delivered at the beginning or on the first day of a library conference, often by a prominent person in or from outside the profession, usually on a topic related to the overall theme of the conference. The keynote address is intended to stimulate thought and set the tone for subsequent discussion.

Keypad

A small handheld infrared device used in large screen demonstrations of online systems to enable the instructor to control electronic equipment installed on the demonstration console.

Keyword Index

A type of subject index in which significant words, usually from the titles of the works indexed, are used as headings. When a string of keywords is rotated, such an index is said to be permuted.

Keyword(s)

A significant word or phrase in the title, subject headings, contents note, abstract, or text of a record in an online catalogue or bibliographic database that can be used as a search term in a free-text search to retrieve all the records containing it.

Most online catalogues and bibliographic data-bases include an option that allows the user to type words that describe the research topic and retrieve records containing the search terms in the data fields the system is designed to search whenever the keywords option is selected. One disadvantage of a key-words search is that it does not take into account the *meaning* of the words used as input, so if a term has more than one meaning, irrelevant records may be retrieved.

Kickstool

A step stool designed to move on casters when gently pushed, often available in the stacks of libraries that have shelving too high to be reached by persons of average height. Many libraries in the United States favour a circular metal design with casters that retract under the downward pressure of a person's weight, a rubber bumper around the bottom that grabs the floor for steadier footing, and a non-skid plastic top tread for safety. Some models also have a rubber belly band to protect adjacent furniture from scratches and dents. Metal kickstools are available from library suppliers in a variety of colours to match interior decor.

Kilgour, Frederick G.

A chemistry major at Harvard University, Frederick Kilgour worked at the Harvard University Library from 1935 to 1942, then as chief of the Interdepartmental Committee of the Office of Strategic Services (OSS), where he applied his knowledge and experience to the problem of importing strategic enemy publications for military use during World War II. He served in the intelligence branch of the U.S., State Department after the war, then worked as librarian at the Yale Medical Library from 1948 to 1965 and was Associate Librarian for Research and Development at the Yale University Library in 1967 when offered the position of executive officer of the fledgling Ohio College Library Center (OCLC), an initiative of the Ohio College Association to make the books and journals of academic libraries in Ohio available to students and faculty at all the state's colleges and universities.

To achieve this goal, an online union catalogue of the holdings of 37 Ohio academic libraries was created in 1971, dramatically decreasing the cost of catalogueing in Ohio and later throughout the United States when the system was expanded. In 1978, an Interlibrary Loan Subsystem was added to the union catalogue. OCLC evolved into the Online Computer Library Center and has grown into the largest bibliographic utility in the world. Kilgour ended his career as distinguished research professor at the University of North Carolina at Chapel Hill.

Kinescope

A motion picture made by filming the images displayed on a television monitor.

Kinetoscope

From the Greek *kineto* ("movable") and *skopos* ("watcher"). The first motion picture viewer, invented by Thomas Edison and his assistant W.K.L. Dickson, demonstrated in 1893 at the Brooklyn Institute of Arts and Sciences, consisting of a large upright wooden cabinet housing a 50-foot loop of 35mm perforated film that revolved on a series of spools at a constant speed by means of an electrically driven sprocket wheel. The viewer, looking through a peephole in the cabinet, perceived a moving image. The camera in which the film was exposed was called a *Kinetograph*.

Kiosk

A small circular pavilion, usually located near the entrance to a library, used for displaying announcements, dust jackets removed from new books, reading lists, comments and suggestions from library users and other information concerning library operations and programmes.

Kipskin

A leather, sometimes used in hand book-binding, made from the skin of young or small cattle, intermediate in grade between calfskin and cowhide.

Kirkus Reviews

Published since, 1933 under various titles, *Kirkus Reviews* is a semimonthly review publication covering books for adults, young adults, and children. ISSN: 0042-6598.

Kit

A set of related materials in more than one medium designed to be used as a unit with no single medium predominating, often stored in a container to keep the parts together. The category includes laboratory kits and packages of curriculum materials.

KLIATT

Published from 1967 to November 2008, *KLIATT* reviewed paperback books, hardcover fiction, audiobooks, and educational CD-ROMs and software recommended for libraries and class-rooms serving young adults.

Knowledge

Information that has been comprehended and evaluated in the light of experience and incorporated into the knower's intellectual understanding of the subject.

Known-item Search

A search in a library for a specific work, as opposed to a search for *any* work by a known author or for works on a particular subject. If the title of the work is known, the easiest way to locate a copy is to search a library catalogue or bibliographic database by title. When the user is uncertain of the precise wording of the title, the best strategy may be to search by author's name. If at least two or three significant words in the title are known with certainty, a keywords search may retrieve an entry for the work.

Köchel Number

Opus Number

Kollêsis

The joint of overlap along which two sheets in a roll of papyrus are glued together. Plural: *kollêses*.

Koran

Qur'an.

Kraft Paper

A heavy, unbleached grade of coarse paper, usually mocha brown in colour, used for paper bags and wrapping paper because of its strength and fold endurance and also for the outer wrapper on magazines to protect the glossy cover from damage in mailing. In binding, a narrow strip of kraft paper may be used as a liner to reinforce the layer of thin fabric applied with adhesive to the binding edge of the sewn sections to hold them firmly together.

Kunstlerroman

From the German word *Kunstler* and the French word *roman*, a novel that traces the growth of a writer's creative genius from childhood to maturity, with particular attention to major trials and obstacles and their influence on the development of the artist's character and work.

KWAC

An acronym for *Keyword and Context*, an algorithmically generated index in which keywords from the title of a document are printed as headings along the left-hand margin of the page, with the portion of the title or text following each keyword indented under the heading, followed by the portion of the title or text preceding the word. Unlike KWOC indexing, this method preserves multiword terms and phrases in the alphanumeric sequence of headings. Compare with KWIC.

KWIC

An acronym for *Keyword in Context*, a type of permuted index in which the title of a document is used to illustrate the meaning of a keyword used as an entry. Tagged by hand or extracted from the document algorithmically, keywords are printed in alphabetical order at a fixed position in a line of fixed length, so that they appear in a column, with as much of the context as can be accommodated preceding and following each word. The keywords in the column may be distinguished typographically to make them easier to read. Keyword and context are usually coded to identify the document indexed. Compare with KWAC and KWOC.

KWOC

An acronym for *Keyword out of Context*, a variation on the KWIC (Keyword in Context) index, in which keywords extracted algorithmically from the title of a document (and sometimes the text) are printed as headings along the left-hand margin of the page, with the titles or portions of text containing each keyword indented under the corresponding heading. A symbol may be substituted for the keyword in the string of text. Unlike KWAC indexing, this method does *not* preserve multiword terms and phrases in the alpha-numeric sequence of headings.

L

LA
Library Association.

Lab
Instruction lab.

Large Print (LP)
Any type size larger than 16-point.

Large-scale Map
A systematic representation on a two-dimensional surface of a relatively small land area, at a representative fraction of 1:75,000 or greater, showing a considerable amount of detail.

Laser Disk
Optical disk.

Latin
A general term used in typography to refer to all typefaces that have their origin in the Latin alphabet, as opposed to those that do not.

Laubach Literacy (LL)
ProLiteracy Worldwide.

Lavage
Erasure by washing a sheet, roll, or leaves to remove the ink. In Antiquity and the early Christian period, the method was applied to papyrus manuscripts. To erase text written on parchment or vellum, rubbing with an abrasive such as pumice was required.

Law of Scatter
Bradford's Law.

Lay
Lai.

Layer Tint
Hypsometric tint.

LBI
Library Binding Institute.

LC
Library of Congress.

LCA
Library Copyright Alliance.

LCC
Library of Congress Classification.

LCCN
Library of Congress Control Number.

LCRI
Library of Congress Rule Interpretations.

Leading
In printing, the amount of vertical space allowed by the typesetter between lines of type in a column or on a page. Pronounced "ledding."

Leaf Book
A book written about another book, with a leaf from the subject volume included.

Learning Resources Center (LRC)
Synonymous in the United States with school library.

Learning Style
Cognitive style.

Leased Line
Dedicated line.

Leasing Plan
Book lease plan.

LEC
Limited Editions Club.

Ledger Binding
Stationery binding.

Legal Value
Archival value.

Legend
A visual aid that explains to the reader the symbols used on a map, chart, or diagram.

LES
Literature in English Section.

Letter Signed (LS)
A manuscript letter signed but not written in the hand of the correspondent. Compare with autograph letter signed.

Lettered
Inscribed with letters of the alphabet, especially the title on the spine of a book, usually done in letters of contrasting colour or gilt. *Lettered direct* means inscribed directly on the material covering the spine, not on a label attached to the spine.

Letterhead
A heading printed on business or personal stationery, which may include name of institution, personal name, street address, e-mail address, phone number, and institutional logo or some other small decorative element.

Lettering Piece
A label, usually of thin leather, often of contrasting colour, affixed to the spine of an old book, on which information about the contents is given in lettering.

LHRT
Library History Round Table.

LI
Library Issues.

LJ *Index of Public Library Service*
The *LJ* Index is a national rating system designed to recognize and promote America's public libraries, to help improve the pool of nationally collected library statistics, and to encourage library self-evaluation

LIBER
Ligue des Bibliothèques Européennes de Recherche.

Libraire
Stationer.

Library Advisory Committee
The Library Advisory Committee

is a reporting committee of the UCF Faculty Senate that provides advice to the Libraries concerning materials and services needed by faculty and students in their teaching and research endeavors.

Library and Book Trade Almanac

A reference serial published annually by Information Today, Inc., *Library and Book Trade Almanac* is a compilation of practical information and informed analysis of issues and topics of interest to the library, information, and book trade community. It includes news of the year; reports from federal agencies, national libraries, and national associations; developments in library legislation, funding, and grants; library research and statistics; average book prices; information on library and information science education, placement, and salaries; a directory of organizations; and a reference section that includes lists of distinguished books and literary award winners. Many libraries receive *Library and Book Trade Almanac* on continuation order. Formerly *The Bowker Annual Library and Book Trade Almanac*. ISSN: 2150-5446.

Library Journal

LIS journal.

Library Law

Library Legislation.

Library Management System (LMS)

In automated systems, an integrated set of applications designed to perform the business and technical functions of a library, including acquisitions, catalogueing, circulation, and the provision of public access. In alphabetical order, the leading vendors of library management software are: Auto-Graphics, EOS International, Ex Libris, Follett, Innovative Interfaces, Polaris Library Systems, SirsiDynix, TLC, and VTLS. Synonymous with *integrated library system (ILS)*.

Library Management

Library Administration.

Library Media Center

School Library.

Library Newsletter

A publication of no more than a few pages issued by a library to its clientele on a regular or irregular basis to inform them of the availability of services and resources, describe new and ongoing initiatives, and announce up-coming events, exhibitions, etc.

Library of Congress Catalogue Number

Library of Congress Control Number.

Library Orientation

Bibliographic Instruction.

Library Rate

Library Mail.

Library Rep

Library Representative.

Library Representative

A publisher's sales representative responsible for calling on libraries, usually within an established territory, to solicit orders for titles on the publisher's list. Contacts are made, usually by telephone or in person, with librarians responsible for collection development and acquisitions.

Library Trustee
A member of an appointed or elected board responsible for overseeing the growth and development of a library or library system, including long-range planning and policy making, public relations, and fund raising. Trustees are usually library advocates but may sometimes be political appointees.

Library without Walls
Virtual library.

Librettist
A writer to specialises in writing the text for operas, operettas, oratorios, cantatas, or other works for the musical stage, whether spoken or sung in recitative or aria. Some composers write their own libretti.

Libweb
A very comprehensive worldwide directory of Web homepages for all types of libraries, updated daily on the Berkeley Digital Library Web site.

Licence
Licensing agreement.

Life Expectancy
In archival terms, the length of time for which an item is expected to remain intact and useable when stored under normal conditions in a typical office environment.

Ligature
Two or more letters joined together in printing, such as *ff* joined at the cross-stroke in some fonts.

Light Bleaching
A conservation technique used to restore prints, drawings, and other paper materials that have become discoloured. After washing and drying, the paper is placed on a light table where it receives carefully regulated exposure to tungsten lights, gradually lightening the discolouration.

Light Box
A box with a glass or translucent plastic surface that can be illuminated from within, on which film is placed for close examination without projection, often with the aid of a magnifying eyepiece called a loupe.

Light Pen
A metal stylus equipped with a light sensor on one end for scanning barcodes at the circulation desk. Some models require an external decoder. Synonymous with *bar code wand*.

Light
Ambient light.

Lightface
A typeface in which the characters are the same size as medium-weight and boldface type of the same font but composed of thinner strokes that do not appear as dark on the printed page.

Lilliput Edition
Miniature Edition.

Limitation

The statement that certifies the total number of copies printed in a limited edition, usually appearing on the verso of the leaf preceding the title page. The statement usually notes any special qualities of the edition and provides a blank space for the number of each copy to be entered by hand. In some limited editions, the statement is signed by the author and/or illustrator.

Limp Binding

A book bound without stiff boards in flexible leather, vellum, or cloth covers, lined or unlined, a style used mainly for diaries, devotional works, and light verse. The squares in limp binding often extend further beyond the edges of the sections than in a normal binding. Inexpensive and surprisingly durable, limp bindings were used as early as the late Middle Ages for books not considered worth the expense of full binding. Vellum covers had a tendency to curl under warm conditions.

Line

In cartography, a shape that has length and direction but lacks area, used on maps and charts to represent features too narrow to be displayed as having area at the given scale and linear features that have no area at all. Compare with point.

Line Art

In printing, an illustration of reproduction quality done in black and white, as opposed to a halftone in which the range of tonal values in the original is rendered by converting the image into a field of minutely graded dots.

Line Drawing

A drawing executed entirely in lines without the use of shading, hatching, or some other graphic technique to add depth or volume to the image. Cartoons, caricatures, and diagrams are often done in this style. In printing, any drawing that can be reproduced without using halftone.

Linear Scale

Bar scale.

Line-item Budget

A method of budgeting used in some libraries and library systems in which anticipated expenditures are divided into discrete functional categories called "lines" for the purpose of systematically allocating resources and tracking operating expenditures.

Liner

A strip of kraft paper glued to the back of a book, to reinforce the layer of thin gauzy fabric, called *crash* or *super*, applied to the binding edge of the sections as lining.

Lining

Material applied with adhesive to the binding edge of a book, following rounding and backing, to hold the sewn sections together securely, usually a piece of thin, loosely woven fabric called crash. In better quality bindings, a strip of kraft paper called a liner is added as a second layer for extra strength.

Link Checking

The process of testing the links in an HTML document to determine if they are functioning properly. Software has been developed to check links automatically. Without regular checking and updating, URL changes and dead links may accumulate in a Web page.

Link Counter

Computer software designed to track the number of times a link within a Web page is used by visitors to the site. Link counters have also been developed that use Web search engines, such as *Google, Yahoo!*, and *AltaVista*, to count how many Web pages on the Internet contain links to a given Web address (URL). Link counters can often be downloaded as free Web widgets.

Link Resolution System

Link resolver.

Link Source

An information resource, such as an abstracting and indexing database, capable of detecting that the user has an available link resolution system and of sending citation information in the form of an OpenURL to the system.

Link Target

An information resource that can be linked via a link resolver. Link targets are often collections of full-text electronic journal articles but may also be abstracting services, citation indexes, document delivery services, library catalogues, and other useful sources of information.

Linocut

A relief print similar to a woodcut, made by inking a block covered with a sheet of linoleum into which the design has been cut. In colour printing, a separate block of linoleum is used for each colour or, in the reduction method, the artist removes more material from the block for each new colour to be printed. Linoleum is much easier to cut than wood, but the pressure exerted in the printing process causes the plate to degrade faster.

Linson

The manufacturer's trade name for an exceptionally strong paper used in edition binding. Often embossed to imitate linen cloth or grained leather, it is available in a variety of colours.

Lion and the Unicorn, The

Published since, 1977, *The Lion and the Unicorn* is a theme and genre-centered journal of international scope, devoted to scholarly discussion of children's literature. Published three times a year by Johns Hopkins University Press, each issue includes a book review section, and some issues include interviews with authors, editors, and other major contributors to the field. The publication is available online in full-text as part of *Project MUSE*. ISSN: 0147-2593.

Liquid Gate Printing

Wet gate printing.

LIRT

Library Instruction Round Table.

LIS Journal
A professional journal devoted to the publication of articles about library and information science, librarianship, and related fields. Many LIS journals also publish reviews of new publications, including books of professional interest to librarians.

LIS
An abbreviation of Library and Information Science and Library and Information Studies.

LISA
Library and Information Science Abstracts.

List
All the publications currently available for purchase from a given publisher, including the frontlist, backlist, and forthcoming titles. Publishers of trade books in hardcover and paperback generally issue seasonal lists twice a year in the spring and fall, or three times a year.

Listening Room
A special soundproof room or area in a library, equipped with playback equipment for listening to audiorecordings.

LISTSERV
Mailing list management software that runs on a variety of platforms, designed to scan incoming e-mail messages for the words "subscribe," "unsubscribe," and other housekeeping commands and update the subscriber list automatically. Also used as a general term for any mailing list that runs on LISTSERV software. *Tile.Net/Lists* is a online directory of e-mail newsletters and discussion lists.

LITA
Library and Information Technology Association.

Literacy Volunteers of America (LVA)
ProLiteracy Worldwide.

Literal
Following the exact words and ordinary meaning of a text or speech, without taking into account possible figurative or symbolic use of language, as in a literal interpretation of a passage from the Bible. The interpretation of words or statements according to their denotation rather than their connotation.

Literary Form
A mode of literary expression characterised by elements of internal structure, rather than by content, for example, drama, poetry, fiction, essay, etc. The major literary forms are further subdivided.

Literary Magazine
Little magazine.

Literary Prise
Literary award.

Literati
Men of letters. Scholarly, learned, and/or well educated people.

Literature
Enduring works of poetry or prose that express ideas and emotions of universal human interest in a form and style embodying excellence.

Literature Search
An exhaustive search for published information on a subject

conducted systematically using all available bibliographic finding tools, aimed at locating as much existing material on the topic as possible, an important initial step in any serious research project. Compare with ready reference.

Lithotint
A lithograph given the appearance of a wash drawing by the use of ink diluted with turpentine in the process of creating the image on the printing stone or plate, a technique introduced in the 1840s, not the same as a lithograph with a background tint produced by the use of a second stone.

Littera Bastarda
Bastarda.

Littera Florissa
A pen-flourished initial or letter in a medieval manuscript and early printed books, embellished with tracery in geometric and/or foliate patterns.

Litterateur
A man of letters, especially one who devotes himself to the study and writing of literature in the capacity of an amateur or dilettante.

Little Press
Small press.

Live Action
A motion picture or video-recording made by photographing sequences of action that occur in the living world, as opposed to one in which the optical illusion of motion is created through the use of animation techniques. A bibliographic item may consist of a combination of live action *and* animated sequences.

Live Recording
A sound recording of an actual performance made at the performance venue before a live audience, as opposed to a studio recording made in the controlled environment of a recording studio. Production quality varies.

Livre d'Artiste
Artist's book.

Livre De Chasse
French for "Book of Hunting." A category of secular medieval manuscript devoted to the subject of hunting for sport, often illustrated with hunting scenes and miniatures of various species of game animal. Hunting manuals were commissioned largely by wealthy aristocrats. The best-known example is the *Le Livre de la Chasse* composed between 1387 and 1389 by Gaston III, Count of Foix and Béarn.

LJ
Library Journal.

LLAMA
Library Leadership and Management Association.

LMP
Literary Market Place.

LMS
Learning management system, library management system, and library media specialist.

Loan Character
A character from one writing system used in writing another lan-

guage, for example, the Chinese characters used by the Japanese to write their own language (Kanji).

Loan Desk
Circulation desk.

Loan Status
The type of loan in effect at a particular time for a specific item in a library collection. In public and academic libraries, most items are available for general circulation, but some may be on reserve or on loan to other libraries via interlibrary loan. Noncirculating items such as reference books are for library use only.

Lobby Card
A motion picture advertisement printed in black-and-white or full colour for display in a theater lobby or showcase window, often a smaller version of a movie poster. In 1909, the Motion Pictures Patent Company established 11 × 14 inches as the standard size. As collectibles, their value depends on age, condition, and rarity. The Beinecke Library at Yale University provides online access to its *Western Silent Films Lobby Card Collection, 1912-1930.*

Loc cit.
An abbreviation of the Latin phrase *loco citato*, meaning "in the place cited."

Local Area Network (LAN)
A communications network restricted to a relatively small geographic area, often within a single building or group of adjacent buildings such as a college, university, or corporate campus, consisting of at least one high-speed server, client workstations, a network operating system, and a communications link. LANs handling communication over the Internet use optical fibre as a transmission medium.

Local Bibliography
A bibliography of books and other materials about a specific geographic area smaller than a country, usually covering material about the history, geography, architecture, and environment of the area, as well as works about the people born or residing in it. Useful in genealogical research.

Local Collection
A library collection of books, prints, maps, photographs, and other materials related to a specific geographic area and its inhabitants, usually the community in which the library is located, useful in historical and genealogical research.

Local History
Materials of historical interest concerning the people and events in a small geographic area, such as a city, county, or town, including news-paper clippings, maps, photographs, posters, diaries, personal papers, community records, etc. Some libraries and historical societies are digitizing their local history collections.

Local Serial Control Number
A unique identification number assigned by a library to a specific serial title, used as a code for serials control within the library but not in data exchange or com-

munication outside the library or local system. Compare with International Standard Serial Number.

Location Code
Location symbol.

Location Map
A small-scale ancillary map inset in or appearing outside the neat line of a map on a larger scale, showing the main map in relation to its vicinity, to help the reader locate its correct geographic position.

Location Symbol
A code consisting of a few letters or a word displayed in a catalogue record or added to an entry in a bibliography, indicating the specific location or collection in which the item is shelved. In a union catalogue, location symbols are used to indicate the libraries in the system or consortium owning at least one copy of the item. Synonymous with *location code.*

Locative Relation
Semantic Relation.

Locked
In film production, the work in its final form, the editing process having been completed.

Locked Up
Said of assembled type and display matter made up into pages and imposed in a chase once it has been tightly secured by adjusting small expandable wooden or metal boxes called *quoins* positioned between the imposed type and the sides of the chase. The resulting forme is ready to be placed on the bed of the press for printing.

LOCKSS
An acronym for Lots of Copies Keeps Stuff Safe, an application designed to create low-cost, persistent digital "caches" of electronic journal articles, housed locally at institutions that have authorised access to the content and elect to preserve it. The idea behind LOCKSS is that e-journal content is more likely to be preserved if there are many distributed copies of the material. If a particular document ceases to be available from the publisher's site, it can be accessed from the LOCKSS cache.

Lo-fi
An abbreviation of *low fidelity*. Recorded music of sound quality below commercial standard, usually due to the use of low-budget do-it-yourself recording techniques and home-based recording equipment. In the 1980s, when cassette technology such as Tascam's four-track Portastudio became widely available, lo-fi became a musical genre.

Log Book
A blankbook in which the daily activities of an expedition, voyage, mission, or other under-taking are noted chronologically as a matter of record, usually by the person in command or a designated person, with the date included in each entry. Because log books provide an account of events as they occurred, the information contained in them can be of considerable historical value. Also spelled *logbook*.

Logoff
The procedure by which the user

closes or terminates communication with a remote computer system. The opposite of log on. Also spelled *log-off* or *logoff*.

Logon
The procedure by which the user gains access to and initiates communication with a remote computer system, usually by typing or entering an authorised username and/or password. The opposite of log off. Also spelled *log-on* and *logon*.

Logogram
A symbol or character that stands for an entire word, for example, $ for *dollar* and # for *number*.

Logotype
In letterpress, a unit of type cast in one piece, bearing two or more characters on the body, not tied together as in a ligature, for example, the frequently used Qu letter combination.

LOMS
Library Organisation and Management Section.

Long Discount
The standard discount given by a publisher to a bookseller on trade books, usually 40 percent.

Long Page
In printing, a page containing more lines of type matter than specified. In books, a typesetter may add an extra line to avoid setting an orphan or widow.

Loop
Film loop.

Loose Hinge
Hinge.

Loose
Sheets of paper, parchment, etc., that are unbound, usually filed in a folder or container. The opposite of *bound*.

Loose-back
Hollow back.

Lossless
A conversion from one format to another that does not result in the loss of data or information. The opposite of *lossy*.

Lossy
Lossless.

Lost
A code used in a library catalogue record to indicate the circulation status of an item no longer available because it was checked out to a previous borrower and never returned. Most libraries bill the patron an amount based on the cost of replacement after a number of overdue notices have been sent without result. In some libraries, the charge may be refundable if the item is found and returned within a reasonable period of time. Compare with missing.

Lot
A regular shipment of books, periodicals, or other printed material sent by a library to a bindery for binding or rebinding. The phrase "closing the lot" refers to the point in time after which no further items are added to a shipment. Only when the lot is closed can the necessary paperwork be prepared to accompany the shipment.

Loudspeaker
Speaker.

Loupe
A pocket-sized magnifying eyepiece used to examine photographic prints and slides, motion picture film, graphic artwork, fine jewellry, etc.

Low-budget Movie
B-movie.

Low-demand
Demand.

LP
Large print and long-playing record.

LPSS
Law and Political Science Section.

LRC
Learning resources center.

LRRT
Library Research Round Table.

LS
Letter signed.

LSCA
Library Services and Construction Act.

LSO
Library security officer.

LSP
Library Statistics Programme.

LSSC
Library Support Staff Certification.

LSSIRT
Library Support Staff Interests Round Table.

LSSPS
Libraries Serving Special Populations Section.

LSTA
Library Services and Technology Act.

Lyric Sheet
A typed or printed copy of the words to a song, usually used in conjunction with a lead sheet. A lyric sheet may also give the song title; the author's name, street address, and telephone number; and notice of copyright. Lyric sheets may also be handwritten.

Lyric
In classical Greece, a song or poem performed to the accompaniment of a harp-like stringed instrument called a *lyre*. In contemporary usage, a relatively short poem in which a single speaker expresses a personal emotion or state of mind, as opposed to narrating a sequence of events. The form includes sonnets, elegies, odes, and hymns. Compare with lyrics.

Lyricist
One who specialises in writing the words for songs, usually in collaboration with a composer who writes the melody. Which comes first? In songwriting, the answer is both: a lyricist may write the lyrics and then turn them over to the composer, who adds the music, or *vice versa*. Or, the two artists may work in closer collaboration. Compare with librettist.

M

Mac
Macintosh.

Machine-readable Records
In archives, records created and maintained in a medium that requires some kind of machine to access their content. Compare with electronic records.

Machine-readable
Data in a form that can be recognised, accepted, and interpreted by a machine, such as a computer or other data processing device, whether created in such a form or converted from a format that a machine cannot read. Usually refers to digital information stored on hard disk, floppy disk, or magnetic tape.

Macro
In computing, a method of customizing user input in which a series of recorded keystrokes, commands, or menu options is assigned a brief name or key combination to enable the user to execute a predetermined sequence of steps quickly by simply typing the name or key combination. Also called *keyboard macro.*

Macroform
A general term for any storage medium bearing text and/or images large enough to be easily read without the aid of magnification. Macro-forms can be transparent or opaque.

Macrophotograph
A photograph of unusually large proportions in which objects are shown life-size or larger. The opposite, in this sense, of microphotograph. Also, a photograph that enlarges a small object, often taken through a microscope, revealing details not visible to the unaided eye.

Made-up Copy
A copy of a book assembled from parts taken from one or more defective copies of the same edition, or a copy in which imperfections are corrected by adding or substituting parts taken from other copies of the same edition. In the antiquarian book trade, the practice is not considered unethical as long as the manner in which the volume is composed is revealed rather than concealed.

MAES
Measurement, Assessment, and Evaluation Section.

Magazine Pagination
Numbering the pages of a periodical, starting with one at the beginning of each issue. Magazines and trade journals are usually paginated in this way, making it more difficult to locate a specific article in a bound volume by page number, than in a publication that uses journal pagination.

MAGIRT
Map and Geospatial Information Round Table.

Magnetic Declination
Declination.

Magnetic Disk
A rewritable computer storage medium consisting of a revolving platter on which digital data is encoded as tiny magnetic spots arranged in tracks. Data is read by a mechanical arm designed to move a read-write head across the surface of the platter. Usually encased in a rigid, protective case, a magnetic disk can be either fixed or removable. Compare with optical disk.

Magnetic Sound Track
Sound track.

Magnetic Strip
A thin magnetised strip of plastic firmly affixed to a book or other bibliographic item at the time it is processed, which can be set to trigger a security alarm whenever someone attempts to remove the item from the library without checking it out. Synonymous with *magnetic detection strip, security strip,* and *tattle-tape.*

Magnetic Stripe
In a composite print of a motion picture, the thin coating of magnetic oxide capable of carrying the sound track, applied in a narrow band along the film edge and on some films to the opposite edge as a *balance stripe* when the film is wound on a reel or core. Also used synonymously with data strip. Abbreviated *magstripe.*

Magnum Opus
Latin for "great work." A literary or artistic work considered by discerning critics to be of major importance, usually the crowning achievement of its author, composer, or creator. Not all authors and artists produce a work that is considered superior to their others. The opposite of opuscule.

Mailing List
An e-mail discussion forum that allows individuals to subscribe and automatically receive messages posted to the list by other subscribers. Participants may also post their own messages and replies for distribution to the other subscribers to the list. A mailing list may be *moderated* or *unmoderated. Tile.Net/Lists* is a comprehensive general directory of e-mail discussion groups. Synonymous with *electronic discussion list.*

Main Class
One of the highest-level divisions of a classification system. In Library of Congress Classification (LCC).

Main Entry

The entry in a library catalogue that provides the fullest description of a bibliographic item, by which the work is to be uniformly identified and cited. In *AACR2*, the main entry is the primary access point. In the card catalogue, it includes all the secondary headings under which the item is catalogueed. For most items, main entry is under name of author. When there is no author, main entry is under title.

Main Heading

In pre-coordinate indexing, the first part of a composite heading divided by at least one sub-heading, usually separated from the first sub-heading by a dash or other mark of punctuation. In the Library of Congress subject heading Information science—Research—Methodology, the term *Information science* is the main heading and *Research* and *Methodology* are sub-headings.

Main Library

Central library.

Main Map

A map that is supplemented or augmented by the inclusion of one or more smaller maps inset within the neat line and/or ancillary maps placed in the margin or else where on the sheet.

Main Schedule

The list of classes used by a cataloguer or indexer, individually or in combination, to classify documents by subject under the rules of a given classification system, arranged in the order of their symbolic notation. In a hierarchical classification system, the logical divisions, sub-divisions, etc., of the main classes are displayed. Compare with auxiliary schedule.

Mainframe

A large computer system capable of supporting many terminals that do not have independent processing capability, used to run complex applications that require a considerable amount of computing power. Main-frames are classified by size. Compare with microcomputer, mini-computer, and supercomputer.

Maintenance Contract

A formal agreement in which an outside company agrees to check designated equipment on a regular basis after any warranty has expired and to maintain it in good working order, including major repairs as needed, in ex-change for payment of a monthly or annual fee, an arrangement common in libraries that own their own photocopiers, reader-printer machines, computer equipment, etc.

Makeready

The process of preparing the printing press for a press run, including adjustment of the forme or plates to produce a uniform impression.

Make-up

In letterpress printing, the process of removing type from the galleys and arranging it in page format, including the positioning of text, illustrations, notes, and running heads in accordance with the typographer's layout, done by a worker known as a compositor. Also spelled *makeup*.

Mammoth Plate
An outsise photographic format used during the second half of the 19th century, especially by view specialists, with 16 × 20, 18 × 22, and 20 × 24 inches being the most common sizes. Artists who used this format include Carleton E. Watkins, Mathew Brady, William Henry Jackson, and Eadweard Muy-bridge. The term includes both the wet collodion glass plate negatives and the prints made from them.

MAN
Metropolitan area network.

Mandatory (M)
In OCLC documentation, a field or subfield of the MARC record in which data must be entered to meet OCLC input standards for a given encoding level. Compare with optional and required if applicable and readily available.

Mandatory Retirement
Compulsory retirement.

Mandatory Rights
Compulsory rights.

Mandorla
A decorative motif in the shape of a pointed oval, used in bookbinding, usually as a centerpiece.

Manicula
Fist.

Manifesto
A public declaration, in speech or writing, of beliefs, motives, plans, and/or intentions, made by an individual, group, organisation, or government.

Manila
A thick, durable buff-coloured paper, originally manufactured from Manila hemp fibre, used mainly for file folders, mailing envelopes, and cards. Also spelled *manilla*.

Mansell
National Union Catalogue (NUC).

Manufacturer
In library catalogueing, the agency responsible for actually making a bibliographic item. In the case of books and other printed publications, the printer is the manufacturer. Compare with producer.

Manuscript Map
A map on any scale produced entirely by hand, rather than by printing or some other mechanised process. Old and rare examples may be aesthetically pleasing and of considerable value to collectors.

Manuscript Society, The
Founded in 1948 as the National Society of Autograph Collectors, the Manuscript Society has since, grown to a membership of over 1800 scholars, authors, dealers, private collectors, librarians, archivists, and curators. Its membership also includes historical societies, museums, special libraries, and academic libraries with manuscript collections. The Society publishes the quarterly journal *Manuscripts* and the newsletter *Manuscript Society News*.

Map Case
A library furnishing, usually made of wood or metal, containing a number of wide, shallow drawers in which large sheet maps can be stored flat, with a wide, smooth, flat top on which they can be spread for examination.

Map Data
Specific cartographic information plotted in relation to base data, for example, population density in relation to geographic area. The same data can be plotted by the use of different map symbols, for example, vertical relief by the use of contours, hypsometric tint, spot elevations, etc.

Map Index
An alphabetical list of the place names written or printed on a map or series of maps, giving the location of each feature, usually as grid coordinates.

Map Series
Two or more sheet maps of uniform size, drawn to the same scale and specifications, utilizing standardised symbols and encompassing a clearly defined geographic area in a systematic pattern when complete. Also, two or more maps of the same geographic area, showing a succession of events occurring over a given period of time, sometimes at fixed intervals. A map series is identified collectively by the mapping agency that produced it.

Map Symbol
A letter, character, abbreviation, graphic, or diagram used on the face of a map, chart, or globe, by convention or with reference to a legend, to represent a specific characteristic or type of feature. Points, lines, and area designators used to represent map data are also considered symbols, but place names and other text are not.

Mapping Agency
An organisation that produces and publishes maps and other cartographic information, usually under the sponsorship of a national government or its armed forces. The largest mapping agency in the United States is the U.S., Geological Survey. UNESCO provides an online list of National Mapping Agencies. In *AACR2*, name of mapping agency is given in the statement of responsibility area of the bibliographic description of a cartographic item.

Maquette
The designer's drawing or model for the proposed binding or layout of a book. The maquette typically evolves from a preliminary version by intermediate stages to the final version.

Marbled Paper
Marbling.

MARC
Machine-Readable Cataloguing.

MARC 21
The version of Machine Readable Catalogueing that superseded USMARC in 1999 with the harmonisation of U.S., and Canadian MARC formats. MARC 21 is supported by OCLC and is the

current official MARC standard in the United States, Great Britain, Canada, Australia, and numerous other countries.

MARC Record
Machine-Readable Cataloguing.

MARCese
The jargon used by librarians who work extensively with MARC records and fall into the habit of using content designators instead of words and phrases to refer to areas and elements of bibliographic description.

Margaret A. Edwards Award
Established in 1988 under the sponsorship of *School Library Journal*, the annual Margaret A. Edwards Award honours an author for his or her significant and long-lasting contribution to young adult literature. Administered by the Young Adult Library Services Association (YALSA), the award recognises the author's achievements in helping adolescents become aware of themselves and of the importance of their role in relationships, society, and the world.

Marginal Data
Information of standard or variable nature written or printed in the margin outside the neat line or border of a map or chart, usually symbols, diagrams, explanatory notes, etc., enabling the reader to identify and interpret its content and/or indicating the source.

Marginal Drawing
A small figure, diagram, or design made by hand in the margin of a manuscript, related or unrelated to the content of the adjacent text. In medieval manuscripts, marginal drawings are sometimes hand-tinted.

Marginal Map
Ancillary Map.

Marginal Note
Side Note.

Marine
A visual work in which the primary subject is ships, shipbuilding, or a harbour, as distinct from a seascape depicting the ocean or some other large body of water, in which the water is the dominant element.

Mark Up
In publishing, to prepare copy for printing by specifying details of typeface, fonts, layout, etc., in a code comprehensible to the compositor or typesetter.

Mark
A visible trace or impression made in or on or applied to the surface of a work, not considered part of its visual imagery, often a sign or symbol helpful in dating the work or establishing its provenance.

Marker Work
A drawing or other work made in water-based or petroleum-based ink, using a pen with a felt, nylon, or ceramic tip.

Married
In bookselling, two related pieces or items brought together, though not originally sold as a unit, for the purpose of making a single item or set complete as published, for ex-

ample, a book and dust jacket, a book and CD or CD-ROM, or two or more volumes in a set.

Married Print
Composite print.

MARS Emerging Technologies in Reference Section
The section of the Reference and User Services Association (RUSA) within the American Library Association (ALA) representing librarians actively engaged in the electronic delivery of reference services or who have an interest in issues concerning digital reference. MARS publishes an annual annotated list of *Best Free Reference Web Sites*.

Martyrology
A liturgical book containing narratives of the lives of Christian saints and their martyrdoms, from the earliest period of Church history, arranged in the order of their feast days, for reading in the Divine Office at the canonical hour of prime. The earliest martyrologies simply list the saints and their feast days.

Mass Media
Media.

Master Negative
In microfilm, the first-generation negative, developed from the film used to shoot the image, from which at least one print master is made, usually stored in a separate location under controlled conditions and used as little as possible.

Master
In reprography, the plate, stencil, negative, or document from which copies are made, usually more than once. The quality of a master copy usually deteriorates with extended use.

Mastering
In sound recording, the process by which the tracks on an album are equalised and balanced in relation to each other and then transferred to a digital or analog storage device from which subsequent copies are manufactured for distribution.

Masterpiece
A work of art, crafts-manship, or writing universally recognised as embodying the highest skill of a great master or group of masters. An artist, composer, or writer may produce a single masterpiece or more than one masterpiece in a lifetime.

Mat
Two pieces of board hinged along one edge for mounting a print, photograph, etc., the bottom piece providing support and the top piece cut in the shape of a window through which the image is viewed. In quality framing, prints are often *double-* or *triple-matted* in boards of contrasting colour. The Florida Bureau of Archives and Records Management provides the online tutorial on *How to Mat a Piece of Art*. Also spelled *matt*

Matching Grant
A grant made by a foundation, government agency, or individual, contingent on the recipient raising sufficient funds to match the donor's contribution. Although the ratio of grant funds to contributions

may vary, most are dollar-for-dollar up to a fixed amount, with a time limit imposed on fund-raising activities. Some federal LSTA grants-in-aid are structured in this way.

Material Specific Details (MSD)

A generic term for the area of the bibliographic record reserved for elements of bibliographic description specific to certain types of material, recorded in field 254 of the MARC record for music, field 255 for cartographic materials, and field 362 for serials.

Material Type

An option available to users of some online catalogues and bibliographic databases that allows search results to be limited to materials of a specific physical format. In catalogueing, material type is assigned to the item from a list established by the local library or library system and is not necessarily the same as the item type used for circulation purposes.

Materials Budget

The portion of a library's operating budget allocated for the purchase of books, media, serials, and other information resources for the use of its clientele and staff, as opposed to expenditures for salaries and wages, equipment, supplies, and services. Some libraries include electronic resources in the materials budget; others make a separate allocation.

Mathematical Data

The field within the materials specific details area of a bibliographic record in which mathematical elements in the bibliographic description of cartographic materials are entered.

Matte

Paper that has a dull unreflective finish, easier on the eye of the reader than glossy finish but not as visually appealing for pictorial content. Also spelled *matt*.

Matter

In printing, copy in the process of being set in type or already set. *Live matter* has yet to be used in printing; *dead matter* has been used and is ready to be *broken up*. The terms *fat matter* and *lean matter* refer to the proportion of white space or broken lines on a page. Printers also differentiate between body matter and display matter.

Mauchline Binding

A decorative technique that originated in the 1830s in the Scottish town of Mauchline in which a transfer print of a wood engraving, often a colour design was applied to a lacquered wooden object, such as the boards of a bookbinding. In the 1860s, photographs and stencils began to be used in the design process. Mauchline ware reached a peak of popularity in the 1880s, disappearing in the 1920s.

Maximize

A feature of a graphical user interface that allows the user to enlarge a window to its fullest size by clicking on a small button in the upper-right-hand corner of the window. The opposite of minimize.

Mazarin Bible
Gutenberg Bible.

McNaughton Plan
Book lease plan.

Mean Line
In typography, the imaginary horizontal line running along the tops of the x-height lowercase letters of a type font that lacks ascenders. Synonymous with *x-line*. Compare with cap line.

Mean Sea Level (MSL)
The average height of the surface of the sea for all stages of tide, observed hourly over a 19-year cycle, with reference to a suitable reference surface or datum, called the *geoid*. MSL is often used as a vertical datum on maps and charts, as on this topographic map of Ansonia, Connecticut. In meteorology, MSL is used as the reference surface for the measurement of altitude in upper atmosphere work; in aviation, it is the level above which altitude is measured by a pressure altimeter.

Measure
In printing, the width over which a line of type is set. A *full measure* extends across the entire width of a line in a column or on a page, without indention.

Mechanical Binding
A form of binding in which the leaves of a publication are held together by some type of mechanism, usually metal or plastic wire or rings threaded or inserted through holes or slots punched along the back margin parallel to the binding edge, to allow the volume to open flat. The category includes loose-leaf binding, comb binding, and spiral binding.

Mechanical Drawing
A design drawing or diagram prepared according to strict scale, conventions, proportions, and methods of projection with the aid of one or more mechanical instruments, such as a compass, ruling pen, T-square, or other drafting tool.

Mechanical Reproduction
The duplication or manufacture of sound recordings by mechanical means, as opposed to digital sound transmission.

Mechanical Work
A graphic work that includes movable parts, such as pop-out or sliding sections, wheels that rotate, or flaps that unfold to reveal hidden features. The term also includes works requiring a specific action by the viewer to reveal the entire image or another image.

Medallion
In books, a decorative element in the form of a panel or tablet, circular or oval in shape, containing a design, inscription, portrait, figure, or group of figures, sometimes made to appear in relief. Commemorative medallions almost always include an inscription, often incorporated into the curved border.

Media
A generic term for non-print library materials. Microforms are not considered media because they are reproductions of print docu-

ments. The person responsible for managing a media collection and associated equipment is a media specialist. Reviews of newly published media titles are indexed annually by type of medium in *Media Review Digest*. Synonymous with *audiovisuals*. In a more general sense, material in *any* format that carries and communicates information content.

Media Center

A facility within an educational institution responsible for providing a full-range of media resources, equipment, and services, staffed to assist students and instructors in utilizing its collections, usually supervised by a media specialist. A media center can be a separate facility, a separately administered unit located in the same building as a library, or an integral part of the library. Synonymous with *learning resources center*.

Media Kit

A packet of promotional materials, including biographical information, photographs, clippings, background information, press releases, etc., distributed to the media to generate publicity for an event, publication, or product. Formerly called a *press kit*.

Media Literacy

The ability to access, analyse, evaluate, and create messages in a variety of forms based on an informed, critical understanding of the nature of mass media, the techniques used by producers of media, and the impact of those techniques on the individual and society. An interdisciplinary field, media literacy has evolved as a necessary response to the complex, pervasive, ever-changing electronic communication environment of the 21st century.

Media Mail

A special rate available from the U.S., Postal Service to businesses and the public for mailing books of at least eight pages, film, printed music, printed test materials, sound recordings, play scripts, printed educational charts, loose-leaf pages and binders containing medical information, and computer-readable media, lower than the rate charged for parcels of comparable weight that do not contain such items. Advertising restrictions apply.

Media Specialist

A librarian or other individual with specialised training in the creation, selection, organisation, maintenance, and provision of access to media of all kinds, who may also be responsible for supervising a media center or the media department of a library, including collections, equipment, and facilities for listening and/or viewing, and any service personnel.

Mediated Search

A systematic search in which a trained intermediary, such as an online services librarian or information broker, assists the end-user in locating desired information, by helping to formulate and execute appropriate strategies for searching online catalogues and databases and by using more traditional bibliographic finding tools. Compare with end-user search.

Mediation

An extra-judicial procedure for resolving disputes, in which two or more parties voluntarily employ another party to find common ground on which a compromise can be negotiated. Usually less costly and time-consuming than arbitration, mediation is usually confidential and the parties are free to terminate the process at any point.

Medical Book

A book published in print, on CD-ROM, or online for the use of medical practitioners, researchers, and/or students or for laypersons with an interest in health care. The category includes textbooks, reference works, and consumer guides, often published in successive editions. Currency is essential in maintaining medical collections used by practitioners.

Medical Library Association (MLA)

Founded in 1898, MLA has a membership of librarians and other individuals engaged in professional library or bibliographic work in medical libraries and allied scientific libraries. An affiliate of the American Library Association (ALA), MLA publishes the quarterly *Bulletin of the Medical Library Association (BMLA).*

Medical Library

A type of special library maintained by a university medical school, hospital, medical research institute, public health agency, or medical association to serve the information needs of students, researchers, and practitioners in the health sciences with collections that include print and online resources related to medicine and allied health. The largest medical library in the United States is the National Library of Medicine, located in Washington, D.C. Medical librarians are organised in the Medical Library Association (MLA). Synonymous with *health science library.*

Medical Subject Headings (MeSH)

The thesaurus of controlled vocabulary used by the National Library of Medicine of the United States. *MeSH* subject headings are used in the NLM's *MEDLINE* data-base in *Index Medicus,* and in bibliographic cataloguing records. *MeSH* headings are published in print by the NLM in an alphabetically arranged annotated list and in tree structures.

Medium

In information storage and retrieval, the physical substance or material on which data is recorded or through which data is transmitted. In a more general sense, the material or technical means by which any creative work is expressed or communicated, in print or non-print format. Plural: *media.*

In printing, a typeface of intermediate weight, as distinct from lightface or boldface. Medium type is standard for printed text.

Medium of Performance

The voice(s) and/or instru-ment(s)

for which a musical work is composed, recorded in the note area of the bibliographic description in the order given on the actual item.

Mediumistic Writing
A written work transmitted through a psychic medium who claims to have received it as a communication from the spirit of a dead person or entity. In libraries, such works are catalogueed under the name of the medium with an added entry under the name of the purported author.

MEDLARS
An acronym for *Medical Literature Analysis and Retrieval Service*. Originally responsible for maintaining and leasing of a collection of National Library of Medicine databases to libraries and research institutions, the MEDLARS Management System (MMS) has expanded its scope to include database development, management, testing, and quality assurance aimed at enhancing access to health information for health professionals and the public.

Medley
A musical composition consisting of a string of wellknown melodies or passages from various pieces that share a common characteristic, arranged so that the end of one coincides with the beginning of the next, with no break in continuity.

Meeting Room Policy
A written statement of the conditions governing the use of a public meeting room on the premises of a library, including reservation procedures and any restrictions on use. Meeting room policies have been challenged at some public libraries in the United States, particularly over issues of free speech and separation of church and state.

Meeting Room
A room in a library that is available to the library's users for meetings, usually by reservation in advance of the meeting date. Most are equipped to handle a fairly large group, with portable chairs and tables, a podium, projection equipment, and in some cases a small kitchenette for serving food. Maximum capacity is usually posted. To avoid misunderstandings, conditions governing use are best stated in written policy or guidelines. Compare with conference room.

Megabook
Blockbuster.

Megabyte (MB)
Byte.

MegaHertz (MHz)
A measurement of the transmission speed of electronic devices, named after the German physicist Heinrich R. Hertz. One MHz equals 1 million cycles per second. In computing, a MegaHertz is usually equal to 1 million bps. When used in reference to a computer's clock, the number of MHz indicates the speed of the central processing unit (CPU).

Melainotype
Tintype.

Member Rate
The price paid by a member of a society or association for a sub-

scription to one of its serial publications, usually lower than the rate charged non-members.

Memo
Memorandum.

Memoir
The record or report of a person's investigations in a specialised field, especially one prepared for presentation to members of a scholarly society. Also, a record of research or observation issued by a scholarly society or institution. Synonymous, in the plural, with proceedings and transactions.

Memorabilia
Materials of sentimental or historical value to the person who created or collected them, including personal books and papers, clippings, photographs, sketches, correspondence, diaries, journals, notes, invitations, badges, etc. Memorabilia are usually added to special collections, in accordance with a library's collection development policy.

Memorandum
A formal note distributed internally to one or more persons in a company, agency, organisation, or institution, with a header indicating the date it was sent and stating to whom it is addressed (To:), from whom it is sent (From:), and the subject of the text (Re:). Unlike a letter, a *memo* does not require a full salutation or signature at the end of the text—the sender may simply initial his or her name in the header. Also, an informal note jotted down, sometimes in haste, as an aid to memory. Plural: *memoranda*.

Memorandum of Agreement (MOA)
A formal document out-lining the mutual responsibilities of a depository library and a library or other institution receiving selectively housed materials from the depository on extended loan. Signed copies of the MOA are sent to the regional librarian and to the Library Programmes Service (LPS) of the U.S., Government Printing Office (GPO). A sample MOA is contained in the FDLP's *Instructions to Depository Libraries*.

Memorial Photograph
A photograph made to commemorate a deceased person who appears in the image while still alive, as distinct from a post-mortem photograph made of the body after death. Memorial photographs are often black-bordered and may be accompanied by verse or vital statistics concerning the life of the deceased. They are sometimes mounted on old tomb-stones. The category includes *morteotypes*.

Memorial Work
Prints, cards, black-edged stationery, and other graphic items produced in memory of a deceased person or to mark the anniversary of the death of an important public figure.

Mending
Minor restoration of a book's condition not requiring replacement of material or removal of the bound sections from the cover. When

mending of library materials is done in-house, the job should be given to a person who is properly trained, to avoid permanent damage to items in need of attention.

Mental Map

A map depicting a geographic area of any extent according to the subjective perceptions of a particular person or group of people, rather than in relation to physical reality, for example, a New Yorker's view of the United States west of the Hudson River.

Mentor

An experienced, trust-worthy person who willingly provides useful advice to a new member of a community, profession, or organisation to assist the person in achieving success in his or her new position and environment. Mentoring relationships can either be established informally by the participants or under the formal sponsorship of an organisation. Mentoring of recent library school graduates can be arranged through the New Members Round Table (NMRT) of the American Library Association (ALA).

Menu

In computer systems, a display of two or more options from which the user may select by typing letters or numbers or by clicking on a link, icon, text label, etc., with a mouse or other pointing device. *Main menu* options often lead to lower-level *submenus* in a hierarchical display. Also, a written or printed list of the dishes and beverages that may be ordered at a restaurant or other eating establishment or that are to be served at a banquet or other occasion, often divided into categories to facilitate selection. Menus are considered a form of ephemera and are collected by libraries and archives mainly for their historical value.

Menu Bar

In computing, a list of menu names, usually displayed horizontally below the title bar in a graphical user interface, with corresponding menu options hidden from view. When the user selects one of the menu names, the appropriate list of options is displayed in a drop-down, popup, or sidebar menu.

Menu-driven

A computer interface that provides a hierarchical sequence of lists of possible choices from which the user must make appropriate selections to accomplish the desired result. Menu-driven interfaces are easier for novices to negotiate but slower and less sophisticated than command-driven systems and consequently less attractive to experienced users.

Merge

To combine in logical sequence two or more separate files of information into one, either manually or by an automated process. When such a combination includes the recognition and removal of duplicate files, the process is known as *merge/purge*.

Merger

The combination of two or more serials into one. A note is included in the bibliographic record for the new serial indicating the titles of the publications that merged, and a companion note is added to the record for each of the serials that merged indicating the title(s) with which it merged and the title of the publication created as the result of the merger. The opposite of split. Compare with absorption.

Meridian

In cartography, an imaginary line through any point on the surface of the earth circling the planet perpendicular to the equator and connecting the geographic poles, where it meets all other meridians. On most modern maps, the 0 meridian runs through Greenwich, England but on early American maps, the prime meridian often runs through Philadelphia, Pennsylvania, or some other city. The relative position of a meridian is measured in degrees, minutes, and seconds of longitude, ranging from 0 to 180 degrees east or west of the prime meridian, with notation indicating direction. Synonymous with *longitude line.*

MeSH

Medical Subject Headings.

Meta-analysis

Statistical analysis of the results of a number of studies of related research hypotheses, intended to yield a quantitative aggregate summary of all the findings. Best results are achieved by including only methodologically sound studies, because sources of bias in the original studies are not controlled in meta-analysis.

Metadatabase

A database of databases, usually formed by aggregating two or more smaller databases to allow the user to search their contents *as a whole,* instead of repeating the same search in each separately. The pace of aggregation has accelerated as very large vendors have dominated the market for access to periodical databases, but however helpful "one-stop searching" may be in interdisciplinary research, segmentation still offers significant advantages for the experienced researcher.

Metadictionary

A search engine that allows the user to search for the definition(s) of a word or phrase in multiple online dictionaries simultaneously. *OneLook Dictionary Search* is an example that indexes English words and phrases from over 900 dictionary Web sites, with translation to other languages.

Meta-index

An index of indexes.

Metal Binding

A bookbinding made of one or more metallic substances usually by a jeweller or skilled metalworker, often in the form of surface decoration mounted on the boards.

Metal Point

A pointed implement made of metal used from the 11th century on for ruling and writing annotations in manuscripts, and for under-drawing. It leaves a trace more discreet than pen-and-ink but more visible than hard point. The colour of the mark left on the writing surface varies with the type of metal used: a brownish mark from a ferrous point, a gray line from silver or lead, and a grayish-green trace from copper. Instructions to illuminators and binders' notes written in metal point are sometimes detectable in early manuscripts.

Metallic Ink

Printing ink to which finely ground particles of metal have been added to produce a decorative metallic effect, used mainly in display work. During the Middle Ages, powdered gold was added to the ink used in chrysography and gilding.

Metamorphic Picture

A graphic image that can be transformed by the viewer, mentally or physically, into one or more other images by turning, folding, or sliding a section and pictures with interchangeable parts, such as parts of the body, which can be mixed and matched to show different figures.

Metapublisher

A third-party electronic service provider in the business of enabling primary publishers to outsource some or all of the text conversion, reference linking, hosting, and gateway services that traditional publishers do not have the resources to provide in-house. Examples include HighWire, Ingenta, and MetaPress.

Method Book

An instruction manual for a particular musical instrument or voice, designed to help aspiring students develop technique and musicality. Often geared to a specific skill level, some are written by accomplished players and teachers.

Methods Journal

A scholarly periodical devoted to disseminating information about the development of new techniques in scientific research and the refinement of existing methodologies.

Metonymy

A figure of speech in which the name of one thing is used for another to which it is related, of which it is an attribute, with which it is associated, or which it suggests. *Reverse metonymy* is the use of the name of a thing to refer to one or more of its attributes, for example, a reference in Shakespeare by a monarch to another by the name of the country, rather than the personal name and title.

METS

Metadata Encoding and Transmission Standard.

MIC

Moving Image Collections.

Michael L. Printz Award for Excellence in Young Adult Literature

Named for a school librarian in Topeka, Kansas, who was a long-time active member of the Young Adult Library Services Association

(YALSA), the Michael L. Printz Award, sponsored by *Booklist*, a publication of the American Library Association (ALA), has been given annually since, 2000 for literary excellence in young adult literature.

Microclimate
The isolated environment within a small confined space such as a display case, enclosed bookcase, drawer, box, or other storage container, easier to control than a large storage area when conservation is a high priority.

Microcomputer
A generic term for a programmable computer designed to handle relatively small operations, usually a desktop machine containing a single-chip microprocessor on a printed circuit board, which may be part of a larger computer system or connected to a network. The term may have been coined to distinguish personal computers from more powerful mini-computers.

Microdrive
Originally a brand name for a miniature, one-inch, 170 MB hard disk designed by IBM and launched in 1999 to fit in a CompactFlash (CF) Type II slot, the term has since, been applied to similar drives manufactured by other companies. Some have licensed the name in order to sell re-branded versions. Although microdrives may consume more power than flash memory, they offer some advantages in the way data is stored and manipulated. In 2006, Hitachi introduced an 8 GB microdrive.

Microfiche Envelope
A small paper envelope, open at the top and right end, or at the top only, with a high throat for storing and protecting one or more sheets of microfiche so that only the title strip on the first sheet is visible. Archival quality microfiche envelopes are made of acid- and lignin-free paper.

Microfilm Exchange
The replacement by a library of issues or bound volumes of a serial publication with micro-film, usually to conserve space or preserve titles that are very heavily used, printed on acid paper, or subject to a high rate of mutilation or loss.

Microfilm Jacket
A transparent plastic holder into which short strips of microfilm are inserted, designed as a unitised format for storing microimages of documents that require periodic updating. Jackets are available in a variety of sizes for both 16mm and 35mm microfilm, plain or colour-coded to facilitate filing. The standard 4 × 6-inch size holds up to 60 images. Compare with aperture card.

Micrographics
A general term for the techniques used to photographically reduce text and/or graphic images to a size too small to be read by the human eye without magnification, usually for the purpose of preservation or compact storage, as in the conversion of newspaper and periodical back files from print to microfilm or microfiche. Micrographic for-

mats also include microopaque and aperture card. Compare with micrography.

Micrography
The art and practice of writing in microscopically small characters.

Micromanagement
A top-down management style in which the manager closely observes and attempts to control the work of his or her subordinates, often devoting excessive attention to minute details at the expense of more important problems. Unable to delegate authority, micro-managers typically discount the ideas of others or accept creative suggestions only when they can put their own spin on an innovation, creating a work environment of distrust and hostility.

Microphone
A device designed to convert acoustic sound vibrations into electrical signals, which are usually fed into an amplifier, recording device, or broadcast transmitter. Abbreviated *mic* or *mike*.

Microphotograph
A photograph of objects shown at so great a reduction in size as to require a magnifying device for viewing. Microphotography was invented in 1839 by John Benjamin Dancer, a manufacturer of optical and scientific equipment in Manchester, England, who used the "wet plate" collodion process to produce a microimage on collodion film for viewing through a microscope. The category includes microfiche and microfilm. The opposite of macrophotograph. Compare with photomicrograph.

Microprocessor
A central processing unit (CPU) etched or printed on a single silicon microchip. To function as a computer, a microprocessor requires a power supply, a clock, and memory. Microprocessors are used in most digital devices.

Microscopic Printing
Printing done in a very small type size. Although the first works printed in Europe were in large type, early printers soon realised that with smaller typefaces more matter could be fitted on a page. By 1825, the French typefounder Henri Didot had cast type that produced 25 lines to the inch. Because the casting of extremely small type has physical limitations, most microscopic reduction is now done photographically.

Microslide
A slide consisting of a single mounted frame of microfilm, not to be confused with a microscope slide.

Middleware
A computer programme designed to mediate between two otherwise separate application programmes, which may be running on different operating systems, allowing data to be exchanged between them. Middleware is also used to facilitate distributed processing—the interconnection of multiple applications, usually over a network, to create a larger, often more complex application. Some functionality, formerly provided by separately marketed middleware, has been incorporated into operating systems.

Migrated Archives
Removed archives.

Migration
A move from one hardware platform or software system to another, usually because the purchaser or lessee believes the new system to be superior. In libraries, the most common example is from the catalogue or database software of one vendor to that of another. Such a change may or may not require the conversion of data from one format to another. Compare with upgrade.

Millboard
Binder's board.

Milling
Cutting away a small portion of the binding edge of a book to prepare the sections for adhesive binding or oversewing, an operation done in a bindery by moving the inner edge of the clamped text block over the rotating blades of a *milling machine.* In first-time binding, the back folds of the sections are cut away, producing loose leaves. In rebinding, the old adhesive, thread, staples, etc., are cut away along with the folds to prepare the leaves for reattachment.

MIME
An acronym for Multi-purpose Internet Mail Extensions, a specification that allows non-ASCII files to be formatted so that they can be transmitted over the Internet via e-mail. Supported by many e-mail clients, MIME extends the SMTP protocol to allow the exchange of graphics, audio, and video files, and messages in character sets other than ASCII.

MIME Media Type
A designation used in Web browsers and other application software to determine file characteristics, consisting of two parts, a type and subtype, separated by a slash. The official list of MIME media types is maintained by the Internet Assigned Numbers Authority (IANA). Synonymous with *MIME type.*

Miniature
A colourful hand-painted standalone illustration in a medieval manuscript or early printed book, often illuminated in gold or silver and enclosed in an ornamental border or painted frame. In printing and reprography, a document conceived on a very small scale or a greatly reduced copy of a document, designed to be read or reproduced with the aid of special optical equipment.

Miniature Book
A book conceived on a very small scale, measuring no more than three inches along its greatest dimension, usually printed in 6-point type or smaller and illustrated on the same scale. Not uncommon, miniature books include Bibles, almanacs, poetry, classics, juvenile literature, tokens, etc.

Miniature Edition
An edition of a book in which the copies are of very small size, usually printed in 6-point type or smaller and illustrated on the same scale. Synonymous with *lilliput edition* and *microscopic edition.*

Miniature Score
A music score printed in small type to allow the pages to be re-

duced to pocket size. Miniature scores are designed to be used by music lovers for study and enjoyment, not for performance.

Miniature Work
A graphic work that is very small in comparison with the usual size for the genre or physical type, but large enough to be viewed without magnification, for example, a gem photograph or miniature painting.

Minicomputer
A medium-size computer introduced in the 1960s capable of serving up to several hundred users. A dedicated minicomputer is used to run the online catalogue in many libraries. Synonymous with *midrange computer*. Compare with mainframe, micro-computer, and super-computer.

Minimal Level Cataloguing (MLC)
An encoding level that allows more severe limitations on the description and classification of an item than in core level cataloguing, resulting in a less than complete bibliographic record. MLC was designed to provide access to materials unavailable due to cataloguing arrears, as well as items worthy of retention but not considered worth the expense of full level cataloguing.

Minimize
A feature of a graphical user interface that allows the user to reduce a window to a tab in the taskbar, or to an icon on the desktop, by clicking on a small button in the upper-right-hand corner of the window. The opposite of maximize.

MIS
Management information system.

Misbound
A book in which a map or illustration, a number of leaves, or a complete section has been folded incorrectly, gathered in incorrect sequence, bound in upside down, or omitted. The publisher will normally send a replacement if such a copy is returned by a bookseller or retail customer.

Miscellany
A collection consisting of an assortment or medley of writings on diverse subjects, usually published in a single volume.

Misinformation
Information that is erroneous or inaccurate.

Misprint
Typographical error.

Mixed Authorship
Mixed Responsibility.

MLA
Medical Library Association and Music Library Association.

MLC
Minimal level cataloguing.

Mnemonic
From the Greek *mnemon*, meaning 'mindful.' A code in which the abbre-viation(s), symbol(s), or formula(s) are easy to remember. Also, a word or rhyme composed by a person to be used as a mental aid in recalling something.

Mnemonic Notation
A classification notation in which the characters representing the classes are directly linked to the name of the class, making it easier for the user to learn and recall the way the classification system is organised. Most notations used in library catalogueing and indexing are *not* mnemonic.

MOCAT
Monthly Catalogue of United States Government Publications.

Model
An accurate three-dimensional representation of the physical appearance of a real object, for example, a globe representing the earth or another celestial body. A model can be the same size as the original object but is usually done to scale. They are often used by curators to plan exhibits and by stage designers. Models are particularly useful in depicting very large objects. Some are used as toys. Compare with mock-up and realia.

Model Book
A book in which a medieval artist recorded a repertoire of designs for decorated initials and other ornamental motifs of the artist's own invention or collected from other sources, sometimes with notes concerning execution, for use in under-drawing.

Modelling
In medieval manuscript illumination, the technique of giving three-dimensional appearance to objects by the use of shading and highlighting, as in this example.

Modern First Edition
In the book trade, the first edition of a book published for the first time within the 20th or 21st century.

MODS
Metadata Object Description Schema.

MOLA
Major Orchestra Librarians' Association.

Monetary Value
Archival Value.

Monochrome Plate
An illustration printed separately from the text in a *single* colour, usually listed by number with any other plates in the front matter of a book. Compare with colour plate and duotone.

Monogram
A single character or design artfully composed of two or more letters used to ornament custom-printed stationery and other items of personal use. Monograms are sometimes found on the bindings of fine books or incorporated into the decoration and/or illustration of medieval manuscripts and early printed books.

Monographic Series
A series of monographs, usually issued under a collective title by a university press or scholarly society. Each volume in the series may contain more than one monograph, each with its own title in addition to the series title.

Monoline
A typeface in which the strokes of

the characters, whether straight or curvilinear, are all of the same thickness, including any serifs. Compare with block letter.

Monthly

Issued once a month with the possible exception of one or two months, usually during the summer. Many magazines and some journals are published monthly.

Morality Play

A form of drama popular during the Middle Ages and Renaissance in which the characters are engaged in an allegorical struggle over the condition of the human soul. Unlike mystery plays and miracle plays, which were presented on mobile wagons, morality plays were usually performed on a stationary platform. One of the longest and best preserved English morality plays is *The Castle of Perseverance.*

Moralised Bible

Bible Moralisée.

Mosaic Binding

A style of decorative book-binding, dating from the 16th century but more closely associated with 19th century French binders, in which small pieces of leather of various colours are inlaid or onlaid, usually forming regular patterns on one or both covers. The pieces are often gold-tooled around the edges to conceal the join and heighten the effect.

Motif

A term borrowed from art and music to refer to a textual element that symbolically represents a specific theme in a literary work by virtue of repetition, usually presented in the opening verse, chapter, or paragraphs and subsequently elaborated. In medieval illuminated manuscripts, a visual theme used in the painting of ornamental borders, initial letters, and miniatures, for example, the putto, the griffin, or the acanthus leaf.

Mottled Calf

Calfskin used in book-binding, dabbed or sprinkled with coloured dye or tanning acid to give it a decorative spotty appearance.

Mould

Mold.

Mounted

An illustration or photograph tipped onto a blank page in a book or album. Also, a fragile or damaged leaf, illustration, map, etc., strengthened with backing made of paper, card, or thin cloth.

Movie

From "moving picture."

MPA

Music Publishers Association.

MRDF

Machine-readable Data File.

MSL

Mean Sea Level.

MU

Music.

Mull

Crash.

Multicast

In telecommunication, to transmit

data simultaneously to more than one individual or site connected to the same network, for example, to all who subscribe to an e-mail mailing list, as opposed to broadcasting messages to all who own the appropriate receiving equipment.

Multidisciplinary Journal

A scholarly periodical that publishes articles of interest to researchers in a wide range of academic disciplines. Compare with interdisciplinary journal.

Multimedia Item

A bibliographic item containing two or more categories of material in which no single medium predominates (*AACR2*). The general material designation [kit] or [multimedia] may be used in the bibliographic description if the item has a collective title.

Multimedia Map

A map available electronically that includes audio, video, and/or animation, in addition to graphic images and text.

Multitracking

A method of recording that allows sound from different sources to be recorded separately on parallel tracks on the same tape and later mixed down to one or two tracks.

Multivolume Work

A work published in two or more numbered or unnumbered volumes under a single title sometimes over an extended period. A multivolume work is catalogueed as a single entity, with the volumes owned by the library listed in the holdings statement. Compare with multipart volume and series.

Music Score

Score.

MX

Mixed materials.

Mylar

The brand name of a very strong, flexible, heat resistant polyester plastic film, introduced by Dupont in the 1960s, used as a base for the thin layer of ferrous oxide in which data is magnetically recorded on audiotape and videotape.

N

n.d.
No date.

n.p.
An abbreviation indicating that *no place* of publication is provided in the imprint.

NACO
Programme for Cooperative Catalogueing.

NAGARA
National Association of Government Archives and Records Administrators.

NAICS
North American Industry Classification System.

NAL
National Agricultural Library.

Name Authority File
An authorised list giving the preferred form of entry for names (personal, corporate, and geographic) used as headings in the library catalogue and any cross-references from variant forms.

Nameplate
Flag.

NAMTC
National Association of Media and Technology Centers.

NAP
Normal administrative practice.

NARA
National Archives and Records Administration.

Narrowcast
Selective use of communication media to target a highly specialised audience, in contrast to a mass media broadcast intended to reach as many listeners or viewers as possible.

NASIG
North American Serials Interest Group.

NASLIN
North American Sport Library Network.

National Biography
A publication containing biographical information about people of note-worthy accomplishments living in or associated with a particular country. Most national

biographies are multivolume reference works.

Example:

- *American National Biography* in 24 volumes, edited by John A. Garraty. New York: Oxford University Press, 1999.

National Board of Review of Motion Pictures (NBR)

Founded in 1909 to protest New York City Mayor George McClennan's revocation of moving picture exhibition licenses on Christmas Eve 1908, NBR is a non-profit organisation, without ties to the commercial motion picture industry, dedicated to supporting film (domestic and foreign) as both art and entertainment. To avoid government censorship, NBR became the unofficial clearinghouse for new films and from 1916 until the 1950's thousands of motion pictures contained "Passed by the National Board of Review" in their titles. NBR presents film awards annually in over 25 categories, provides educational film programmes, and awards scholarships and grants to promising film students and directors.

National Book Award

An honour awarded since, 1950 by the National Book Foundation, a consortium of book publishing groups, to enhance public awareness of exceptional books written by Americans. Awards are given in five categories: fiction, non-fiction, poetry, young people's literature, and the Medal for Distinguished Contribution to American Letters. Decisions are made by an independent panel of five judges. The prise in each category is $10,000 and a crystal sculpture.

National Book Festival

Organised annually since, 2001 by the Center for the Book at the Library of Congress, the National Book Festival is a two-day event held on the Mall in Washington, D.C., usually in early autumn. Nationally published authors, illustrators, and poets are invited to lecture, read from their works, give interviews, and sign their books, and librarians from libraries across the United States are invited to represent their states. Usually hosted by the First Lady, the National Book Festival is funded by the Institute for Museum and Library Services (IMLS), the National Endowment for the Humanities (NEH), and corporate sponsors.

National Circulation Interchange Protocol (NCIP)

Information standard Z39.83, developed by the National Information Standards Organisation (NISO) to support circulation activities among independent library systems, including patron and item enquiry, and to update transactions in circulation and inter-library loan (hold, reserve, checkout, renew, and check-in), self-service applications, online payment, direct consortial borrowing, and controlled access to electronic resources. The NISO Standards Committee based its work on the Standard Interchange Protocol (SIP) developed by the 3M company to support self-checkout systems.

Implementation is expected to facilitate the development of open systems in information exchange.

National Commission on Libraries and Information Science (NCLIS)

An independent agency within the executive branch of the U.S., federal government, established in 1970 to advise the president and Congress on national library and information policy, conduct studies of library and information needs, assess the adequacy of current resources and services, promote research, develop plans for meeting the nation's information needs, and help coordinate library-related activities at the federal, state, and local levels. In 2008, the activities of the Commission were consolidated into the Institute of Museum and Library Services (IMLS).

National Digital Information Infrastructure and Preservation Programme (NDIIPP)

A programme led by the Library of Congress and partially funded in 2000 by the U.S., Congress to assess the current state of digital archiving and preservation and to develop a national strategy for the preservation of digital content. Sometimes shortened to *Digital Preservation Programme.*

National Film Preservation Board (NFPB)

Established by the *National Film Preservation Act* of 1988, NFPB is an advisory board authorised to assist the Librarian of Congress in preserving archival materials related to 25 films selected each year for the National Film Registry as culturally, historically, and aesthetically significant.

National Film Preservation Foundation (NFPF)

A non-profit organisation created by Congress to support nationwide efforts to preserve the film heritage of the United States and improve access to film for study, research, education, and exhibition, NFPF began in 1997 with the support of grants from the Academy of Motion Picture Arts and Sciences and the Film Foundation. In 2000, the organisation began distributing federal matching grants to film archives to preserve endangered films and collections.

National Film Registry (NFR)

A list of up to 25 films selected each year by the Librarian of Congress, with the assistance of the National Film Preservation Board, for preservation in the archives of the Library of Congress. The films must be at least 10 years old but need not be feature-length or have been released to a theater audience to be eligible for selection. The *National Film Preservation Act* of 1988 authorises the Board to consider the broadest possible range of films in its deliberations.

National Genealogical Society (NGS)

Founded in 1903 with headquarters in Arlington, Virginia, NGS is a service organisation devoted to collecting, preserving, and disseminating genealogical information, encouraging interest in genealogical research, fostering careful documentation of genealogical data, and promoting education and training in the field of genealogy. NGS publishes the journal *NGS Quarterly* and the *NGS News-magazine.*

National Library of Australia (NLA)

Established in 1901, the NLA moved from Melbourne to Canberra in 1927, following the opening of the Federal Parliament building, and in 1968 to its new and permanent home on the shore of Lake Burley Griffin, uniting collections formerly dispersed around Canberra. In addition to its Main Reading Room, the NLA has separate reading rooms for collections of Asian materials, manuscripts, maps, pictorial works, rare books, newspapers, oral history, music, and ephemera. The national library also has an active publishing programme and is a member of the MARC Advisory Committee.

National Library of Education (NLE)

The largest library in the world devoted solely to the collection, preservation, and effective use of research and other information in the field of education. Located in Washington, D.C., the NLE was established with the purchase of the private collection of Henry Barnard, the first U.S., Commissioner of Education following his resignation in 1870. Since, then, its growth has been funded by the federal government. It serves the U.S., Department of Education, Congress, and the Office of the President, as well as the general public, and is the center of a national network of libraries, archives, and other information providers in education.

National Library Symbol

Originally designed by Ralph E. DeVore for the Western Maryland Public Libraries, the generic figure of a human being reading a book was endorsed at the 1982 annual conference of the American Library Association (ALA) as the standard symbol representing all types of libraries in the United States to increase public awareness of libraries as an institution by its utilisation on directional signs and promotional materials. In 1985, the symbol was accepted by the Federal Highway Administration for inclusion in the manual setting standards for highway signs.

National Library Week (NLW)

Sponsored for the first time in 1958 by the National Book Committee and the American Library Association (ALA), National Library Week is an officially recognised seven-day period in the spring of each year during which special attention is given to promoting libraries of all types in the United States. Most public libraries celebrate the event by displaying posters and exhibits, issuing press releases, and sponsoring book talks and other promotional activities. In the United Kingdom, a similar event, National Libraries Week, is celebrated in the fall of each year.

National Library Workers Day (NLWD)

A special day during National Library Week (NLW) reserved for formal recognition of the contributions of all library workers (librarians, support staff, and others), NLWD was established in 2003 by an ALA-APA Council resolution adopted at the annual conference of the American Library Association in Toronto.

National Library

A library designated and funded by a national government to serve the nation by maintaining a comprehensive collection of the published and unpublished literary output of the nation as a whole, including publications of the government itself. Most national libraries are also responsible for compiling a national bibliography, and some serve as the legal depository for works protected by copyright in the country. The national library of the United States is the Library of Congress, located in Washington, D.C. Three other libraries—the National Agricultural Library, the National Library of Education, and the National Library of Medicine—contain national collections in specific subject areas.

National Medal for Museum and Library Service

Honourary awards made annually by the federal Institute of Museum and Library Services to outstanding institutions that make significant and exceptional contributions to their communities. To be selected, an institution must demonstrate extraordinary and innovative approaches to public service, exceeding the expected levels of community outreach and core programmes generally associated with its services. The National Museum and Library Services Board reviews nominations and makes recommendations to the IMLS Director, who makes the final selection. Winners are announced in the fall of each year.

National Music Publishers Association (NMPA)

The largest music publishing trade association in the United States, with over 800 members, the National Music Publishers Association is devoted to protecting, promoting, and advancing the interests of small and large music publishers and their songwriter partners.

National Public Radio (NPR)

Created in 1970, following passage of the *Public Broadcasting Act of 1967*, NPR is a privately and publicly funded non-profit membership media organisation providing mainly news and cultural programming to a national syndicate of almost 800 public radio stations in the United States. The individual member stations are not required to broadcast all NPR programmes that are produced.

National Science Digital Library (NSDL)

A digital library of collections and services funded by the National Science Foundation and intended to become a comprehensive, online source of digital resources for use in science, technology, engineering, and mathematics education.

National Survey
A government agency that specialises in mapping, surveying, and providing scientific information about the topography, geology, and natural resources of a country. In the United States, the national surveys are the U.S., Geological Survey (USGS) and the National Geodetic Survey (NGS).

National Telecommunications and Information Administration (NTIA)
Established in 1978, NTIA is the agency within the U.S., Department of Commerce responsible for advising the President on telecommunications and information policy issues. NTIA's policies and programmes are largely devoted to expanding broadband Internet adoption and access in the United States and to ensuring that the Internet continues to enhance innovation and economic growth.

National Union Catalogue of Manuscript Collections (NUCMC)
A cooperative cataloguing programme sponsored by the Library of Congress since, 1959, *NUCMC* provides cataloguing of archival and manuscript materials at no charge to repositories in the United States that meet its eligibility guide-lines. MARC records are created by *NUCMC* cataloguers in the *RLIN* national-level database, based on catalogueing data supplied by eligible repositories.

Natural Scale
Representative fraction.

Nautical Atlas
A book of charts of seas, coastlines, or other water-ways, often rendered in uniform style and sometimes accompanied by text.

Nautical Chart
A special-purpose map designed to meet the special requirements of navigation at sea or on some other waterway, by indicating soundings, currents, and characteristics of the bottom; showing adjacent coastal areas, islands, ports, and known navigational hazards; and providing other information of interest to mariners, such as tidal data, magnetic variation in the charted area, etc.

Navigation Bar
A series of options, usually in the form of clickable buttons, icons, or text links arranged in a row across the top or bottom of the screen or window, or along the right- or left-hand side, indicating the main categories under which the information contained in the subpages of a Web site is organised. In a well-designed site, the navigation bar is repeated on each subpage to enable the user to select from the list of main options without having to return to the initial page. Compare with toolbar.

Navigation
The use of hypertext links, icons, menu options, and search engines displayed on a Web page to move to other resources available on the Internet or to other pages within

the same Web site. When the user proceeds in a casual way, the activity is called surfing; when the approach is purposeful, it is a search.

NBC
National Board Certification.

NBPTS
An abbreviation of National Board for Professional Teaching Standards.

NDLTD
Electronic theses and dissertations.

NDNP
National Digital Newspaper Programme.

NE
New edition pending.

Nearline
Data stored offline in a digital storage and retrieval system, but available for online use in a comparatively short time due to the nature of the storage device (usually removable hard drive, CD-ROM, or DVD-ROM). Nearline retrieval is not instantaneous, normally requiring a few seconds.

Neat Line
A line, usually grid or graticule, marking the outer edge of a map or chart, separating its detail from any border or margin. The neat line on a quadrangle map is formed by the meridians and parallels marking its outer limits

Nebula Awards
Awards given for the best works of literary and dramatic speculative fiction published in the United States, presented annually since, 1965 by the Science Fiction and Fantasy Writers of America (SFWA) in five categories: novel, novella, novelette, short story, and script. There is no cash prise—winners receive a transparent block containing a glittering spiral nebula.

Necklace Book
A small miniature book, usually containing blank leaves covered in leather or metal, made to be worn about the neck as a pendant suspended from a chain, ribbon, or thong, sometimes as a piece of jewelry.

NED
National Elevation Data-set.

Negative
The image that results when standard photographic or motion picture film is developed, producing tonal values (black, gray, and white) that are the reverse of the original subject and of any positive print of the same image. Negative colour film reverses not only the tonal values but also the colours of the subject, making them appear complementary to the original hues (red as green, blue as yellow, etc.).

Negative Print
A photographic print in which the tonal values are the opposite of those of the subject (light for dark and dark for light).

NEH
National Endowment for the Humanities.

Nemeth Code
Braille.

Neologism
A new word coined from an existing term or terms (*example*: netiquette from "network" and "etiquette"), or a new meaning given to an existing word (*example*: "quark" from *Finnegans Wake* used in physics as the name of a subatomic particle). Acronyms are neologisms. Also refers to the use of such a new word or meaning.

Net
A shortened form of Internet.

Terms of sale in which a publisher specifies that a book must be offered at *no* retail discount or reduction in price. Synonymous with *net published price*.

Net Borrower
A library that borrows more items via interlibrary loan than it lends to other libraries over a designated period of time. Small libraries are more likely to be net borrowers than large libraries. The opposite of net lender.

Net Price
A bookseller's cost for a book or other publication, usually the publisher's list price or suggested price, less any discounts or allowances. Cost of shipping is usually added to net price.

Net Pricing
In bookselling, a method of price setting in which no cover price is printed on the item or on the dust jacket. Instead, the publisher sets the wholesale price without reference to a suggested retail price, and each bookseller or jobber is free to establish its own resale price, which may vary from one seller to another. According to *The Bookman's Glossary* (Bowker, 1983), this controversial practice began in 1979 and is used most often in the college textbook market.

Netcast
Webcast.

Netiquette
A neologism formed by shortening the phrase *network etiquette*. The rules of civility and good manners that apply to communication via the Internet, an environment in which the visual cues available in face-to-face communication and the auditory cues perceptible in voice communication are lacking.

Netspeak
The argot of Internet enthusiasts ("netiquette," "flaming," "mouse potato," etc.). Other examples can be found in *NetLingo: The Internet Dictionary*. Net-speak's peculiarities include selective in attention to current norms of spelling and grammar, use of all-lowercase letters, infrequent punctuation, informality of tone, frequent use of abbreviations and acronyms, and turning nouns into verbs ('blogging,' 'spamming,' etc.).

New Adult Reader
A person of mature years who has recently learned to read, usually by enrolling in an adult literacy programme. Public libraries try to meet the needs of new adult readers

by selecting materials appropriate to their reading level and by developing services to acquaint them with available information resources.

New Book
A new title issued for the first time, usually in hardcover, announced by the publisher in book trade journals and review publications and promoted through book signings, author interviews, etc. Recently published titles make up a publisher's frontlist. Some new books make the bestseller list. Compare with backlist.

New Edition
Revised edition.

New Edition Pending (NE or NEP)
A code used on a publisher's invoice to indicate that a new edition of the title ordered is in preparation but has not yet been issued.

New Release
A media item (motion picture, videorecording, audiorecording, etc.) that has just been issued, shown, or offered for sale to the general public for the first time.

New Series
In *AACR2*, a term used in the numeric and/or alphabetical, chronological, or other designation area of the bibliographic record to indicate that a serial publication has been given a new numbering sequence without a change in its title proper.

New Title Notification
A free service offered by some book publishers and vendors, informing prospective buyers via e-mail of the availability of new publications on a prepublication or on-publication basis. Some sellers allow the customer to limit notifications to a specific interest profile.

New Title
New book.

New York Review of Books (NYRB)
Published since, 1963 in 20 issues per year by NYREV, Inc., *NYRB* provides in-depth commentary on literature, culture, politics, and science in the form of lengthy book reviews written for the educated reader by well-known authors and scholars. *NYRB* also includes announcements of new books published by trade and university presses. ISSN: 0028-7504.

New York Times Book Review (NYTBR)
One of the most influential review publications in the United States, *NYTBR* is published weekly as part of the Sunday edition of the *New York Times* newspaper. It is also available by subscription as a separate section. Reviews are long and scholarly, written for the educated reader by well-known writers and scholars. Some publishers consider it the most important medium in the country for advertising new trade books. ISSN: 0028-7806.

New York Times Co. v. Tasini
Tasini decision.

Newbery Medal
A literary award given annually

since, 1922 under the auspices of the American Library Association (ALA) to the author of the most distinguished children's book published in the United States during the preceding year. Sponsored by the family of Frederic G. Melcher, the medal is named after John Newbery (1713-1767), the British publisher who first issued books written specifically for children.

Newbie

A slang term for a person who is a newcomer to e-mail, electronic mailing lists, newsgroups, the World Wide Web, or the Internet in general, or to any computer application or system.

Newsbook

As censorship weakened during the English Civil War of 1642-1651, publication of news as a profit-making industry began with broadsides and small pamphlets from four to forty pages in length, called "news-books". Generally devoted to a single topic per issue, newsbooks provided accounts of current events (politics, natural disasters, murders and other crimes) in much the same manner as a tabloid newspaper.

Newscast

Information about current events and topics of general interest transmitted over television airwaves or cable transmission lines.

Newsgroup

An Internet message board, usually devoted to a specific topic, to which a participant may post comments or queries, then view the replies of other participants, responses to the replies, and so on. A sequence of related postings is called a discussion thread. The most common types are *Usenet* and *NetNews*, which use the Network News Transfer Protocol (NNTP). Unlike e-mail mailing lists, most news-groups are unmoderated, so postings are not filtered on the basis of content, nor are they limited to a list of registered subscribers.

Newsletter

A serial publication consisting of no more than a few pages, devoted to news, announcements, and current information of interest primarily to a specialised group of subscribers or members of an association or organisation who receive it as part of their membership, for example, *The National Teaching and Learning Forum* available in print and online. Newsletters are listed in the *Oxbridge Directory of Newsletters*. Most periodical indexes and bibliographic data-bases do not cover news-letter content.

Newsmagazine

A general interest magazine devoted to the publication of news and editorial comment, usually on a wide range of subjects, from politics to entertainment (*examples*: *U.S., News and World Report* and *Maclean's* in Canada). Most newsmagazines are published weekly and sold at newsstands, in bookstores, and by subscription. Some are available in an online version (*examples*: *Bloomberg Businessweek* and *Time Online Edition*).

Newspaper Index
A list of the editorial content (news stories, articles, editorials, and columns) published in one or more newspapers, usually arranged alphabetically by subject (including names). Indexes to major U.S., dailies are available in print (*example*: *New York Times Index*). Newspaper indexes are also available online (*DataTimes* and *Newspaper Abstracts* in OCLC *FirstSearch*).

Newspaper Library
Morgue.

Newspaper Rod
Stick.

Newsprint
A grade of coarse, absorbent, unsised paper made primarily from groundwood pulp, used in printing newspapers and newsletters to keep costs down. Because newsprint is bulky, yellows quickly, and becomes brittle with the passage of time, libraries convert news-paper back files to microfilm or microfiche and provide reader-printer machines for enlarging and making hard copies.

News Story
An article published in a newspaper, newsmagazine, or online news service, reporting the details of a current event or the latest information on a topic of general interest. News stories are usually short and often unattributed.

NFAIS
National Federation of Abstracting and Information Services.

NHPRC
National Historical Publication and Records Commission.

Nib
In bookbinding, a stublike extension along one edge of a folded map, chart, diagram, etc., by which it is tipped into a book along the gutter, allowing the illustration to be fully viewed when the volume is open. Also refers to the writing point of a pen.

Niche Database
An electronic database designed to provide information about a very specific topic, as opposed to a range of topics, usually for a limited audience. An example is Thomson's *SDC Platinum*, providing current and historical data on mergers and acquisitions of domestic and international companies, new issues, and venture capital funding.

Niche Publishing
The activities of small presses and divisions within large publishing companies that limit their scope to a relatively narrow subject area (*example*: auto repair manuals or travel guides) or type of literature (genre fiction), producing publications intended to meet the needs of a specific market segment. Some niches are broader than others.

Nickname
A familiar name of a person, usually a diminutive form of the full given name (*example*: Bill for William). Also, a popular name sometimes given in derision or to high-

light a special attribute of the person (Wild Bill). Corporate entities can have nicknames (Big Apple for New York City). Information on nicknames can be found in the latest edition of the *Pseudonyms and Nicknames Dictionary* published by Gale. Compare with conventional name.

Nihil Obstat

A Latin phrase meaning "nothing hinders" appearing on the verso of the title page of works that have been examined by officials of the Roman Catholic Church and found to contain no offence that merits censorship, still used in books that present official Catholic doctrine (*example*: *New Catholic Encyclopaedia*).

Nipping

In bookbinding, the step in which the text block and case (or covers) are pressed firmly together to expel air from between the leaves, giving the volume its desired shape. When done after sewing to reduce swell before the covers are applied, the process is called *smashing*.

NISO

National Information Standards Organisation.

Nitrate Film

Cellulose nitrate.

NLC/NIC

Library and Archives of Canada.

NLM

National Library of Medicine.

NLS

National Library Service for the Blind and Physically Handicapped.

NLWD

National Library Workers Day.

NMRT

New Members Round Table.

NNTP

Newsgroup.

Nobel Prise in Literature

A highly prestigious literary award established and funded in 1900 by Alfred B. Nobel, who made his fortune from the invention of dynamite. The Nobel Prise in Literature is given annually by the Swedish Academy in Stockholm to "the person who shall have produced in the field of literature the most distinguished work of an idealistic tendency."

Node

From the Latin *nodus*, meaning "knot" or "knob." In botany, the point on the stem of a plant from which a leaf or twig grows. In communications, a junction point in a network, such as a personal computer connected to a LAN or a terminal connected to a mainframe. Each node has its own unique network address and the capacity to send, receive, and store messages. In an indexing language, the point in a tree structure at which two or more lines meet.

Noise

In physics, any unwanted or unmodulated energy (audible or inaudible) accompanying a signal, especially random and persistent disturbance that obscures or interferes with transmission. Intensity is expressed as *signal-to-noise ratio*. In communication, any distortions, distractions, irrelevancies, etc., that interfere with the transfer of desired information.

Noise Management
Techniques used in libraries to mitigate the level of noise caused by high traffic and by users who do not regard the library as a quiet refuge, such as the designation of specific spaces for group study, establishment of "quiet zones" (including private study rooms), improvement of signage, and use of furniture designed to encourage quiet study and construction materials that deaden sound.

Nom De Plume
French for pen name, a name assumed by a writer, usually to disguise identity. Synonymous with pseudonym. According to *The Bookman's Glossary* (Bowker, 1983), the term is also used in reference to a fabricated byline adopted by one or more writers.

Non-adhesive Binding
A method of binding used mainly in conservation in which no adhesive is used in direct contact with the book block. Some forms of non-adhesive binding use no adhesives at all.

Non-current
Recurring information, materials, or records that are no longer up-to-date, for example, corporate annual reports from previous years or earlier editions of a reference serial, often retained in libraries and archives for their archival value. Non-current holdings of print newspapers and periodicals, called back files, are often converted to micro-film or microfiche to conserve space. The opposite of current. Compare with outdated.

Non-fiction Film
A motion picture that presents actual rather than imaginary (fictional) people and situations. The category includes documentaries, educational films, ethnographic films, nature films, travel films, promotional films, newsreels, and some animated and cartoon films.

Non-gap Break
A hiatus in the publication or numbering of a serial title despite the fact that no items issued are missing. This may occur when publication ceases temporarily and later resumes under the same or a different title, sometimes with a change of numbering. Compare with gap.

Non-net
Copies of a work (usually a text-book) that a book-seller is permitted by the publisher to sell in bulk quantities to schools for educational use at a discretionary discount. Compare with net.

Non-print
Materials published in a format other than writing or print on paper, including microfiche and microfilm, slides, film-strips, films, videorecordings, audiorecordings, and information in digital formats such as machine-readable data files. Most non-print library materials require special

equipment for listening and/or viewing. Compare with non-book.

Non-reader

A person who is unable to read, usually due to mental or physical disability or poor reading skills, or who chooses not to read, having never acquired the habit or for lack of motivation. Some non-readers enjoy looking at publications, such as magazines, graphic novels, and comic books, that contain an abundance of pictorial content. Also spelled *non-reader*.

Non-repeatable (NR)

A MARC field that may appear only once in the same bibliographic record, for example, the 250 field reserved for the edition statement and other information pertaining to edition. A non-repeatable subfield may occur only once in a field. The opposite of repeatable.

Non-resident's Card

A borrower's card issued to a person who does not reside within the legal boundaries of the district or geographic area served by the library or library system, usually upon payment of a modest fee, renewable at regular intervals.

Non-subscription Serial

A serial publication not available on subscription or standing order because the publisher requires that each part or volume be ordered individually.

Non-trad

Non-traditional Student.

NOP

Not Our Publication.

North Pointer

A standard graphic device in the form of a small cross or arrow pointing to the north, printed on maps, charts, blueprints, plans, etc., usually in or near the legend to indicate com-pass orientation.

NOS

Not On Shelf.

Not Returnable (NR)

A term used on a publisher's invoice to indicate that a book or other item cannot be returned once it has been received by the library or bookseller placing the order.

Not Yet Published (NYP)

A term used on a publisher's invoice to indicate that the title ordered cannot be immediately supplied because it is in the process of being published and will be available at some time in the future.

Notable Book

Best books.

Notched Binding

In some adhesive bindings, shallow parallel grooves are cut into the binding edge of the sections perpendicular to the spine to enlarge the surface area exposed to the adhesive. Although *notching* strengthens the binding of a book, the additional adhesive has the disadvantage of restricting open ability.

Notching

Making a 'V' cut into the edge of motion picture film to remove damaged perforations, rather than making the repair with a splice, a practice that should be avoided because, by weakening the stock, it often leads to further damage.

Note Area
The area following the physical description in a bibliographic record giving the contents of the work, its relationship to other works, and any physical characteristics not included in preceding areas of bibliographic description. Each note is given a separate paragraph in fields 5×× of the MARC record (with ×× in the range of 01-99), for example, the 520 field reserved for the annotation or summary note.

Notorious Book
A written work that has acquired a reputation, usually unfavourable. A prime example is *Malleus Maleficarum* ('The Hammer of Witches') by Hein-rich Kramer and Jacob Sprenger, first published in 1487 (University of Sydney Library). For 300 years, it was the leading manual used by Catholic and Protestant clergy in the detection and persecution of witches and witchcraft.

Novelette
A novel of 30,000 to 50,000 words (*example*: *Sweet Smell of Success* by Ernest Lehman). Synonymous with *short novel*. Compare with novella.

Novelty Binding
A bookbinding of unconventional shape and/or covering material (carved ivory, papier-mâché, mother-of-pearl, fur, snakeskin, etc.), fashionable during the 19th and early 20th centuries.

Novelty Work
A work made from materials uncommon for its format, with unusual attachments, in an unconventional shape, or with other uncommon features (*Thesaurus for Graphic Materials II: Genre and Physical Characteristic Terms*), for example, a postcard made of leather, a luminescent poster, or a hidden image work. Novelty works are often collectible. Synonymous with *exotic work*.

NPR
National Public Radio.

NRPB
National Recording Preservation Board.

NRR
National Recording Registry.

NSDL
National Science Digital Library.

NSN
National Storytelling Network.

NT (or N)
Narrower Term.

NTIA
National Telecommunications and Information Administration.

NTIS
National Technical Information Service.

NUC
National Union Catalogue.

NUCMC
National Union Catalogue of Manuscript Collections.

Number Book
A form of book, common in the 18th and 19th centuries, published in numbered parts or installments, usually at regular intervals.

Numbered Copy
A copy of a book published in a consecutively numbered limited edition, bearing a copy number assigned by hand by the publisher, as well as an indication of the total number of copies printed, usually in the colophon or in a certificate of issue on the verso of the leaf preceding title page.

Numbering
The identification of each of the successive items of a publication (issues, parts, volumes, etc.) by the assignment of a numeral, letter, or other character, or combination of characters, with or without an accompanying word ('volume,' 'number,' etc.) and/or chronological designation (*AACR2*). Not all serial publications are numbered.

NYP
Not yet published.

NYPL
New York Public Library.

NYRB
New York Review of Books.

NYTBR
New York Times Book Review.

O

OAI
Open Archives Initiative.

OAIS
Open Archival Information System.

OBA
Open Book Alliance.

Obiit
Latin for "died," usually abbreviated *ob.* before a date to indicate the year of a person's decease (*ob. 1922*).

Object
In *AACR2*, a three-dimensional artifact, replica of an artifact, or naturally occurring entity. In the British list of general material designations, the term also includes dioramas, games, microscope slides, models, and realia.

Oblong
A book wider than it is high.

OC
Order Cancelled.

OCA
Open Content Alliance.

Occasional
A document or publication issued on an irregular basis, sometimes numbered sequentially by the publisher (*example*: *Occasional Publications in Archaeology and History* of the Massachusetts Historical Commission).

OCLC Four-Figure Cutter Tables
Cutter Table.

OCLC
Online Computer Library Center.

OCR
Optical character recognition.

Octateuch
The first eight books of the Old Testament of the Bible (the Pentateuch plus the books of Joshua, Judges, and Ruth), sometimes produced as a separate manuscript by medieval scribes.

ODC
Opening Day Collection.

OED
Oxford English Dictionary.

OFD
Office for Diversity.

Off the Record
A statement or comment that the speaker does not wish recorded or made publicly known. At meetings, such remarks are not included in the minutes and may not be expressed if the proceedings are tape-recorded.

Off-Broadway Theater Awards
Obie Awards.

Office for Diversity (OFD)
The executive office of the American Library Association (ALA) charged with serving as a key resource on professional issues related to diversity as a fundamental value and action area for the Association, the OFD serves as the liaison to the Committee on Diversity and its subcommittees and administers the Spectrum Initiative, a scholarship programme designed to improve library service through the development of an ethnically diverse workforce.

Official Name
The legal name of a company, agency, organisation, institution, etc., which may differ from the form of the name used in its publications or in catalogueing them for a library collection.

Official Publication
A document issued in multiple copies by an official body, such as a government agency or intergovernmental organisation, under its legal name, often retained by libraries for reference purposes (*example*: *Budget of the United States Government* issued annually by the Office of Management and Budget). U.S., federal government documents fall into this category.

Official Records
The formal written documents in which the ongoing activities of a company, government, organisation, or institution are recorded, usually retained in archives for their evidential, legal, informational, or historical value, in accordance with instructions contained in a disposition schedule (*example*: *Congressional Record*).

Official Title
The full title appearing on the title page of a book or other printed publication, used by librarians in catalogueing the item.

Offset
A rotary printing process in which ink is applied to a thin plate wrapped around a rotating cylinder, which transfers the image to a second rubbercoated cylinder from which an impression is made on a sheet or roll of printing paper. Offset is faster, less expensive, and capable of printing much finer detail than letterpress.

OGR
Office of Government Relations.

OHA
Oral History Association.

OIF
Office for Intellectual Freedom.

OITP
Office for Information Technology Policy.

OLAC
Online Audiovisual Cataloguers, Inc.

Old Map

A map produced at some time in the past, which no longer serves the purpose for which it was made, often because the information it contains is outdated, but which may be of artistic or historic interest. An old map that is rare may be of considerable value in the collector's market.

Older Adult

An elderly person who may require special assistance in accessing and using the facilities, services, and collections of a library. Because the proportion of older adults is increasing in many communities across the United States, public libraries must focus more attention on providing outreach to seniors.

Oleograph

A chromolithograph printed with oil paint on canvas or a similarly textured surface to imitate an oil painting. The process was used in the late 19th century to produce inexpensive reproductions of oil paintings.

OLOS

Office for Literacy and Outreach Services.

OLUC

OCLC OnLine Union Catalogue.

Omnibus Bill

A piece of proposed legislation that serves more than one purpose, packaging several measures into one or combining diverse items or particulars in a single bill. Appropriations are often handled in this manner. When passed, such legislation becomes an *omnibus act*.

Omnibus Reference

A crossreference directing the user from a single heading to multiple headings in an index, as in the following example from the *Library of Congress Subject Headings* list:

Example:

* Bibliographical co-operation *see* Bibliography, International; Catalogueing, Co-operative; International cooperation; Union catalogues

Omnibus Review

An evaluative article in which a reviewer discusses and in some cases compares two or more books or other publications of a certain type, on a specific subject, in a particular field of study, or that have some other characteristic in common.

On Approval

An arrangement with a publisher or jobber that allows a prospective buyer, such as a library, to examine newly published items before deciding to purchase. Materials sent for inspection must be returned within a designated period of time if the recipient does not intend to purchase.

On Loan

Checked out.

On Order

A term used in library acquisitions to describe an item ordered but not yet received from the vendor. Once the item is received and processed, the order record created by the library at the time the order was placed can be purged. In some online catalogues, the status of an item on order is displayed in a temporary catalogue record.

On Sale or Return
Terms given by a publisher to a bookseller allowing the return for credit of copies that remain unsold. The bookseller's account is normally charged for the sale, but payment is not expected until the items have sold or a designated time limit has expired.

On-duty
Time when an employee is expected to be at work, particularly the hours of a scheduled shift at a public service point, such as the circulation desk or reference desk. The opposite of off-duty.

One-of-a-kind Book
A book created in a single copy, as opposed to a production book issued in multiple copies. Artist's books created for display are usually of this type.

One-on-one
Services provided by a librarian or other library staff member working alone with a single patron, usually involving a high degree of interaction, as in most transactions at the reference desk.

One-person Library (OPL)
A library or information service operated and managed by a single individual, usually with minimal assistance, more common in special libraries than in other types of libraries. In public library systems, small branch libraries are often run by a solo librarian or paraprofessional, sometimes with the help of volunteers from the community. Bookmobiles are nearly always operated by a single person.

Onionskin
A very thin, tough, lightweight, translucent paper with a smooth glazed or cockle finish, used for airmail stationery, tracing paper, etc. Also spelled *onion skin*.

ONIX
Online Information Exchange.

Onlay
One or more panels or thin pieces of cut leather or paper, often of more than one colour, mounted in relief on the cover of a book, usually forming a design, often with tooling around the edges to secure them to the surface (and for decorative effect).

Online Book Club
A group of readers who select a book on a regular basis and exchange comments about it via an online mailing list or Web blog (*example*: BookTalk.org). The advantages are no set meeting times, relative anonymity, and accessibility to readers unable to travel. The disadvantages are lack of face-to-face interaction and slower communications.

Online Bookstore
A commercial enterprise that markets and sells books and non-print media (videos, CDs, DVDs, CD-ROMs, etc.) electronically over the Internet, with payment by credit card (*example*: Amazon.com). BookSpot.com provides links to online bookstores.

Online Public Access Catalogue
OPAC.

Online Reference
Digital reference.

Online Services
In libraries, the branch of public services concerned with selecting and providing access to electronic resources, such as online catalogues and bibliographic databases, including mediated searching, often handled by an *online services librarian*. Compare with systems librarian.

OnLine Union Catalogue (OLUC)
OCLC OnLine Union Catalogue.

ONLINE
A magazine providing feature articles, product reviews, case studies, and informed opinion to assist information professionals in selecting, using, and managing electronic information products, including online databases, CD-ROMs, and Internet resources, published bimonthly since, 1977 by Information Today, Inc. ISSN: 0146-5422.

On-the-job
Occurring in the course of one's employment, for example, *on-the-job training* as opposed to learning that takes place outside the normal work routine.

Ooze Leather
Calf or split sheepskin given a soft velvet or suede finish on the flesh side, used mainly for binding volumes of poetry, belles lettres, etc.

Op. cit.
Latin for *opere citato,* meaning "in the work previously cited." An abbreviation used in notes and bibliographic citations that allows a quotation or idea from the work previously cited to be referenced simply by giving the new page number(s).

OP
Out of Print.

OPAL
Online Programming for All Libraries.

Opaline Photograph
A photographic print mounted under bevelled glass, to make it resemble an opalotype.

Opalotype
A type of early photograph, popular from the 1880s to the early 1900s, made on opaque white ("milky") glass, called *opal glass,* by one of two methods: transferring a carbon print onto glass or exposing a light-sensitive emulsion on the surface of the glass to a negative

Op-ed page
The page of a newspaper, usually opposite the editorial page, on which a variety of opinions are expressed concerning issues of the day, often written by syndicated columnists whose view-points may differ from the editorial position of the paper. Political cartoons are also printed on the op-ed page.

Open Archives Initiative (OAI)
The Open Archives Initiative

(OAI) is an attempt to build a "low-barrier interoperability framework" for archives (institutional repositories) containing digital content (digital libraries). It allows people (Service Providers) to harvest metadata (from Data Providers). These metadata are used to provide "value-added services", often by combining different data sets. Over time, however, the work of OAI has expanded to promote broad access to digital resources for eScholarship, eLearning, and eScience.

Open Back
Hollow back.

Open Catalogue
A library catalogue in which there are no restrictions on the addition of new bibliographic records, and existing records are revised and corrected as the need arises.

Open Order
In acquisitions, an order for library materials that remains active because it could not be completely filled by the seller at the time it was placed, usually because one or more items are temporarily out of stock.

Open Reserve
A reserve collection shelved in an open stack to afford library users unrestricted access.

Open Stacks
Shelving in a library to which users have unrestricted access. Synonymous with *open access*. The opposite of closed stacks.

Open Tear
A tear in a book or other printed publication which may have some material missing.

Openability
A binder's term for the ease with which the binding on a book can be opened at any page. In hardcover bindings, a volume with a hollow back can be opened more easily than one with a tight back. In adhesive bindings, an Otabind binding opens flat more easily than a perfect binding. In perfect bindings, an unnotched binding is easier to open than a notched binding. Most mechanical bindings are designed to open flat.

Opened
Said of a book left uncut in binding whose pages have been slit by hand with a paperknife, usually by the person who purchases the volume or receives it as a gift.

Open-end index
An ongoing index covering a single serial publication (*example*: *New York Times Index*), works of a particular form (*Biography Index*), or the published literature of a specific subject (*Index Islamicus*), academic discipline (*Art Index*), or group of related disciplines (*MEDLINE*), updated continuously or at fixed intervals.

Opening
Any two facing pages in an open book or other printed publication. The right-hand page is called the recto; the left-hand page, the verso.

Operating Budget
Funds allocated, usually on an

annual or biennial basis, to cover the ongoing expenses incurred in running a library or library system, including the payment of salaries and wages and the purchase of materials, equipment, supplies, and services.

Operational
Said of equipment and/or systems that are running in good working order.

Operations
A management term encompassing all the activities and details involved in running a library or library system on a day-to-day basis, as opposed to functions requiring a long-range view of the institution's direction and priorities, such as planning and budgeting, policymaking, fund-raising, and public relations.

Operetta
A short, amusing musical play, often satirical. Also, a genre of light opera in which music and subject matter generally are not serious, a precursor of today's musical comedy. The works of Johann Strauss, Jr., in German and of Gilbert and Sullivan in English are prime examples.

OPL
One-person library.

OPP
Out of print at present.

OPS
Out of print, searching.

Optical Center
In printing, the point slightly above the mathematical center of a page that the human eye perceives as the center. In page layout, the typographer fools the eye by designing around the optical center, rather than the mathematical center. The same rule applies in Web page design for computer screens.

Optical Disk
A high-density direct access storage medium consisting of a specially coated disk on which data is encoded in a pattern of tiny pits burned into the surface with a laser, to be read by a device that reflects a laser beam off the pitted surface, then decoded by a micro-processor into digital signals. Optical disks can be read-only (audio CDs, CD-ROMs, DVDs, photo CDs, videodiscs), write once (WORM disks), or rewritable. They have far greater storage capacity than magnetic disks and are more robust.

Optical Scanner
Scanner.

Optical Sound Track
Sound track.

Optical Spacing
In typesetting, the technique of adjusting the distance between the individual letters in a line of capitals to create the optical illusion of even spacing, which requires placing some letter combinations closer together than others.

Optional Number
In Dewey Decimal Classification (DDC), a class number listed in parentheses in the schedules or tables that is an alternative to the standard notation for the class.

Also, a class number created by following an option in the schedules or tables.

Optional
A field or subfield of the MARC record in which data may be entered at the discretion of the cataloguer but is not required to meet OCLC input standards for a given catalogueing level. Compare with mandatory and required if applicable and readily available.

In *AACR2*, a unit of data that may be added at the catalogueer's discretion to the bibliographic description of an item but is not required, for example, the name of the releasing agent in the publication, distribution, etc., area of the bibliographic record representing a motion picture.

Opus
Latin for "a work." In the most general sense, any creative work or composition. In music, the term is usually followed by an opus number assigned by the composer or publisher to one of several works, or a collection of works related in form or medium, to indicate its place in the sequence in which they were composed or issued. Abbreviated *op.* Plural: *opera* or *opuses*.

Opuscule
A book or treatise of small size. Also refers to a musical work or literary composition of little significance.

Orchestral Score
The full score of a musical work composed for orchestra, giving the parts for all the instruments.

Order Canceled (OC)
A term used on an invoice to indicate that the order for a book or other item has been canceled by the seller, usually because copies are no longer available.

Order Form
A preprinted card or sheet sent by a publisher or vendor with a promotional mailing, as an insert in a periodical, or as part of a trade catalogue, providing blank spaces for the customer to fill in the names or titles of items to be ordered. In online sales (*e-commerce*), the order form is often called a "shopping cart." Most libraries use a purchase order when ordering materials.

Order of Precedence
Preference order.

Order of Preference
Preference order.

Ordinal
A term that applies to two types of liturgical books used in services of the Catholic Church:

- A guide setting forth the order in which the liturgy is to be celebrated, including instructions for the clergy concerning the performance of liturgical actions, and
- A book giving the rules and form of service to be followed in the ordination of a deacon or priest, the consecration of a bishop, or the coronation of a king.

Organisational Culture
The prevailing values, expectations, and conventions within an

organisation or institution, often unspoken and persistent. Advancement may depend on sensitivity to such norms.

Origin
The place in which a manuscript was produced, seldom recorded unless mentioned in the colophon. Codicologists must determine origin by carefully studying the volume's contents, patronage, methods of production, and provenance. According to the British Library's *Catalogueue of Illuminated Manuscripts*, the "use" of a liturgical manuscript is not necessarily evidence of its geographic origin, since, eventually the major uses came to be widely distributed.

Original Binding
A term used in the antiquarian book trade to indicate that a book retains the binding in which it was first issued, which may show definite signs of wear if the volume is an old one. Synonymous with *primary binding*.

Original Catalogueing
Preparation of a bibliographic record from scratch, without the aid of a pre-existing catalogue record for the same edition, more time-consuming for the cataloguer than copy catalogueing.

Original Language
The language in which a work is first written or produced, as distinct from the language in which it is translated. In library cataloguing, the original language of a translation is entered in the 765 field of the MARC record. In the bibliographic description, the note *Translation of:* is followed by the title in the original language or a transliteration of it.

Original Order
The principle in archives that records should remain in the sequence in which they were maintained when in active use, unless the method of accumulation is determined upon inspection to have been so unsystematic as to render retrieval difficult, if not impossible. Existing relationships are preserved when documents remain as originally arranged, making it easier to prepare finding aids. Original order also has evidential value.

Original Parts
A descriptive term used in library catalogueing to indicate that a copy of a work first issued in installments has survived in its original form without having been rebound.

Orihon
A manuscript or printed document in the form of a continuous length of papyrus, vellum, or paper, folded backwards and forwards accordionstyle between the columns of text to divide the work into pages, which are usually fastened with a cord threaded through holes pierced in the back fold, with or without lacedon covers.

Ornament
Printer's ornament and tooling.

Orphan Work
An out of print work protected by copyright, for which the current

copyright holder is unknown or cannot be located or contacted. The question of who owns the rights to orphan works has been a major bone of contention in litigation over the *Google Books* settlement. Libraries creating digital repositories also face the daunting challenge of identifying orphan works if they are to make them freely available online.

ORS

Office for Research and Statistics.

Orthography

Correct spelling of a written language, usually given in a standard dictionary. British spelling differs slightly from American spelling of certain words (*cataloguing/catalogueing, grey/gray, palaeography/paleography, theatre/theater*, etc.). Also refers to any style or method of spelling and to the study of spelling and its conventions.

Orthophotograph

An aerial photograph of uniform scale on which horizontal distance can be accurately measured, the central perspective of the original conventional photograph having been converted to an orthogonal projection by a process of *rectification,* which removes displacement and distortions, giving the image the spatial attributes of a map.

OS

Operating system and out of stock.

Oscar

Academy Award.

OSI

Open Systems Interconnection.

OSS

An abbreviation of *open source software*.

Out of Circulation

Not available to be checked out or used for reference, for example, library materials in the process of being mended, repaired, rebound, recatalogueed, etc. The opposite of *in circulation*.

Out of Print at Present (OPP)

A term used on a publisher's invoice to indicate that a publication cannot be supplied because current inventory is exhausted but additional copies may be printed at some unspecified time in the future.

Out of Print, Searching (OPS)

A term used on an invoice to indicate that a publication is no longer available from the publisher but the seller is attempting to fulfil the order through other channels.

Out of Series

The unnumbered copies of a book, printed in excess of the number specified by the publisher for a limited edition, usually bound as overs, for use in promotion and for distribution as review copies. Out of series copies are usually not signed by the author unless they are used as complimentary copies. Also spelled *out-of-series*.

Out of Stock (OS)

A term used on a publisher's invoice to indicate that a publication cannot be supplied at the time the order is received because it is not in inventory. Also abbreviated *o.s.* The opposite of in stock. Compare with out of print.

Out
In printing, copy accidentally omitted from a text in typesetting. When a bookseller or retail purchaser discovers a defect of this kind, the publisher will normally send a replacement copy at no charge.

Outcomes Assessment
The systematic, quantitative measurement of the extent to which a library's programmes and services actually change the behaviour of library users with respect to the library's stated goals and objectives, for example, the degree to which a formal information literacy programme improves the research skills of the students receiving instruction. Assessment of learning outcomes is accomplished through testing (pre- and post-), surveys, interviews, and evaluation of the results of student research (bibliographies, term papers, porfolios, etc.).

Outdated
Information that is no longer current. Publications containing such information may be misleading, for example, a superseded edition of a manual of medical diagnosis or prescription drugs. Loose-leaf services are designed to facilitate updating. Books are usually updated in supplements and revised editions. Resources available online may be updated continuously.

Outlay
A sum of money spent, especially in the initial phase of a project, on the expectation that the investment will eventually produce a tangible or intangible return or some other desired result. Public relations expenditures usually fall into this category.

Outline Drawing
A style of medieval manuscript illumination in which the outlines of a figure or scene are drawn in detail in black and/or coloured ink. The technique was sometimes combined with tinted or fully painted design elements.

Outline Letter
A letter printed from a unit of type from which the inside of each stroke has been removed, leaving a black line around the edges enclosing white space in the interior. Synonymous with *open letter*.

Outline Map
A map providing the minimum amount of geographic information necessary to allow the correlation of additional data displayed on it, for example, a map showing political or administrative boundaries.

Outline
A popular treatment of an extensive subject (*example*: *The Outline of History* by H.G. Wells). Also refers to a summary of the main aspects of a topic or a systematic list of the most important points of a speech or written work, often with indention used to indicate logical subordination.

Outtake
A term used in cataloguing mov-

ing images to refer to footage shot for a longer work that is not used in the final cut. Often used in the plural (*outtakes*) to refer to all the footage not used in a completed film. In a broader sense, film or tape rejected in the process of editing a motion picture or a work recorded on videotape or audiotape. Also spelled *out-take*.

Over the Transom

An unsolicited manuscript or book proposal received by a publisher without prior notification, usually directly from the author without the assistance of a literary agent. Publishers generally consign such submissions to a *slushpile*. Very few receive more than a rejection slip, but occasionally a work of exceptional quality is submitted in this way, launching a successful writing career.

Overclassified

A government document assigned a security classification by an agency of the U.S., government, which is more stringent than necessary to protect the national interest, making it difficult or impossible for members of the public to gain access to its content.

Overdubbing

A recording technique in which supplementary sound is added in the studio to previously recorded music, for example, to allow vocalists to sing harmony with themselves, create a choral effect, or add their own instrumental accompaniment. The practice began in the late 1920s when RCA Victor added studio orchestra accompaniment to early recordings of singer Enrico Caruso, originally made with piano accompaniment only.

Overdue Notice

A printed or handwritten notice sent to a borrower's street address requesting the prompt return of items kept past their due date. The first overdue notice may be followed by a second notice, then a final notice, depending on the policy of the individual library or library system.

Overhang

In bookbinding, the portion of covering material that extends beyond the edges of the boards before it is turned in and the endpapers pasted down

Overhead Projector

A tabletop platform device used in presentations and library instruction to project clear transparencies onto a wall screen or other flat, light-coloured surface. Document cameras are superseding overhead projectors in well-equipped library instruction classrooms and labs.

Overhead Transparency

Transparency.

Overleaf

On the other side of the leaf, a term used in captions to refer to full-page illustration on the reverse side of the same leaf.

Overpainting

In manuscript painting, the application of pigment over the surface of a preliminary drawing or underpainting. In medieval manuscripts, illuminators typically sketched a design in metal point, then reworked the underdrawing in greater detail in ink before applying metallic leaf and then pigment.

Overrun
Sheets or copies of a publication printed in excess of the quantity ordered by the publisher to allow for normal spoilage in printing and binding and for distribution as presentation and review copies. Synonymous with *overs*. The opposite of underrun.

Overs
Overrun.

Oversewing
A method of extrastrength binding in which the back folds are removed from the sections by milling and the resulting leaves sewn through the back margin in thin groups, one to another in succession, with the needle held perpendicular to the paper surface in hand sewing or positioned at an oblique angle in machine sewing. Oversewing is also used in some fold sewn bindings to reinforce the first and last sections. The swell added by oversewing may limit a volume's openability.

Overstaffed
Having more than enough employees to accomplish the necessary work, a situation that is usually remedied by reassigning staff to other duties and responsibilities or in extreme cases by laying off personnel. The opposite of understaffed.

Overstock
Excess quantities of a book or other item held in stock for which demand has dropped to a low level or ceased, usually the result of overestimating the sales potential of the work or a returns policy that encourages booksellers to overorder to secure a more favourable discount. To avoid paying tax on inventory, the publisher may dispose of overstock by remaindering.

Overtime
Time worked in excess of the maximum number of regular hours per day, week, or month specified under the terms of employment, for which an employee is normally compensated at a higher rate. Libraries pay their staff overtime only under very exceptional circumstances.

Oxford Corners
A binding decorated with plain, straight border lines that cross at the corners, popular from the 16th to the 18th century. The lines can be tooled in blind or gilt.

P

P2P
Peer-to-peer.

Packing List
Shipping list.

Page Head
Headline.

Paging System
Public address system.

Palmtop
Personal digital assistant.

Pamphlet Binding
A self-cover or paper publisher's binding in which the leaves of a periodical or pamphlet are wire-stitched or stapled, rather than sewn or glued. Also refers to the rebinding of a pamphlet or its enclosure in a specially-made outer binding, usually for purposes of preservation.

Panel
In binding, a square or rectangular compartment on the side of a book cover impressed in the dampened surface and/or enclosed in a border or frame, often stamped with the title or displaying a picture or design. *Panel stamps* were large tools (cast not engraved) incorporating an entire design rather than a repeatable motif. On a large book, several panels might be used to decorate the entire area. According to P.J.M. Marks, panels were used in Antwerp as early as the 13th century, sometimes based on woodcuts (*The British Library Guide to Bookbinding*, University of Toronto Press, 1998). Click here to view a 16th-century example bearing a single blind-stamped panel (Special Collections, Glasgow University Library, BD2-h.2) and here to see a multi-paneled binding of the same period (Princeton University Library). To see other examples, try a search on the keyword "panel" in the British Library's *Database of Bookbindings*. Also refers to a similar design stamped on the spine of a book, often between raised bands on the spine of a hand-bound volume.
In printing, a "list of works by the

same author" appearing in some books on the verso of the leaf immediately preceding the title page, which may include titles out of print or even issued by other publishers.

Also, one of a series of drawings in a cartoon or comic strip created as a sequence of related images to be viewed from left to right.

Panel Back

The spine of a hand-bound book on which the space between two or more of the bands has been enclosed in decorative tooling or panel-stamped with a similar design, in blind or gilt.

Panel Stamp

Panel.

Panel-stamped Binding

Panel.

Paper

A flat fibrous writing or printing surface made by breaking down vegetable fiber, such as wood or rag, into pulp to which a filler is added in water suspension. As the water is drained away on a wire screen, the moist fibers bond with each other at points of contact, forming a homogeneous, felted mat that stiffens as it dries. Paper is graded by content and intended use and by such properties as color, brightness, opacity, finish, strength, density, weight, and chemical stability. It can be coated or uncoated,sized or unsized, handmade or machine-made. The acid content of the paper used in library materials is an issue in preservation. For more information about paper, please see the entry by Derek Priest in the *International Encyclopedia of Information and Library*. Compare with papyrus and parchment.

Also refers to a brief composition, especially one prepared for presentation by the author at a conference or other professional meeting. Conference papers may bepublished in proceedings or transactions. They are indexed in *PapersFirst*, an online database available in OCLC *FirstSearch*. Compare with article.

Paperback

A book published in paper covers, rather than in hardcover, usually adhesive bound. The modern paperback first appeared in the 1930s when Sir Allen Lane, founder of Penguin books, published *Ariel* by Andre Maurois in paper covers. Paperback editions are normally published *after* the hardcover edition of the same title and sold at a lower price, which has made them a staple of the retail market for fiction and nonfiction. Synonymous with *paperbound* and *softcover*. Abbreviated *pb, pbk,* and *ppr*. Compare with paper boards.

Also refers to a form of bookbinding in which hot-melt adhesive is applied to the flat binding edge of the unsewn sections, securing them directly to a heavy paper covercut flush. Durability depends on the capacity of the adhesive to remain flexible over time.

Paper Boards

An edition bound in boards made

of paste-board covered in heavy paper, usually not as durable as cloth binding. Compare with paperback.

Paper Covers
A softcover publication not bound in stiff paper covers, for example, a booklet or pamphlet. The category also includes temporary bindings and wrappers commonly used in the late 18th and 19th century.

Paperback Original
A work of fiction or non-fiction published for the first time in mass-market or trade paperback edition, not previously issued in hardcover.

Paperboard
Fairly rigid sheets of matted fibre manufactured in the same manner as paper but.- 3 millimeter or more in thickness. Various grades are used in the manufacture of cases for publisher's bindings.

Paperbound
Paperback.

Paperless
An automated office or system that relies primarily on electronic media, rather than print on paper, for information transmission and recordkeeping.

Papermark
Watermark.

Paperwork
Routine tasks having to do with matters that must be committed to paper as opposed to work that is more creative or involves other forms of communication.

Papier-mâché Binding
A 19th-century molded binding made from a mixture of paper fibre, plaster of Paris, and possibly antimony, formed in a rigid frame usually made of metal. The designs, mainly in black heavy-relief reflected the Victorian revival of Gothic style in the decorative arts. Patented by the British firm Jackson and Sons, the method required a leather spine.

Parable
A short, simple story, usually written in the form of an allegory, intended to convey an explicit moral lesson or religious principle.

Paradigm
A model, pattern, or example, especially one that revolutionises the standard approach to a subject or conventional modes of thinking in a profession or field of study. In library and information science, paradigm shifts are increasingly driven by technological innovation.

Parallel Edition
Parallel texts.

Parchmenter
Parchment.

PARS
Preservation and Reformatting Section.

Partitive Relation
Semantic relation.

Passionale
Martyrology.

Passive Relation
Semantic relation.

Paste Paper Binding
A book bound in paper decorated by the application of a starch adhesive mixed with pigment to give the surface design and texture.

PAT
Photographic Activity Test.

Patent and Trademark Office
U.S., Patent and Trade-mark Office.

Patent Number
Patent.

Patriot Act
USA Patriot Act.

PBS
Public Television.

PC
Personal computer and political correctness.

PCC
Programme for Cooperatrive Catalogueing.

PCD
Photo CD.
PD public domain.

PDA
Patron-driven acquisition and personal digital assistant.

PDF
Portable Document Format.

Peepshow Book
Tunnel book.

PEG
Public access television.

Pegging
In early bookbinding, the process of attaching the sewing supports, usually cords, to the boards by means of a peg or dowel sunk into the surface of the board at the outer end of each of the channels or grooves in which the cords were recessed.

Perfecting
The process of printing the second side of a sheet. On a *perfecting press,* both sides are printed in a single pass. Synonymous with *backing up.*

Performance Measurement
Performance evaluation.

Period Subdivision
Chronological subdivision.

Permissions Copy
A copy of a book containing quoted or excerpted material sent to the copyright holder at first publication to confirm that passages were used in accordance with the permissions granted.

Personal Video Recorder (PVR)
DVR.

Personnel
Human resources.

PG
Project Gutenberg.

Philately
The collection and study of postage stamps and related materials, usually as a hobby.

Phoenix
A complete revision of a class in Dewey Decimal Classification (DDC). Synonymous with *phoenix schedule.*

Phone Book
Elephone directory.

Piano Score
An arrangement for solo piano of a vocal, instrumental, or orchestral work, written or printed on two staves.

Pictogram
Pictograph.

Pictorial Dictionary
Visual dictionary.

Pictorial Envelope
A category of ephemera consisting of mailing envelopes bearing printed or hand-drawn designs or illustration on the front or back. The images may be geographical, commercial (advertising), commemorative, political, comic, or purely decorative.

Picture Collection
Picture library.

Picture Dictionary
Visual dictionary.

Pierpont Morgan Library
Morgan Library, The.

PII
Personally identifiable information.

Piracy
Copyright piracy and pirated edition.

PL
Personal librarian and public library.

PLA
Public Library Association.

Placard
Poster.

Place Index
Geographic index.

Place Name
Geographic name.

Place of Publication
The geographic location in which an edition of a work is issued, usually given on the title page of a book as the city (or city and state) and sometimes more completely on the verso. In library cataloguing, place of publication is one of the elements recorded in the publication, distribution, etc., area of the bibliographic description.

Place Subdivision
Geographic subdivision.

Plagiary
Work offered as original that has, in fact, been copied (plagiarised) from another source, usually without permission.

Plain Binding
A bookbinding made of ordinary materials, often in a neutral colour, with little or no adornment, generally produced by a job binder.

Planetarium
Planetary model.

Planetary Model
A three-dimensional model of the solar system on any scale, showing the orbits of the planets around the sun and of the moons around the planets. In *AACR2*, planetary models are catalogueed as cartographic materials.

Planimetric Map
A map on any scale showing only the relationships of surface features (locations and distances) on a horizontal plane, with no indi-

cation of vertical relief. Road maps are usually planimetric.

Planisphere
The projection of all or part of a sphere onto a plane surface, especially a map representing the entire surface of the earth or another celestial body, without division into hemispheres.

Platter
A slang expression for phonograph record, derived from its disc shape.

PLGDB
Public Library Geographic Database.

PLIN
Public Libraries International Network.

PLR
Public Lending Right.

PLSS
Public Land Survey System.

Plug
To attempt to boost sales and readership of a book by praising its strengths and ignoring or downplaying its weaknesses. Such an endorsement may be unsolicited by the author or publisher.

Plummet
Precursor to the graphite pencil, plummet was a piece of lead alloy, sometimes mounted in a holder, used from the 11th for ruling and writing annotations in manuscripts and for underdrawing. Before plummet, medieval scribes and illuminators used hard point and metal point. Synonymous with *lead point*.

PMC
PubMed Central.

PMEST
The five main facets in S.R. Ranganathan's *Colon Classification*: personality, matter, energy, space, and time.

PMID
The unique numeric identifier assigned to the bibliographic record representing a source document when the record is entered into the National Library of Medicine's *PubMed* database.

Pocket Bible
A portable bible of small size, written in condensed script or printed in small type, used mainly for home study.

Pocket Computer
Personal digital assistant.

Point of Access
Access point.

Point of Service
Service point.

Post-coordination
Post-coordinate indexing.

Poster Style
A style of pictorial publisher's binding, popular at the end of the 19th and the beginning of the 20th centuries, stamped with a bold design resembling a printed poster, in which the colour of the cloth is often an important design element.

Postliminary Matter
Back matter.

Pounce
Pouncing.

PPO
Public Programmes Office.

PPV
Pay-per-view.

Prebinding
Prelibrary binding.

Prebound
Prelibrary binding.

Preference Order
In Dewey Decimal Classification, the order in which one of two or more numbers is to be chosen when different characteristics of a subject cannot be shown in full bynumber building, indicated in a note, sometimes containing a table of preference (*DDC*). When the class notation can be synthesized to show two or more characteristics, the decision is governed by citation order. Synonymous with *order of preference* and *precedence order*.

PRECIS
Preserved Context Indexing System.

Preliminary Matter
Preliminaries.

Prelims
Preliminaries.

Prepay
Prepayment.

Prepayment Discount
Discount.

Prepub
An abbreviation of pre-publication.

Preservation Survey
Conservation survey.

Preservation Wind
Wind tension.

Princeps Edition
First edition.

Printer's Device
Printer's mark.

Printing Dupe
Print master.

Printout
Text, images, or other data from a computer file printed as output on paper or some other printing surface by a peripheral device called a printer. Compare with hard copy.

Prison Library
Correctional library.

Pristine
A book or other bibliographic item in its original condition, unchanged in any way. Synonymous with *mint*.

PRMS
Public Relations and Marketing Section.

PRO
Public Record Office.

Probation Volunteer
Community service volunteer.

Processing Center
Centralised processing.

Production Company
Producer.

Programme Records
In archives, the records created or received and maintained by an organisation in the conduct of the primary functions for which it is

responsible, as distinct from the house-keeping records related to its administrative operations. Synonymous with *substantive records*.

Promotional Film

A non-fiction motion picture of any length made to publicise or further the interests of a specific business, industry, organisation, cause, etc., for example, Walt Disney's last film, a 1966 preview to EPCOT. Abbreviated *promo film*.

Prompt

A message at a point on a computer screen, usually in the form of a small blinking cursor (with or without explanatory text), indicating that data is to be entered or an operation initiated by the user.

Proof Impression

Proof print.

Proof of Payment

Verification, usually in the form of a canceled check, that an amount due has been paid, normally provided at the request of a vendor or supplier, but the customer may also make such a request.

Proof Print

In printing, an impression of an illustration made from the final plate before the regular impression is published, usually prior to the addition of the title or caption. Synonymous with *proof impression*.

Proportional Circle

Graduated circle.

Provisional Edition

Preliminary edition.

Pseudonym

A fictitious name, especially one assumed by an author to conceal or obscure identity (see this example, courtesy of the British Library). The classic example in American literature is Mark Twain whose real name was Samuel Langhorne Clemens. The writer François-Marie Arouet (Voltaire) probably holds the record for the most pseudonyms, with Daniel Foe (Defoe) a close second. Prior to the mid-19th century, women writers often used male pseudonyms (pseudandry) to get their workspublished and to attract readership (*example*: George Sand whose real name was Amandine-Aurore-Lucile Dupin Dudevant), although there were notable exceptions (Jane Austen and the Brontë sisters). A *joint pseudonym* is one shared by two or more collaborators in a work (Rosetta Stone used by Dr. Seuss and the illustratorMichael K. Frith). U.S. copyright law permits a person to register works pseudonymously. Click here to connect to *a.k.a.*, an online dictionary of pseudonyms, or try theList of Pseudonyms provided by *Wikipedia*. Abbreviated *pseud*. Compare with allonym.

PTDLA

Patent and Trademark Depository Library Association.

PTO

U.S., Patent and Trade-mark Office.

PTRC

Patent and trademark resource center.

Public Access Policy
NIH Public Access Policy.

Public Broadcasting System (PBS)
Public Television.

Public Use File
Disclosure-free extract.

Published Price
List price.

Publisher's Cloth
The original cloth cover of an edition binding as issued by the publisher, as distinct from the cloth cover of a custom binding.

Publisher's Device
Publisher's Mark.

Publisher's Mark
A device printed in a book to identify its publisher, in the same way that a printer's mark represents the printer. Some early publisher's marks included a motto. Synonymous with *publisher's device.*

Publishing Season
Season.

PubMed
MEDLINE.

Pull-out
Throw-out.

Pulp Magazine
An inexpensive popular magazine of the early 20th century devoted to sensational stories of love, adventure, mystery, or intrigue, usually printed on newsprint.

PURL
Persistent URL.

PVA
Polyvinyl acetate.

PVC
Polyvinyl chloride.

PW
Publishers Weekly.

QR Code
An abbreviation of *Quick Response code*. A type of two-dimensional barcode invented in 1994 by a subsidiary of Toyota for use in the automotive industry. QR codes have far greater data storage capacity than standard UPC barcodes and can be decoded at high speed. QR codes storing addresses and Uniform Resource Locators (URLs) may appear on almost any object (books, periodicals, signage) to direct users to additional information (example).

Q

Quad
Quadrangle.

Quad-centered Photograph
The second exposure in a series of three consecutive aerial photographs taken of the area covered by a quadrangle used as a unit in mapping. The first exposure is taken directly above one of the boundaries of the quadrangle, the second directly above the center of the quad, and the third above the opposite boundary. The quad centered exposure is made from an altitude that permits coverage of the entire area of the quad.

Quadrangle
A four-sided area of the earth's surface bounded by parallels of latitude and meridians of longitude, used as a unit of area in mapping. The dimensions of a *quad* are not necessarily the same in both directions. The 1:24,000 7.5-minute topographic quadrangle is the base map used by the U.S., Geological Survey, the largest mapping agency in the United States. Each USGS quad bears a name, often based on a distinctive feature of the area mapped. The Earth Sciences and Map Library at UC Berkeley is working to provide online access to the historic topographic quadrangles produced by the U.S., Geological Survey from 1895 to the present. Map-tech provides historic topographic quads for the northeastern United States.

Quadraphonic
Sound reproduced by an audio device simultaneously from four separate channels with four amplifiers or speakers. Because quadraphonic sound separation produces a more realistic result than monaural or stereophonic sound recording, its developers envisioned it replacing stereo but it failed to do so.

Quadrennial
Issued every four years. Also refers to a serial publication issued every four years.

Quadrilinear Script
Minuscule.

Qualification
Evidence that a person applying for employment has passed the requisite examinations or acquired the education, experience, and skills necessary to meet the requirements stated in the position description. Usually used in the plural: *qualifications*.

In Dublin Core and some other metadata schemes, the process of using qualifiers to provide additional information about a metadata element.

Qualifier
In Dublin Core and some other metadata schemes, a term added to provide information about the value of a metadata element. In Dublin Core, qualifiers may refine the meaning of an element or identify encoding schemes that aid in interpreting the element value.

Quality of Service
The degree to which the services provided by a library or library system meet the needs of its users and the standards established by the profession, usually assessed statisticcally and on the basis of qualitative feedback (user surveys, suggestion box, etc.). Quality of service is affected by budgetary constraints, management policies, design and condition of facilities, personnel decisions, and employee morale. Abbreviated *QoS*.

Quality Paperback
Trade paperback.

Quantity Discount
A discount offered by a publisher or jobber to booksellers and libraries on orders for a minimum number of copies of the same item or a minimum number of assorted titles. Large libraries are usually in a better position than small libraries to take advantage of such offers.

Quarter Binding
A style of bookbinding in which the spine is bound in a different material than the sides, usually a more durable covering such as leather, often in a contrasting colour, extending no more than one-eighth of the width of the boards.

Quarter Cloth
A book with the spine bound in cloth and the rest of the cover in some other material, such as paper, often in a contrasting colour. Compare with half cloth.

Quarter Leather
A book with the spine bound in leather and the rest of the cover in some other material, such as cloth, often in a contrasting colour. Compare with half leather.

Quarterly
Issued four times a year. Also refers to a serial issued every three months, usually in spring, summer, fall, and winter. Most scholarly journals are published quarterly (*examples*: *Shakespeare Quarterly* and *Quarterly Review of Film and Video*).

Quarto (4to)
A book, approximately 13 inches in height, made by folding a full sheet of book paper in two right-angle folds, producing signatures

of four leaves (eight pages). The precise size of each leaf in a quarto edition depends on the size of the original sheet. Some early editions are known by the number of leaves in their sections, for example, the *Quarto Edition* of Shakespeare's plays. Compare with folio, octavo, duodecimo, and sextodecimo.

Quasi-synonym
A word or phrase not precisely the same in meaning as another term, which is nevertheless treated as synonymous in a given indexing language, for example, the term 'Library science' used for (UF) 'Librarianship' in the *Library of Congress Subject Headings* list. Synonymous with *nearsynonym.*

Quatern Book
In hand-binding, the binder traditionally bound the thirteenth book at no charge, presumably as an incentive to place larger binding orders, but by the early 19th century, this custom was restricted in England to all the copies of a single title delivered to the bindery at the same time and was not carried over into machine binding.

Quaternion
In bookbinding, a gathering consisting of four sheets of paper, parchment, or vellum folded once to create eight leaves, used in assembling some manuscript books and early printed books.

Quatrefoil
An ornament or illustration resembling a fourlobed leaf or flower, commonly used in medieval architecture (especially in stained glass windows) and in miniatures painted in illuminated manuscripts.

Query
A request submitted as input in a search of an online catalogue or bibliographic database to retrieve records or documents relevant to the user's information need(s). Some information storage and retrieval systems allow queries to be submitted in natural language, but most systems require the user to formulate search statements in the artificial language used for indexing and in syntax acceptable to the search software. The query is an approximation of the information need that provides the impetus for the search.

Questionnaire
A list of written questions carefully formulated to be administered to a selected group of people for the purpose of gathering information (feedback) in survey research. In libraries, patrons are sometimes asked to fill out a questionnaire designed to assess the perceived quality and usefulness of services and resources. The results are then compiled and analysed for use in self-assessment and planning.

Queue
A temporary storage location in a computer, reserved for data awaiting processing, usually organised chronologically (first-in-first-out) or according to some other pre-established priority. Also refers to a line of people waiting to be served or a series of tasks waiting to be ex-

ecuted, usually in the order in which they arrived or were received.

Quill and Quire
A monthly magazine published in Toronto since, 1935, providing news and reviews of books published in Canada. The June and December issues include the *Canadian Publishers Directory* as a free supplement. ISSN: 0033-6491.

Quill Pen
A writing implement made by cutting back the plume and shaping the thick end of one of the flight feathers of a large bird, such as a goose or swan, used prior to the invention of the dip fountain pen in the 18th century for writing documents and for copying manuscripts by hand. Using a quill pen was a two-handed operation in the Middle Ages, with a knife held in the spare hand for making corrections. A quill pen had to be sharpened repeatedly because the nib wears and often breaks with use.

Quinquennial
Issued very five years. Also refers to a serial publication issued every five years (*example*: *Biography and Genealogy Master Index*).

Quinternion
In bookbinding, a gathering consisting of five sheets of paper, parchment, or vellum, each folded once to create 10 leaves, used in assembling some manuscript books and early printed books.

Quire
Originally, a gathering consisting of two or more (usually four) parchment or vellum bifolia nested one inside another to form eight leaves (16 pages), convenient for handsewn books. Michelle Brown notes in *Understanding Illuminated Manuscripts* (Getty Museum/British Library, 1994) that *quire numeration* (numbers written on the final verso to facilitate collation in binding) began in late Antiquity, and *quire signatures* (numbers and/or letters written within a quire to facilitate internal arrangement) began around 1400. When paper came into widespread use after the invention of printing from movable type, its thinness enabled more sheets to be included in a gathering. In modern usage, the term is synonymous with gathering, section, and signature. Also refers to one-twentieth of a ream, equal to 24 sheets of handmade paper or 25 sheets of machine-made paper.

Quorum
The minimum number of members who must be present for business to be conducted at a formal meeting governed by the rules of parliamentary procedure. When a quorum is not present, a meeting may proceed without formally transacting business.

Quotation
Words or passages reproduced from a written work or repeated verbatim from an oral statement. Because words and phrases taken out of context may give a misleading impression of the whole, care must be taken in selecting quotations. A passage quoted incorrectly is a *misquotation*. In publishing, the

accuracy of quotations is checked by the editor. Collections of literary quotations are available in the reference section of most libraries. Bartlett's *Familiar Quotations* is available online from *Bartleby.com*. In printing, brief quotations are set in the text, enclosed in 'quotation marks.' Long quotations, called *block quotations*, are set apart from the main text by indention and/or printed in a smaller type size without quotation marks, preceded and followed by a blank line. A very long quotation is an excerpt. To avoid copy-right infringement, quotations in a written work should be documented in footnotes or endnotes. In an oral statement, the source should be verbally acknowledged as a courtesy to the original author. Synonymous with *quote*. In acquisitions, a general term for a library's request that a publisher or vendor state the price of an item, and for the seller's response.

Qur'an

Arabic for 'recital.' The sacred text of the Muslims, consisting of revelations made by Allah through the angel Gabriel to Mohammad, who delivered them orally from A.D. 610 until his death in 632. Put into writing after his death and canonised by the Third Caliph, Uthman, in the codex of Medina, the *Qur'an* is made up of 114 *surahs* or chapters. Like the Christian Bible, the Arabic text, copied in many forms, has served as a vehicle for the development of the arts of calligraphy, illumination, and fine binding.

R

RA
Readers' advisory.

Rag Book
Cloth book.

Rag Paper
Paper made from cotton and/or linen rags, stronger and more permanent than paper made from wood pulp and most other fibres but also more expensive. Rag content is usually indicated as a percentage. Paper made from 100 percent rag fibre is called *all-rag*.

Ragged
Refers to a page of type with lines of variable length, usually *ragged right*, set flush (aligned) with the left-hand margin but unjustified on the right, as in the lines of a poem.

Railway Edition
An inexpensive edition of a popular work (fiction, biography, history, etc.), often printed in pocket-size format, for sale to train travellers at book-stalls in railroad stations during the 19th century. Synonymous with *railway library edition*.

Raised Bands
Narrow, slightly elevated ridges visible at intervals across the spine of a hand-bound book, produced by the underlying sewing supports to which the sections are attached.

Raised Capital
In printing, an initial letter, usually at the beginning of the first paragraph of a chapter, projecting above the line of type on which it appears. Synonymous with *cocked-up initial*.

RAM
Random Access Memory.

Range Line
One of the two north-south boundaries of a township in the United States surveyed under the Public Land Survey System (PLSS). Range lines are numbered east and west of the principal meridian used in the survey.

RAP
Regional Alliance for Preservation.

Ratings
Content rating and library rating.

Raw Stock
Stock.

RBB
Reference Books Bulletin.

RBMS
Rare Books and Manu-scripts Section.

RCL
Resources for College Libraries.

Reading Habits
Reading preference.

Read-only Memory (ROM)
A memory chip containing instructions and/or data that cannot be changed or erased because the manufacturer created it in unalterable form. Usually contains the programmes required to start the computer.

Read-only
A digital storage medium capable of being read but not modified or erased, used for data that is to be retained permanently, for example, ROM (read-only memory) and CD-ROM. The opposite of rewritable.

Real Time
Happening immediately, in the present moment, for example, a report on or record of events made simultaneously with their occurrence. In computing, an electronic process, operation, or routine that occurs quickly enough to affect or respond to a related process taking place simultaneously in actual time, for example, *chat reference.* The opposite of asynchronous.

Rebacked
A book given a new spine and mended hinges, usually because the spine was cracked or the hinges weakened. Original materials are used where possible, but when new cover material is required, a close match is usually attempted by the binder. Rebacking is not as extensive as rebinding since, some of the original binding (usually the boards) is retained.

Reboot
To cause the files in the operating system of a computer to be re-executed, usually by selecting the option to "Restart" or "Reset" or by pressing Ctrl+Alt+Del on the keyboard. This procedure is sometimes helpful in getting a computer "unstuck" after it locks up unexpectedly during processing. If it fails, the user can cold boot the system, but powering down will result in the loss of unsaved data. Synonymous with *warm boot.*

Recatalogueing
The process of making substantial revisions in bibliographic records for items that have already been catalogueed, usually in response to changes in the needs or policies of the library, for example, the addition of contents notes to records representing anthologies and other collected works. Also spelled *re-cataloguing.*

Receipt
A written document stating that something has been received, usually in exchange for payment of an

amount noted in the acknowledgment. Sometimes found among personal and family papers, receipts may contain information of historical importance.

Receiving
In acquisitions, the initial processing of an item shipped to the library by a publisher, jobber, or vendor, including verification that the correct item was shipped with all parts included, routing the invoice to the appropriate accounting office for payment, and updating the order record, usually with date received, number of parts received, and an indication of where the item was sent for the next step in processing.

Recension
A revision of the text of a work, often a literary classic, based on a critical examination of earlier texts and authoritative sources, usually undertaken only after a consensus has developed among leading scholars concerning the weight of evidence.

Recessed Monitor
Monitor.

Reciprocal Agreement
A mutual understanding between libraries, usually concerning fees for lending via interlibrary loan, typically 'We will not charge you if you do not charge us.'

Recon
Retrospective conversion.

Reconfigure
To change the way data is structured in a computer system.

Reconnaissance Map
A map that is the result of a preliminary survey or exploratory examination of a geographic area, usually less accurate than the cartographic product of a subsequent survey in which more rigourous methods are employed.

Reconstruction
A graphic image intended to show how something, such as a building, street, complex, or city, may have appeared at a previous time, usually based on historical, archaeological, or other evidence.

Record Club
In the music industry, a commercial company that markets recordings at discounted prices, usually via mail order catalogues (*example*: Columbia Record Club, established in 1955). Incentives, such as bonus records, may be offered to attract customers.

Record Jacket
Album cover.

Recorded Book
Audiobook.

Records Schedule
Disposition schedule.

Reduction
A reproduction or copy produced on a smaller scale than the original, usually indicated as a percentage of the initial size (a 50 per cent reduction of an 8 × 10 inch original produces a copy measuring 4 × 5 inches). Most photocopiers available in libraries have reduction capability for the convenience of users. The opposite of enlargement.

Refereed
Peer-reviewed.

Reference Matter
Back matter.

Refresh
Reload.

Refurbishing
In conservation, the basic cleaning and reconditioning of an old book, including the application of leather dressing and minor repairs, intended to improve appearance and retard deterioration.

Reimburse
To pay back money spent by another person or to compensate someone for damages or expenses incurred, usually upon presentation of a receipt verifying the amount. In libraries, employees may be reimbursed for work-related travel expense, office supplies purchased out of pocket, etc.

Reinforced Binding
A publisher's binding that has been strengthened, usually by adding a strip of cloth to each hinge and using stronger thread to sew the sections, but that does not meet the standards for prelibrary binding.

Reinstate
To return something to a former condition, or a person to a position from which he or she has been removed, sometimes in compliance with the outcome of a grievance procedure or lawsuit.

Reissue
A second or subsequent impression of a previously published edition in which the text remains substantially the same, but the title page may be redesigned and the front matter and back matter altered. When a mass-market paperback is reissued, the cover design of the earlier edition is often changed.

Rejection Rate
In journal publishing, the percentage of the total number of articles submitted for publication during a given period of time that are rejected or returned to the author (or authors) for revision as a condition of acceptance, usually following the process of peer-review.

Rejection Slip
A printed slip sent by a publisher with a returned manuscript informing the author (or authors) that the work has *not* been accepted for publication.

Rejoint
In binding, to repair a broken joint by the application of a cloth or paper strip, preserving the original covers and spine. Not an especially strong method, but it can be used to keep a worn book in circulation when rebinding is not cost effective.

Related Work
Dependent work.

Relative Humidity
Humidity.

Releasing Agent
The person or agency responsible for the initial distribution (release)

of a motion picture. In *AACR2*, the name is recorded optionally in the publication, distribution, etc., area of the bibliographic description following the name of the publisher.

Relevance Ratio
Precision.

Relievo Binding
In Italian *relievo* means "relief." A binding made from leather that is softened, then molded and deeply embossed, a technique used in 19th century England to introduce designs reflec-ting the Victorian revival of Gothic style.

Remainder Binding
Remainders.

Remote Storage
Off-site storage.

Removed Archives
Archives taken from the country in which they were originally accumulated, often under unusual circumstances, for example, by one of the combatants during a war or in its aftermath.

Removes
A printing term for notes or quotations set in smaller type at the foot of a page of text, for example, a book set in 12-point might have footnotes or endnotes set in 10-point or smaller type.

Renaissance Librarian
A librarian who cultivates a broad and deep under-standing and appreciation of, and lively interest in, all aspects of librarianship, despite having developed at least one specialisation.

Replevin
The recovery of archived property (records, manuscripts, documents, etc.) by an organisation or institution claiming ownership. Also refers to the writ or legal action by which such property is recovered.

Replica
A reproduction or copy of a work of art, especially one made by the artist who created the original or produced under the artist's supervision.

Residuum
The portion of an author's total body of work considered by scholars and critics to be of lasting value.

Respondent
A candidate for an academic degree who must defend, against one or more opponents, a thesis proposed by a faculty moderator acting as the praeses in a formal disputation.

Restrike
In printmaking, to make one or more additional impressions from the same plate or block after the original edition of the print has been issued. Restrikes are usually unsigned and unnumbered.

Retail Price
List price.

Retention Schedule
Disposition schedule.

Review of the Literature
Literature review.

RF
Representative Fraction.

RFC
Request for Comments.

RFID
Radio frequency identification.

RFP
Request for Proposal.

RIAA
Recording Industry Association of America.

Rights Metadata
Administrative metadata.

RLG
Research Libraries Group.

RLIN
Research Libraries Information Network.

Rocaille
A style of bookbinding popular in France in the 19th century featuring a panel framed by elegantly curved, often foliate shapes, usually tooled in gold or silver, with or without a centerpiece.

Rock Drawing
In cartography, the stylised rendering of rock faces for terrain too steep to be shown by other methods of representing relief.

ROI
Return on investment.

Role Indicator
In indexing, a code used to indicate the syntactic relationship between two or more index terms (subject headings or descriptors) assigned to a document to facilitate retrieval by subject (adapted from the *ASIS Thesaurus of Information Science and Librarianship*, Information Today, 1998).

ROM
Readonly memory.

RSI
Repetitive Stress Injury.

RT (or R)
Related term and running title.

Rubbing
An impression made by moving charcoal, graphite, chalk, crayon, or a similar substance back and forth across a sheet of paper placed over a surface, portions of which are in raised relief.

RUSA
Reference and User Services Association.

Rush Processing
In acquisitions, an item sent to catalogueing to be processed as soon as it is received, usually a rush order or an item for which a patron is waiting.

S

S.n.
Sine nomine.

SA
An abbreviation of *see also.*

SAA
Society of American Archivists.

SACO
Programme for Cooperative Catalogueing.

SAILS
Project SAILS.

SALIS
Substance Abuse Librarians and Information Specialists.

Salt Print
Salted paper print.

SAN
Standard Address Number.

SASS
Systems and Services Section.

Sawnin Cords
Sunk bands.

SBU
Sensitive but unclassified.

Scatter Border
Strewn border.

Scattered
Completeness.

SCBWI
Society of Children's Book Writers and Illustrators.

Schadograph
Photogram.

Schedule
Classification schedule.

School Librarian
Library media specialist.

School Library Media Center
School library.

School Prise Binding
Prise binding.

SCL
Society of Composers and Lyricists.

Screen Capture
Screencast and screen-shot.

Scrinium
A container in the shape of a cyl-

inder with a removable lid, used by the ancient Romans for storing manuscripts in the form of scrolls.

Scrip
A category of ephemera consisting of money issued as a substitute for legal tender (currency) by a business, military organisation, or local government, usually as a form of credit against wages or as small change when real money is not available, for example, in time of war or severe economic crisis

Scriptura Continua
Scriptio continuo.

Scroll Map
A map of elongated format made in the form of a roll, usually showing a linear feature such as a road, mountain range, or coastline.

Sculptural Binding
A bookbinding in the form of an object, natural or manmade, often related in theme to the content of the book.

SDI
An abbreviation of *selective dissemination of information.*

Sealskin
Seal.

Seascape
An scene, made by photographic or artistic means, in which the ocean or seashore is the principal subject; the maritime equivalent of a landscape. Also, a genre of art in which the principal subject is the maritime environment.

Seasonal Catalogue
Season.

Secondary Entry
Added entry.

Secondary Values
In archives, the values of records for the activities of users other than the office of record or its successors.

Secondhand Book
Used book.

Secondhand Bookstore
Used bookstore.

Section Title
Divisional title.

Security Strip
Magnetic strip.

See
A cross-reference in a library catalogue, index, or reference work directing the user from a synonym (or other equivalent term) to the preferred heading or descriptor for a given name, place, or subject. Synonymous with *search under.*

SEES
Slavic and East European Section.

Segmentation
In Dewey Decimal Classification, the indication of logical breaks in a number by means of a typographical device, such as a slash or a prime mark used to indicate the end of an abridged class number or the beginning of a standard subdivision (*DDC*).

Seismic Upgrade
Renovation of an existing library fa-

cility to meet current safety standards intended to minimize potential damage or loss caused by a major earthquake. When structural changes are required, a seismic upgrade can be costly, but for older library builidings in earthquake-prone areas (*e.g.*, parts of California), it is often necessary.

Selective Dissemination of Information (SDI)
Current awareness service.

Selector
Selection.

Self End
In bookbinding, an end-paper that is not separate from the text but rather part of the first or last section and therefore of the same paper stock as the text.

Self Work
A literary or other work of which the subject is the life of its author/creator. The category includes autobiographies, diaries, journals, logs, common-place books, keepsakes, scrapbooks, etc.

Self-checkout
An automated circulation system that allows registered borrowers to check out circulating materials on their own without the assistance of library staff, usually by means of barcodes attached to the item and appearing on the patron's library card. Self-checkout is part of a trend towards self-service in library operations.

Self-citation
Reference made in a written work to one or more of the author's previous publications (book, periodical article, conference paper, etc.), an accepted practice in scholarly communication, provided important works written on the subject by other authors are not neglected or ignored.

Self-cover
A pamphlet or periodical covered in the same paper stock used to print the text, rather than a heavier grade of paper.

Self-wrappers
Wrappers.

Semantic Relation
The connection in meaning between two or more concepts and between the terms (subject headings or descriptors) used to represent them in an indexing language.

Semé
The past tense of the French verb *semer*, meaning "to sow." A style of bookbinding in which the surface of one or both covers is decorated in a pattern created by the regular repetition of one or more small ornamental motifs, usually in gilt, against an open ground. A fleuron is often used for this purpose.

Semiannual
Issued at intervals of six months. Also refers to a serial issued every six months. Synonymous with *half yearly* and *twice yearly*. Compare with biennial.

Semicurrent
Archival materials too old to be considered current but still useful and therefore retained for a certain period, usually in a location re-

served for intermediate storage, pending final disposition.

Semi-limp
A binding in boards made of thin, flexible card or some other material that bends easily (bibles are often bound in this way). The flexible boards are not always attached to the covering material.

Semimonthly
Issued twice each month or every two weeks. Also refers to a serial issued twice a month, with the possible exception of certain issues (*example*: *Library Journal*). Synonymous with biweekly.

Semiotics
The systematic study of the linguistic and non-linguistic signs and symbols used in both natural and artificially constructed languages. The three branches of semiotics are:

- Pragmatics (how signs are used by those who make use of them),
- Semantics (relation-ships of meaning between signs and their referents), and
- Syntax (how signs are combined). Each of the branches has theoretical, descriptive, and applied aspects.

Semipublished
Works such as reports, internal documents, theses, etc., that are difficult if not impossible to purchase through regular market channels because they were never intended for publication, but which may be obtainable via interlibrary loan, document delivery service, or some other method of retrieval.

Semiweekly
Issued twice each week. Also refers to a serial publication issued twice a week. Synonymous with *twice weekly*.

Send
To transmit data from one node to another on a computer network, as in the exchange of e-mail messages or the export of bibliographic data from an online catalogue or bibliographic database to an e-mail account. Also refers to the command in a computer programme that initiates such a transmission. The opposite of *receive*.

Senior
Older adult.

Seniority
The numerical position of an individual with respect to longevity of employment, which may be a factor in certain personnel decisions (assignment of duties and responsibilities, promotion, layoff, etc.).

Sentencing
The application of the appropriate disposition schedule to a group or collection of archival records.

Separately Paginated
Numbering the pages of each volume or part of a set, or of each issue of a single volume of a periodical, in a separate sequence, starting with number one.

Separately Published
An item issued by a publisher or

distributor as an independent entity, usually under its own title and copyright, as opposed to a work published in a collection or as a serial, for example, the individual works in a monographic series, each published under a separate title.

Septennial
Issued every seven years. Also refers to a serial publication issued every seven years.

Sequential Locator
Locator.

Sequentiary
A liturgical book (or portion of a gradual or troper) containing extended melodies (*sequences*) sung by a soloist between the Alleluia and the Gospel lesson at Mass. Synonymous with *sequentiale.*

Serial Bibliography
A bibliography published in successive parts, at fairly regular intervals, usually limited to a specialised field of study (*example*: *Bibliography of Asian Studies*, published every one or two years).

Serial Set
U.S., Congressional Serial Set.

Series Area
Series statement.

Series Author
A writer of works separately published as individual titles within a group of items (*example*: J.K. Rowling, author of the Harry Potter series of books for children).

Series Binding
A style of binding repeated by the publisher on all the volumes issued in a series of works.

Serigraphy
Screen printing.

Seriocomedy
Comedydrama.

Service Area
The geographic area served by a public library or library system, from which it derives a major portion, if not all, of its funding, usually through taxation.

Service Book
Liturgical work.

Service Copy
A third-generation micro-film copy, produced from a print master to be catalogueed, stored, and used as an information source in a library.

Set Discount
The price charged by the publisher when all the volumes in a multi-volume set are ordered at the same time, as opposed to the higher price charged per volume when one or more volumes are purchased separately. The price difference is usually 5 to 20 per cent.

Sexennial
Issued every six years. Also refers to a serial publication issued every six years.

Sextodecimo (16mo)
A small book, approximately six inches in height, made by folding each sheet of book paper to form signatures of 16 leaves (32 pages).

SF
Science Fiction.

SFWA
Science Fiction and Fantasy Writers of America.

SGML
Standard Generalised Markup Language.

Sgraffito
A design or writing produced on a surface, such as parchment or plaster, by scratching through an upper coat of pigment to reveal an underlying layer of contrasting colour or the natural colour of the surface.

Shape Book
A book with covers and book block cut to the shape of a picture or design printed on the front cover, a common format in children's board books.

Shared Authorship
Shared responsibility.

Shared Catalogueing
Cooperative catalogueing.

SHARP
Society for the History of Authorship, Reading and Publishing.

Shaved
Said of a book in which the edges of the sections have been trimmed so closely in binding that the text is touched but not cut into. Compare with cropped.

Sheet Map
A map printed on one side of a single sheet of paper, with or without explanatory matter printed on the reverse side. In libraries, sheet maps are usually stored flat or folded in a map case that has wide shallow drawers.

Sheet Music
A musical work written or printed on one or more unbound sheets of paper. Libraries usually place sheet music inside a protective folder or binder in physical processing to keep the sheets together.

Shelf Life
The average length of time an item owned by a library, such as a book, audiocassette, video-cassette, or CD, is likely to remain in usable condition before it must be replaced due to normal wear.

Shelving
Bookshelves.

Short Loan
Reserves.

Short Novel
Novelette.

Short Subject
Short film.

Short Title
An abbreviated title of a book or other publication, usually enough of the full title to enable the item to be identified in a catalogue or bibliography or on a price list or order form. Also spelled *short-title*.

Short
Short film.

Shorts
Short shipment.

Show Print
Release print.

Showcard
Window card.

Shut-in
Homebound.

SIC
Standard Industrial Classification.

SICI
Serial Item and Contribution Identifier.

Sides
The outer surface of the upper and lower boards of a book, usually covered in a protective material such as leather, cloth, or paper.

Sign Language
A method of non-verbal communication devised to assist the deaf, in which a system of manual, facial, and other body movements is used to express words, thoughts, and feelings.

Sign
A lettered board or graphic symbol intended to identify a place or building, provide information, or give directions, notice, or warning

Signatory
A government or agency that has the legal right to sign an official document, such as a treaty or trade agreement. Also refers to the person whose signature appears on such a document.

Signed Edition
An edition (usually a limited edition) in which the individual copies bear the signature of the author or illustrator.

Signet
Register.

Silk Screen
Screen printing.

Silver Print
Gelatin silver print.

Siting
Site selection.

SLA
Special Libraries Association.

Slander
Libel.

SLAS
State Library Agency Section.

Slide Projector
Slide.

Slide Viewer
Slide.

Slip Proof
Galley proof.

SLJ
School Library Journal.

Small Capital
A capital letter of x-height, about two-thirds as large as the full-size capital of the same type size, used for emphasis in printed text. Abbreviated *small cap*. Abbreviated *s.c.*

Small-scale Map
A systematic representation on a two-dimensional surface of a relatively large land area, such as a country, continent, or the world, at a representative fraction of 1:250,000 or smaller, providing only a limited amount of detail.

Smashing
Nipping.

Smooth Spine
The spine of a book that lacks the raised bands produced by unrecessed sewing supports, not to be confused with the flat back of a book not rounded in the process of binding.

SMPTE Code
Time code.

SMTP
Simple Mail Transfer Protocol, the standard TCP/IP e-mail protocol used on the Internet, originally designed for ASCII text but subsequently enhanced to permit the attachment of other file types.

SN
Scope Note.

Snakeskin
Leather made from the tanned skin of one of the larger species of snake (python, water snake, etc.), used as a covering material in hand-binding and for decorative bands on books bound in other kinds of leather.

SOCAN
Society of Composers, Authors, and Music Publishers of Canada.

Social Tagging
A system, developed in 1996, that allows Internet users to store, classify, share, and search lists of bookmarked resources.

Solidus
Slash.

Song Folio
In music publishing, a collection of songs, usually written by the same songwriter, performed by the same vocalist, or of the same genre or time period, offered for sale as a single unit

SORT
Staff Organisations Round Table.

Sound Disc
Compact disc and phonograph record.

Spanish Calf
A bookbinding in calf-skin, acid-stained in large blotches of boldly contrasting colour.

SPARC
Scholarly Publishing and Academic Resources Coalition.

Special Collections
Some libraries segregate from the general collection rare books, manuscripts, papers, and other items that are
- Of a certain form,
- On a certain subject,
- Of a certain time period or geographic area,
- In fragile or poor condition, or
- Especially valuable.

Such materials are not allowed to circulate and access to them may be restricted.

Specs
Specifications.

Speech Recognition
Voice recognition.

Spider
Crawler.

Split Catalogue
Divided catalogue.

Spoilage
In book production, printed sheets or entire copies discarded because they contain imperfections or were damaged in printing or binding. Allowance for spoilage is included in the size of printing and binding orders.

Spot Height
Spot elevation.

Spread
The full expanse of facing pages in an opening in a book or other bound publication. The page on the right-hand side is the recto; the one on the left is the verso.

Sprocket Holes
Perforations.

SPVS
Supervisors Section.

SRRT
Social Responsibilities Round Table.

SS
Serials Section and stock shot.

SSP
Society for Scholarly Publishing.

Stab Sewing
Side sewing.

Stack Aisle
Range aisle.

Stamping
Blocking.

Standard Title
Uniform title.

Staple
On chained books, the metal fitting that attaches the chain to one of the boards, usually at its head.

Stapling
Saddle-stitching.

Star Atlas
Celestial atlas.

Star Map
Celestial chart.

STARS
Sharing and Transforming Access to Resources Section.

Statement of Extent
Extent of item.

Statistical Bibliography
Bibliometrics.

Status
Borrower status, circulation status, and loan status.

Statutory Copy
Deposit copy.

Stave
Staff.

STC
Short-Title Catalogueue.

Stemming
Truncation.

Stereo Map
Anaglyph.

Stereocard
Stereograph.

Stereogram
Stereograph.

Sticker Damage
Surface damage to the cover of a

book or to one of its endpapers or leaves, caused by the rough removal of a price sticker.

Sticker Ghost
Discolouration of the surface of the cover of a book or one of its endpapers or leaves, caused by a chemical reaction with the adhesive from a price sticker.

Sticker Price
List price.

Stilted
A book given wider squares to bring the height of its binding up to that of other volumes in the same set or on the same shelf, when the book block is slightly shorter.

STO
Standing order.

Stock Poster
A poster bearing a generic image, with space left blank for the subsequent addition of text announcing a specific event

Stop List
Stopword.

Stop Word
Stopword.

Storyboard
A series of pictures or rough sketches with accompanying text, used in the production of an audiovisual or multimedia work to help the creators visualise the sequence of its parts.

Storytime
Story hour.

Strawboard
A coarse board sometimes used in case binding, made from unbleached straw and repulped waste fibre. Binder's board is preferred in trade editions because it is stronger.

Stripe
A narrow band of magnetic material applied as a coating along one or both edges of a length of motion picture film on which the sound track is recorded.

STRN
Standard Technical Report Number.

STS
Science and Technology Section.

Subdirectory
Directory.

Subgroup
Record group.

Submenu
Menu.

Subscription Cycle
Subscription period.

Subscription Rate
Subscription price.

Subscription Work
Subscriber's edition.

Subsidiaries
Back matter.

Substitution
The provision of a copy of a document, often in microform, to protect the original from wear or possible damage in use. The copy is considered a surrogate.

Suggested Retail List Price (SRLP)
List price.

Super 16mm
16mm film.

Super 8mm
8mm film.

Super
Crash.

Superintendent of Documents Classification
SuDocs.

Supposed Author
Attributed author.

Surprint
Overprint.

T

T.e.g.
An abbreviation of *top edge gilt.*

T.l.s.
Typed letter signed.

Tailband
Headband.

Tailcap
Headcap.

Talbotype
Calotype.

Talking Book
Audiobook.

Tape Recording
Audiotape.

Tarot Cards
A category of ephemera consisting of pictorial cards, issued in standard sets of 22, for use in forecasting the future and as trumps in tarok, a card game played in Europe since, the mid-15th century.

Tattle-tape
Magnetic strip.

TEACH
Technology, Education and Copyright Harmonisation Act.

Teaching Librarian
Instruction librarian.

Tear Test
Grain.

Teaser
Advertising copy supplied by the marketing department of a publishing company, usually printed on the dust jacket of a new book to entice the reader to open the cover and sample the text.

Techie
Technician.

Technical Illustration
An illustration made or used to show or explain how something works, often published in a reference work or technical manual

TEI
Text Encoding Initiative.

Telecast
To transmit information in the form of electromagnetic signals over television airwaves or cable transmission lines. In a *cablecast,* transmission is limited to a cable system. Also refers to a television progra-

mme transmitted in such a manner. Compare with broadcast.

Telecine

A piece of equipment designed to convert the images and sound track on motion picture film to electronic signals recorded on videotape or as image files on disk, or telecast directly without recording

Telecommute

To work from home using a computer and tele-communication links, instead of traveling to an office to conduct business. Some library functions, such as the design and maintenance of Web sites, can be accomplished from a distance, but most library personnel work on-site.

Teleconference

A live, two-way conference of two or more people using audio and video transmission technology that enables the participants to see and hear each other in real time without having to meet in the same physical location.

Teleplay

A drama written to be recorded in a studio for broadcast on television, rather than to be performed live on stage or filmed as a motion picture. Synonymous with *television drama*. Compare with screenplay.

Template

A tool in the form of a pattern or overlay, used in graphics as a guide in the duplication of letters, shapes, or designs. Compare with stencil.

Temporary Storage

A space within an archive or library facility, or located offsite, where materials, equipment, or supplies are kept for a short time until they can be processed, installed, distributed, transferred to a permanent location, or disposed of in some other way, for example, a large gift collection awaiting examination by selectors.

Tender

Used in the antiquarian book trade to describe the condition of book with a binding that is loosening.

Term

A word, phrase, or symbol, especially one used to represent, in a dictionary, catalogue, index, or database, a subject or other feature of a work.

Terminal Emulation

Emulation.

Termination

The conclusion of a period of employment, whether by mutual agreement, by the employee through resignation, or by the employer through dismissal. The employment contract usually specifies the terms under which an individual or institution may terminate employment and the proper procedures for doing so.

Terminology

Words, phrases, and symbols representing the concepts and subjects used in a specific field of research, study, or activity, for which the meaning (established by convention or explicit agreement among its practitioners) is clearly defined, sometimes in a published glossary or lexicon. Synonymous with *nomenclature.*

Terms of Availability
The conditions under which a bibliographic item is available for sale in the market place, usually the list price, entered in field 020 or 022 of the MARC record.

Ternion
In bookbinding, a gathering consisting of three sheets of paper, parchment, or vellum folded once to create six leaves, used in some manuscript books and early printed books.

Test Guide
Study Guide.

Tetrology
Trilogy.

Text Message
A typed electronic message of less than 160 characters, sent via a wireless network to another person for viewing on a mobile or handheld device. Restrictions on length have led to the widespread use of abbreviations and acronyms in text-messaging. Abbreviated *texting*.

Text Type
Type used to print reading material, for example, the body of a book or other publication, as opposed to the display type used to print headings, running titles, etc., or the extract type used to print notes and long quotations. Synonymous with *body type.*

Textile Design Drawing
A graphic image made for the design and production of woven or non-woven fabric, or to document such work Before the advent of computer-aided design software, textile designers often transferred their drawings to a special type of graph paper called *point paper,* used by weavers in setting up their looms

Texting
Text message.

Textspeak
A developing language of abbreviations used in Internet and cell phone communication, in which letters of the alphabet are used to represent syllables or words, numerals to represent sounds or words, and combinations of letters and numerals to compose sentences (*examples*: RUOK for "Are you OK?" and CUL8R for "See you later").

Text-to-speech (TTS)
Software designed to convert natural language text into synthetic human speech sounds, allowing people with reading disabilities or visual impairments to listen to printed works on a personal computer, e-book reader, or other electronic device. Some libraries provide access to computers with speech synthesizing capability.

Textual Criticism
Close study and comparison of the various texts of a literary work to determine the version that reflects most faithfully the writer's intentions, particularly important in the case of older works for which the original manuscript is missing or

incomplete or for which multiple versions exist.

Textura
Latin for "weaving" or "woven." In printing, the most formal of the gothic or *black letter* type fonts, used for early editions of the Bible.

TF
Term frequency.

TGN
Getty Thesaurus of Geographic Names.

Thematic Index
A list of the major themes in a musical composition, or group of compositions, usually printed in the front or back of the score, with references to the work(s) in which they appear. For short pieces, the theme is usually given as the first few bars. Compare with thematic catalogue.

Thermohygrograph
Hygrometer.

Thermohygrometer
Hygrometer.

Thesaurus of Geographic Names
Getty Thesaurus of Geographic Names.

Thesaurus
A book of synonyms and nearsynonyms in a written language, usually arranged conceptually, although dictionary arrangement is not uncommon. The first thesaurus of the English language, published in 1852, was compiled by Peter Mark Roget.

Thesis Play
A dramatic work in which the playwright consciously attempts to illustrate a social problem and suggests to the reader or audience a possible solution (*example*: *Mrs. Warren's Profession* by George Bernard Shaw).

Thong
A sturdy strip of tawed skin or leather used as a wrap-around fastening or as a sewing support in early bookbinding.

Three on
Two on.

Three-quarter Border
Full border.

Thumb Book
Bibelot.

Thumb Drive
USB flash drive.

Ticket
A category of ephemera that includes small pieces of paper, card stock, or other material, usually bearing printed information indicating that the holder has paid for or is otherwise entitled to a specified service, right, or consideration, for example, admittance or passage. A *season ticket* usually covers a specified period of time and/or number of events.

Tier
One of two or more distinct levels, as of shelves in a section of library shelving, priorities for resource allocation or acquisition, payment or benefit options in a health care plan, etc.

Ties
Narrow strips of leather, cloth, rib-

bon, or other material attached in pairs to the boards of a book, usually along the foreedge but sometimes also at head and foot, enabling the binding to be tied shut when not in use. Cloth ties on older bindings often survive only in traces. Some older bindings have clasps or straps for the same purpose.

Time-expired Records
In archives, temporary records assigned a specific date for destruction that has passed without the occurrence of appropriate action, usually due to a backlog in processing.

Time-lapse Photograph
Motion study photograph.

Timeline
A linear, visual representation of the chronological development of a subject, usually from a given starting point up to the present, often in multiple dimensions (geographic, thematic, etc.).

Tinsel Print
A coloured print, usually depicting actors and/or actresses in costume, decorated by tinsel enthusiasts with diecut metal foils (tinsel) and sometimes bits of fabric, leather, feathers, and other suitable material, an art form popular from about 1815 to 1830.

Tip In
Tipped in.

Tissue
A sheet of very thin paper inserted loose between the leaves of a book or affixed to the inner margin, usually to protect the surface of a plate or prevent the offset of fresh ink onto the facing page.

Title and Statement of Responsibility
In library catalogueing, the area of bibliographic description in which the title proper of a work and information concerning authorship (statement of responsibility) are recorded (field 245 of the MARC record).

Title Block
Synonymous in cartography with cartouche.

Title Index
An alphabetically arranged list of the titles of the works covered in a serial or nonserial publication, for example, the *Book and Film Title Index* to *America: History and Life.* Title and author indexes are sometimes combined.

Title Leaf
The leaf of a book bearing the title page on the recto and, in mocern publications, the publisher's imprint, notice of copy-right, cataloguing-in-publication (CIP), ISBN, and printing history on the verso. In the front matter of a book, the title leaf follows the half title and precedes the dedication.

Title Proper
The primary name of a bibliographic item, usually found on the chief source of information, including any alternative title but not parallel titles and other title information. In *AACR2*, the title proper is entered in the title and statement of

responsibility area of the bibliographic description (field 245 of the MARC record).

TLA
Theatre Library Association.

TLD
Top level domain.

TLS
Times Literary Supplement.

TLS
Typed Letter Signed.

TM
Trademark.

TNA
National Archives, The.

TOC
Table of Contents.

Tome
Originally, any volume of a work published in more than one volume. In modern usage, a book of very large size, also weighty in subject or treatment. Pronounced like 'Rome.'

Tonary
A liturgical book in which antiphons, responsories, and other chants of the Mass and Divine Office are classified according to the eight musical modes of Gregorian chant, to assist in memorisation.

Tool Kit
Toolkit.

Top Term (TT)
The most general term in a hierarchical classification system, indicated by the abbreviation TT in the thesaurus of indexing terms (*example*: *INSPEC Thesaurus*) or by the narrowest indention under the heading to which it applies.

TOP
Temporarily Out of Print.

Topo
Topographic Map.

Topographic scale
Large-scale Map.

Topographic Series
A group of topographic sheet maps showing the geographic features of the surface of a country at scales of 1:10,000 to 1:250,000, usually issued by an agency of civilian or military government, such as a national survey or mapping division of a defence department.

Topographical Postcard
A postcard showing an actual view of a specific geographic place or area. Photographic examples, often locally produced, are preferred to printed views by collectors. Abbreviated *topo postcard*.

Top-stain
Staining.

Tortoise-shell Binding
A style of 17th-century luxury bookbinding with boards and spine covered in thin pieces of polished tortoise shell, often embellished with silver fittings.

TOS
Temporarily Out of Stock.

Touchpad
An electronic pointing device consisting of a small flat surface connected to a computer, which the

user can activate with the touch of a finger, instead of depressing the keys on a keyboard or moving a mouse. Synonymous with *touch panel*.

Tracing

A copy of an image, map, design, etc., made by drawing over its lines on a translucent medium superimposed on the original (as on a light table) or by the use of transfer paper.

Track Listing

A list of the selections on a record album containing more than one selection, usually in the order in which they are arranged on the recording. Track listings are usually printed on the back of the album cover of an LP or on the paper insert or booklet inside the jewel case containing a compact disc (CD).

Tract

A book or pamphlet containing a treatise or discourse on a political, social, or religious topic, usually issued as propaganda or for doctrinal purposes.

Trade Binding

The plain, unlettered calf or sheepskin binding used by booksellers of the 15th to the 18th century on books bound in advance of sale, as opposed to craft binding executed per the customer's instructions. Also used synonymously with publisher's binding.

Trade List

Trade Catalogue.

Trade Name

The name used to designate a specific business enterprise and the reputation it has acquired in the market place (*example*: Microsoft), as distinct from any trademark associated with the firm's products (Windows).

Transactions

The published papers or abstracts of papers presented at a conference or meeting of a society or association, usually including a record of what transpired. The term may also appear in the title of a scholarly journal that publishes articles that have not been presented orally, for example, *Transactions of the American Mathematical Society*.

Transcribe

To make a written or typewritten copy, usually of a conversation, speech, broadcast, sound recording, or other oral presentation, or a copy of notes taken on the content of such a presentation.

Transcript

A copy of an original, usually made by hand or typewritten, particularly a legal document or official record, for example, a student's official academic record. Also refers to the written record of words spoken in court proceedings or in a speech, interview, broadcast, or sound recording

Transfer

A change in the physical custody of archival materials from one location or agency to another, usually without a corresponding change of legal ownership and responsibility, for example, the relocation of records no longer current to temporary storage to await final disposition.

Treatment History
A record of the conservation procedures applied to an item (deacidification, fumigation, rebinding, restoration, etc.), usually including date of application and any details concerning the treatment process that might be of future use to conservators, particularly in cases requiring reversal.

Triacetate
Cellulose Triacetate.

Trial Print
Answer print.

Trial Proof
In printmaking, a print pulled before completion of the accepted impression, usually to enable the artist to check its quality and refine and perfect it to the desired state for the edition. A trial proof is usually unsigned.

Trial User
A person or organisation asked to use a new service or computer system, usually for a limited period of time, to test its usefulness and effectiveness and to help identify problems that need to be corrected before the final version is released for general use.

Trial
A test conducted for a limited period of time to determine the suitability of a new person in a position or the quality or feasibility of a new system, product, or service. Data-base vendors usually offer a free 30-day trial to libraries as an inducement to subscribe.

Triennial
Issued every three years. Also refers to a serial publication issued every three years.

Trilogy
A set of three narrative works related in theme or plot, which together form a larger work (*example*: the *Oresteia* of Aeschylus). Four similarly related works form a *tetrology* (*The Alexandria Quartet* by Lawrence Durrell).

Trim Size
The finished dimensions of a printed sheet or publication after waste has been trimmed away to prepare it for binding, usually indicated in the specifications for the print job.

Trimmed
A term used in the book trade to indicate that the leaves of a book have been cut down to a size smaller than the publication as originally issued.

Trimming
In bookbinding, the process of slicing approximately one-eighth of an inch from the head, tail, and fore-edge of the body of a book to remove the folds of its signatures, done on a machine called a guillotine.

Triptych
Diptych.

Triquarterly
Issued three times a year. Also refers to a serial publication issued three times a year.

Trustee
Library trustee.

TRW
Teen Read Week.

TT
Top term.

TTS
Text-to-speech.

Tunnel Book
A novelty book in which the pages are bound at both sides and separable accordion-style, allowing the user to look through an opening in the front page to view, as if in three dimensions, a scene depicted on subsequent pages. Synonymous with *peepshow book.*

Turntable Hit
In the music recording industry, a vinyl single that achieved success on radio airplay charts, but was not as strong in product sales.

Twice Weekly
Semiweekly.

Twice Yearly
Semiannual.

Type Page
The area or part of a printed page that is printed upon, excluding the margins, headlines, footlines, and page numbers.

Typed Letter Signed (TLS)
A letter written on a typewriter or by the use of word processing software and signed by the correspondent.

Typesetting
In printing, the setting of type from copy by hand or by machine, with attention to the aesthetic presentation of text, accomplished by a person called a *typesetter*. To learn more about type-setting, try *Wikipedia.*

Typical Librarian
Stereotype.

Typo
Typographical error.

U

U.S. Congressional Serial Set
The official U.S., government publication containing the numbered reports and documents of the House and Senate, bound by session of Congress, beginning with the 15th Congress in 1817, sometimes known simply as the 'Serial Set.' The reports are mostly from congressional committees dealing with proposed legislation and issues under investigation, and the documents include all other papers that the House or Senate ordered printed.

U.S. Serial Set
U.S. Congressional Serial Set.

UBCIM
An initialism for Universal Bibliographic Control and Inter-national MARC Core Activity.

UCE
An abbreviation of *unsolicited commercial e-mail,* known unaffectionately as spam.

UCITA
Uniform Computer Information Transactions Act.

UDC
Universal Decimal Classification.

UKSG
United Kingdom Serials Group.

ULC
Urban Libraries Council.

ULS
University Libraries Section.

Ultrafiche
A card-shaped transparent microform with a reduction ratio considerably greater than that of standard microfiche or superfiche (up to 3,000 frames per 4 × 6 inch sheet). A special ultrafiche reader-printer machine is required to view and make hard copies of documents stored in this medium.

Umbilicus
In Antiquity, a knobbed wooden rod attached to one end of a papyrus scroll around which the manuscript was rolled when not in use. A vellum tag was usually attached to one end, noting the title and/or contents.

UMLS
Unified Medical Language System.

Unabridged

A version of a written work that has not been shortened and is therefore considered to be complete. The fact that an edition is unabridged is sometimes indicated on the title page of long works issued in paperback, but unless otherwise stated, a published work is assumed to be unabridged. An unabridged dictionary is the version containing the most words (*example*: *Webster's Third New International Dictionary*).

Unattributed

A work, quotation, or artifact lacking indication of authorship, creator, or source. For example, in journal articles and research papers, the author of the abstract is often not indicated by name or initials, and news stories published in newspapers and online news services may lack a byline. Compare with anonymous.

Unauthorised Biography

A biographical work written without the consent of its subject or the subject's family if the *biographee* is deceased, sometimes more objective in its analysis than an authorised biography because the *biographer* does not have to make concessions to gain access to confidential sources. However, an unauthorised biography may be less detailed or complete if the author was denied important information.

Unauthorised Eition

An edition printed without the consent of the author, the author's legal representative, or the original publisher but not in violation of existing copyright law.

Unbacked

Printed on only one side of a blank sheet of paper, as in a poster or art print. The side printed upon is considered the recto.

Unbound

A printed publication issued without a binding or cover, or a copy that is not and never has been bound, as distinct from disbound. Prior to the 19th century, books were sold in the form of printed sections to be bound to the purchaser's specifications. Also refers to an issue of a periodical or part of a serial that will eventually be bound, usually with others, to form a volume.

Uncial

From the Latin *uncialis*, meaning 'of an inch' or 'inch-high.' A large, full majuscule script probably developed in the Christian monasteries of Egypt and North Africa during the late 2nd or early 3rd century, used in the earliest biblical codices and as a book hand in manuscripts written from the 4th to 8th century, reaching its fullest expression in the 5th century. The calligraphic capital letters of uncial were broad and rounded, probably to enhance speed, with the beginnings of ascenders and descenders suggestive of later lowercase letters. Half uncial gradually replaced uncial as a book hand after the 6th century. The term also refers to manuscripts written in the script.

Uncoated Paper
Paper to which no surface coating has been added to improve appearance and printability. In books consisting mostly of text, the text is usually printed on uncoated paper. Any illustrations printed separately from the text may be done on coated paper to permit greater detail in the graphic image.

Uncorrected Proof
A prepublication printing of a book, usually issued in plain coloured wrappers, intended for editorial use or, in some cases, to be sent out for review.

Uncut
A volume in which the bolts were not trimmed to uniform size in binding, leaving the leaves to be separated by hand by the owner of the book, using a paper knife or similar instrument. Synonymous with *untrimmed.*

Underfunded
An organisaton, institution, or project allocated insufficient monies to accomplish its goals and objectives. Chronic underfunding can lead to a decline in quality of service and is demoralising for staff and management.

Underground Comics
Small press or self-published comic books, often socially satirical in tone, containing content considered outside the mainstream by the Comics Code Authority, usually because drug use, sex, or violence is depicted too explicitly. Robert Crumb's Zap Comix, published in the heady 1960s and 1970s, are an example. Also spelled *underground comix.*

Underground Press
A publisher that issues printed publications unofficially or clandestinely, usually to members of a group or organisaton that opposes the policies of an established government or other authority, more common during periods of civil unrest than in times of peace and prosperity. Eventually, most underground presses either disband or become 'above ground' publishing houses.

Underlining
Words, phrases, or passages of text underscored in pencil or ink by a previous reader, usually for future reference. As a general rule, libraries do not add heavily underlined gift books to the collection. Also refers to a formatting option available in word processing software that can be used to place a line beneath a single character, word, phrase, line, or entire passage of text.

Underrun
A press run that produces fewer copies than the number ordered, sometimes causing a shortage of publisher's inventory. The opposite of overrun.

Underscore
Background music composed to create a mood or support dialogue in radio and television programming, motion pictures, broadcast commercials, newscasts, etc. Underscore music is generally quiet, without a strong melody line be-

cause vocals and lead instruments are absent.

Underserved
Persons within the geographic area or clientele served by a library or library system who use its services infrequently for a variety of reasons, including limited awareness of available resources and services, lack of familiarity with the national language, illiteracy, poor health, lack of transportation, etc. Outreach programmes help bridge these gaps.

Understaffed
Having an insufficient number of employees to do the work required. Signs of overwork (fatigue, absenteeism, arrears, etc.) can be the result of understaffing. Synonymous with *short-staffed* and *short-handed*. The opposite of overstaffed.

Underutilised
A library service, resource, or item used less often than it ought to be, usually because its usefulness is not widely appreciated or because it is not as accessible as other alternatives, for example, collections of theses and dissertations in some academic libraries.

Underwater Photograph
A photographic image made below the surface of a body of water (usually a stream, river, sea, or ocean), using special waterproof equipment or taken from a manned or unmanned submarine vehicle, used extensively in marine biology, oceanography (example), and in exploration and reclamation of submerged vessels (example).

Undocumented
Lacking official papers or other tangible evidence in support of existence, identity, validity, authenticity, provenance, etc.

Unedited
A term used in cataloguing moving images to indicate the form of a work composed of footage recording a live event, for example, a legislative hearing or floor debate, press conference, ceremony involving an important person (coronation, inauguration, funeral), scientific experiment, etc. Except for necessary shifts in camera angle, the shots remain in the sequence in which events occurred, without subsequent editing and with no commentary. Much of the television programming provided by C-SPAN falls into this category.

Unexpurgated
A text or edition that includes passages omitted from other versions or editions, usually because the language or content was considered offensive to some readers.

Uniform Edition
Two or more books printed, bound, and jacketed in the same style to show that they constitute a single entity, such as a multivolume encyclopaedia, or that they are related to each other in some other way, for example, the individual titles in a monographic series or the collected works of an author.

Uniform Style

The appearance of publications printed in the same typographical style on the same grade of paper, issued in a binding of the same size and design. Volumes published as a set or series are usually produced in this fashion.

UNIMARC

Universal Machine-Readable Cataloguing.

Union Case

A shallow, hinged box made to mount and protect an early light-sensitive photographic image by molding a compound of shellac and sawdust or wood flour, often into elaborate decorative patterns, using a thermoplastic process patented in 1854 by Samuel Peck. According to the *Thesaurus for Graphic Materials II,* over 800 design motifs have been recorded. Most union cases are square or rectangular, but novel shapes are not uncommon.

Union List

A complete list of the holdings of a group of libraries of materials (1) of a specific type, (2) on a certain subject, or (3) in a particular field, usually compiled for the purpose of resource sharing (*example: Union List of Serials in the Libraries of the United States and Canada* and its continuation *New Serial Titles,* issued by the Library of Congress). The entry for each bibliographic item includes a list of codes representing the libraries owning at least one copy. Union lists are usually printed, but some have been converted into online databases

Unionisaton

The decision by professional librarians and/or non-professional library staff to join an existing labour union or form a new one, authorised to engage in collective bargaining with the employer on their behalf over issues concerning employment (wages and benefits, working conditions, etc.). In the United States, unionisaton is governed by state and federal labour law.

Unique

A bibliographic item so rare that no other copies are known to exist. Examples include original manuscripts; one-of-a-kind artist's books; artist's proofs; daguerreotypes and autochromes; 8mm, Super 8mm, and 16mm reversal originals; etc. With prints, uniqueness can be difficult to establish.

Unit Cost

The financial expenditure required of a library or library system to acquire and/or process an item, or to deliver a service that can be measured in discrete units, usually calculated as an average amount. For example, the Association of Research Libraries (ARL) includes in the unit cost of an interlibrary loan transaction the costs of staff time, network/communications, equipment, photocopying, supplies, delivery, and borrowing fees (*ARL Bimonthly Report* 230/231, October/December 2003). Economies of scale can be a factor in reducing unit cost.

Unitary Term
A heading or indexing term composed of two or more nouns joined by the conjunction 'and,' treated as a single subject because their meanings overlap to such an extent that the literature about them is not clearly separated.

United Kingdom Serials Group (UKSG)
An alliance of over 600 organisatons concerned with the publication, distribution, and use of printed and electronic serials (and associated technology) and with their role in scholarly communication. UKSG publishes the electronic newsletter *Serials-eNews* and the journal *Serials* thrice yearly in print and online.

United States Newspaper Programme (USNP)
National Digital Newspaper Programme (NDNP).

Universal Copyright Convention (UCC)
An international copyright convention drafted in 1952 under the auspices of UNESCO, revised in 1971 and ratified by over 65 countries, including the United States. Under its terms, each signatory nation extends to foreign works the same copyright protection it gives to works published within its territory by one of its own citizens.

Universal Machine-Readable Cataloguing (UNIMARC)
The most comprehensive version of the MARC format for cataloguing bibliographic items, UNIMARC was first published in 1977 and is currently developed under the sponsorship of the IFLA Universal Bibliographic Control and International MARC Core Activity (UBCIM) programme to facilitate the international exchange of bibliographic records between national bibliographic agencies.

Universal Serials and Book Exchange
United States Book Exchange.

Universal Tranverse Mercator (UTM) Grid
A special grid system adopted by the National Imagery and Mapping Agency (formerly the Defence Mapping Agency) for military use throughout the world based on the transverse Mercator projection. The UTM grid divides the world into 60 north-south (longitudinal) zones, each 6° wide. The zones are numbered consecutively beginning with Zone 1 between 180° and 174° west longitude and progressing eastward to Zone 60 between 174° and 180° east longitude. In the United States, the 48 contiguous states are covered by 10 zones, from Zone 10 on the west coast through Zone 19 in New England. In each zone, coordinates are measured north and east in meters.

University Libraries Section (ULS)
Established in 1937, ULS is the section of the Association of College and Research Libraries (ACRL)

within the American Library Association (ALA) devoted to advancing university librarianship, university library service, and the development of university libraries within institutions that offer graduate programmes. ULS also fosters cooperation locally with university administrators and teaching faculty, and among colleges and universities on issues of mutual concern.

University Library
A library or library system established, administered, and funded by a university to meet the information, research, and curriculum needs of its students, faculty, and staff. Some large universities maintain separate undergraduate and graduate libraries. Large university libraries with comprehensive collections are considered research libraries.

University Press
A publishing house associated with a university or other scholarly institution, specialising in the publication of scholarly books and journals, particularly works written by its faculty (*example*: Johns Hopkins University Press). Most university presses operate on a non-profit basis, relying on a committee of senior faculty members to select manuscripts for publication. The trade association of university presses in North America is the Association of American University Presses (AAUP).

UNIX
An operating system developed at Bell Labs in 1969, UNIX supports multiple users and multitasking and has gone through many versions. It runs on a variety of hardware platforms and remains popular at academic and scientific institutions, particularly those that received it free of charge from AT & T in the early stages of its development.

Unknown Authorship
A work for which the author (or authors) is unknown or cannot be identified with certainty, including works emanating from a corporate body that is unknown or lacks a name. Libraries catalogue such works under the title (*example*: *Chanson de Roland*). In *AACR2*, if the work is attributed to one or more persons or corporate bodies, added entries are made under their names. Synonymous with anonymous.

Unlettered
A binding with neither the title nor the author's name displayed on the spine (or sides), making its content difficult to identify when placed upright alongside other volumes on the shelf. Prior to the 17th century, books were often marked by the owner with the title in ink on at least one edge of the sections to facilitate identification in a period when books were usually stored flat with one edge facing out.

Unopened
A book in which the bolts are left untrimmed in binding, a common practice in the 19th century. Once

the leaves have been slit by hand using a paper knife or other thin-edged implement, the volume is said to have been opened.

Unpaged
Pages of a book or other publication not assigned individual page numbers, usually found in the front matter. The cataloger records the number of such pages in the physical description area of the bibliographic record, as an interpolation inside square brackets (example: [15] p.).

Unpaginated
A book or other publication in which the pages of the text are not numbered or sequentially marked. The total number of pages in an unpaginated work is noted by the cataloger as an interpolation inside square brackets in the physical description area of the bibliographic record (*example*: [118] p.). The opposite of paginated.

Unprintable
A word or phrase considered unfit to be printed, usually for reasons of obscenity, sometimes indicated in text by the first letter followed by an asterisk substituted for each of the remaining letters (h***).

Unprotected
Data accessible to modification or deletion by unauthorised persons because it is stored in a file or on a disk that is not secured.

Unpublished
A work in the process of publication that has yet to be issued. Also, a manuscript or typescript never published, either because it was not intended for publication or because the author was unable to find a publisher.

Unrecorded
A descriptive term used in the antiquarian book trade for a rare book or manuscript unnoticed by collectors and bibliographers (usually for centuries), whose discovery is of sufficient importance to merit recording an account of its existence.

Unsewn
A book in the original folded sheets, never bound. Very high-priced facsimiles are sometimes sold *in quires*, to allow the purchaser the option of custom binding.

Unsigned
A written work, such as an entry in a reference book or article in a magazine, that does not include the name of the author, usually an indication that the piece was written by a paid staff writer. In a more general sense, any written document that does not indicate the identity of the author, especially a letter or legal instrument lacking a signature. The opposite of signed. Compare with anonymous.

Unsophisticated
A term used in the antiquarian book trade to describe a book that has not undergone restoration or been altered with intent to deceive. Such a volume may, however, show definite signs of ownership and use.

Untitled
literary or other work that lacks a title, usually because it was given no name by its creator or publisher, a common occurrence in medieval manuscripts and books printed before it became standard practice to include a title page. Also refers to a person of noble birth who has no title and hence no right to rule.

Untouched
A term describing early printed books (incunabula) that have been neither rubricated nor illuminated.

Update
To make a news story, data file, reference work, or other information source current, usually by revising existing content or substituting new material. Bibliographic databases are updated on a regular basis by adding records representing newly published items. Frequency of update is usually given in the database description. Printed indexes and abstracting services are updated monthly or quarterly in paperbound supplements, usually cumulated annually. Legal publications (statutes, case law, etc.) may also be updated in supplements, but most reference works are revised and republished in a new edition.

Updated
A work from which outdated information has been removed and current information substituted or to which more recent information has been added. Printed publications may be updated in supplements (*examples*: legal statutes and case law) or revised and republished in a new edition. The currency of information provided on a Web site is indicated in the note 'Last updated on [date]' usually displayed near the bottom of the welcome screen.

Updating Database
An electronic database in which the content is revised and/or augmented, usually on a regular basis, to provide current information or to add recently published sources. Most journal databases are updated on a regular basis as new issues are published and indexed.

Upgrade
To improve existing hardware or software by replacing it with a model or version that has new features and/or additional capabilities. Software upgrades are usually indicated sequentially by a decimal number added to the name of the application. In employment, to reclassify a job at a higher grade, usually moving it to a higher pay scale.

Upload
To transmit a copy of one or more files from a local computer to the hard disk of another (usually more remote) computer, such as a mainframe or network server, a process that may require terminal emulation software. The opposite of download.

Uppercase
The capital letters of a type font (A B C D E F G H I J K L M N O P Q

R S T U V W X Y Z), as opposed to its small or lowercase letters (a b c d e f g h i j k l m n o p q r s t u v w x y z). The terms *uppercase* and *lowercase* are derived from the relative positions of the compartments in the wood or metal case containing elements of type bearing capital letters and small letters at a typesetter's bench in the days when type was set by hand (letterpress). Also spelled *upper case.*

Urban Fiction
A type of American crime fiction, especially popular with younger African Americans, in which the characters are often young people drawn by the lure of easy money into drugs, prostitution, and violent crime. Rendered in the evolving language of mean streets, these gritty novels provide a steady diet of explicit sex and violence. The origins of this new genre can be traced back to the ghetto novels of Donald Goines and Iceberg Slim (Robert Beck) published in the late 1960s and early 1970s.

Urban Libraries Council (ULC)
Founded in 1971, ULC is an association of approximately 150 public libraries located in metropolitan areas of the United States with 50,000 or more inhabitants, and the corporations that serve them, organised to solve common problems, take advantage of new opportunities, and foster applied research to improve professional practice. ULC is an affiliate of the American Library Association (ALA).

URL
Uniform Resource Locator.

Usability Testing
Usability Assessment.

Usability
The ease with which a computer interface can be efficiently and effectively used, especially by a novice. The first priority in designing for usability is to provide clear, consistent navigation of content. Some libraries employ usability assessment techniques to evaluate the user-friendliness of their Web pages.

Usage
The number of times a bibliographic item is used by library patrons during a given period of time, including the number of times it is checked out and any in-house use measured by the number of times it is picked up for reshelving from a desk or table located in a public area. In academic libraries, *high-use* materials may be given a shorter loan period or placed on reserve or in the reference section. In some libraries, *low-use* items may be candidates for weeding. Usage statistics are also helpful in collection development.

USBE
United States Book Exchange.

Use Life
The length of time or number of times an item can be used before it becomes so worn that it is no longer fit for use and has to be dis-

carded. For books, use life depends on quality of paper, strength of binding, and actions taken to protect the cover, such as enclosing the dust jacket in a washable plastic sleeve.

USE

An instruction given in an entry in a subject headings list or thesaurus of controlled vocabulary to direct the user from a synonym or quasi-synonym to the preferred term under which items on the topic are cataloged or indexed (*example*: Reading Therapy USE Biblio-therapy in the *Thesaurus of ERIC Descriptors*).

Used Book

A book that has had at least one previous owner. The condition of the cover and leaves is an indication of the amount of use a volume has received. Sometimes used books are found upon appraisal to be rare and valuable, especially copies of a first edition. Titles out of print from the publisher may be available through the used book market. Synonymous with *secondhand book.*

Used Bookstore

A bookstore that specialises in books that have had at least one previous owner, sometimes limited to a particular genre, such as mystery or science fiction. Unless a used book is rare or out of print, it is usually priced on the basis of condition, lower than the list price of a new copy. Some bookstores sell both new *and* used books (*examples*: The Strand in Manhattan and Powell's in Oregon). Used books are also available through online book-sellers, such as Amazon.com. Synonymous with *secondhand bookstore.*

Used for (UF)

A phrase indicating a term (or terms) synonymous with an authorised subject heading or descriptor, *not* used in cataloguing or indexing to avoid scatter. In a subject headings list or thesaurus of controlled vocabulary, synonyms are given immediately following the official heading. In the alphabetical list of indexing terms, they are included as lead-in vocabulary followed by a *see* or USE cross-reference directing the user to the correct heading.

User Area

The amount of floor space in a library that can be assigned for the use of patrons, as opposed to the area required for the use of staff, closed stacks, automation and HVAC equipment, maintenance, storage, etc.

User Education

All the activities involved in teaching users how to make the best possible use of library resources, services, and facilities, including formal and informal instruction delivered by a librarian or other staff member one-on-one or in a group. Also includes online tutorials, audiovisual materials, and printed guides and path-finders. A broader term than bibliographic instruction.

User Experience (UX)

In the ISO 9241 standard covering the ergonomics of human-system interaction, *user experience* is defined as the perceptions and response of a person, resulting from his/her use or anticipated use of a product, system, or service. The term is broader in scope than usability because it includes the user's subjective response (feelings, beliefs, preferences), as well as perceptions of utility, efficiency, and ease of use. Three factors influence user experience: the person's previous experience and inner state at time of use; the properties of the product, system, or service; and context of use.

User Warrant

The addition of a term to an indexing language, or the assignment of an existing descriptor to documents by an indexer, based on the frequency with which it is requested or included in the search statements entered as input by the users of an information retrieval system.

User-Initiated

A service that the library patron may use at his or her discretion without the assistance or mediation of library staff, for example, renewals and holds placed via the online catalogue or requests to borrow materials from another library made via the online catalogue or an electronic interlibrary loan/document delivery system. Although initial instruction may be necessary, most users achieve self-sufficiency with practice.

Username

A permanent code that an authorised user must enter into a computer system to log on and gain access to its resources, usually consisting of the full name (johnwilson) or surname plus the initial(s) of the given name(s) (wilsonj) or plus one or more arabic numerals (wilson001). Synonymous with *user ID*.

USNP

National Digital Newspaper Programme.

Uterine Vellum

A thin, smooth writing material made from the processed skin of an unborn, stillborn, or newborn calf, used sparingly because of its cost when medieval and Renaissance scribes required an especially fine, white unblemished surface

UTF-8

A scheme for encoding Unicode values in sets of 8 bits, facilitating Unicode implementation on UNIX systems.

Utility

A small programme that expands the capability of a computer's operating system by enabling it to perform an additional task, usually something as routine as managing a disk drive, printer, scanner, or other peripheral device. Unlike the basic operating system, utilities can be added and removed as needed. A utility differs from an application programme in being less complex, usually limited to a single function.

UTM

Universal Transverse Mercator grid.

Utopia

A term coined by Thomas More from the Greek *ou* ('no' or 'not') and *topos* ('place'). A literary or artistic work in which the setting is an ideal society, usually existing in a future time or imaginary place (*example*: *Looking Backward* by Edward Bellamy). Utopian literature is created by authors who feel nostalgia for an idealised past or who wish to call attention to the need to reform existing social, political, or economic institutions. The opposite of *dystopia*.

UX

User Experience.

V

V.P.
An abbreviation of *various publishers* and *various places.*

Vacuum Cleaning
The most effective way to prevent the accumulation of dust and dirt when library collections are stored on open shelving. Routine maintenance with an electrically-powered vacuum machine is best done with a soft brush attachment. Protective face mask and gloves are recommended for very dusty collections.

Vacuum Thermal Drying
A conservation procedure by which slightly to very wet books (or other records) are placed wet or frozen in a vacuum chamber and dried at just above 32 degrees F. Because the materials remain wet while drying, the method may produce extreme distortion of the text block and binding in books and blocking of coated papers. According to the Northeast Document Conservation Centre (NEDCC), the method is more cost-effective than air drying for large numbers of water-damaged items, but extensive rebinding or recasing is often necessary.

Vade Mecum
A Latin phrase meaning 'goes with me.' A small book such as a guidebook, handbook, or manual meant to be carried about, used during the Middle Ages by physicians, astrologers, and tradesmen for quick reference and computation. Offten suspended from a girdle or belt, some were designed so that the pages folded out like a map or accordion-style.

Value Added
A service offered to a library by a vendor that enhances the product, thereby increasing its value in the market place, for example, the addition by the vendor of table of contents notes to the catalogue records for titles purchased (additional charges may apply). Also, a supplementary feature designed to facilitate or enhance an existing library service, for example, a search utility that helps users identify and locate fiction in DVD,

video, or laserdisc format via the library's online catalogue. Also spelled *value-added*.

Vandalism

Damage to library collections, furnishings, or facilities that is intentional rather than accidental, usually motivated by anger or malice on the part of the perpetrator. Vandalism detracts from the physical appearance of a library and its resources. The cost of repair or replacement puts an unwelcome burden on the budget. To avoid detection, most acts of vandalism are committed in unstaffed locations or after hours. Some libraries employ a security guard to keep an eye on areas not visible from at least one public service point when the library is open.

Vanilla Text

Text written on a computer, usually with the aid of a text editor or word processing software in a standard font without formatting (boldface, italics, etc.), usually with the extension.**txt** at the end of the filename. Synonymous with *plaintext*.

Vanity Press

vanity publisher.

Vanity Pulisher

A type of publisher, more common in the United States than in other countries, that specialises in producing books at the author's expense, used mainly by writers whose works have been rejected by commercial publishers and by individuals of private means who are convinced they have an important message to impart to the world. In England, vanity publishing is used primarily for poetry. Books published by vanity publishers are avoided by reviewers and rarely purchased by retail booksellers and libraries.

Variable Data Field

A variable field of the MARC record (tagged 1××-9×× with ×× in the range of 00-99) that has two indicator positions following the tag and usually contains textual rather than coded information, consisting of one or more elements of bibliographic description, each recorded in a separate subfield preceded by a two-character subfield code.

Variant Edition

An edition that includes changes made in the work by the author, sometimes ranging from first composition all the way to publication in a definitive edition, allowing the reader to see the evolution of the text. Compare with variorum edition.

Variant

A copy of a book that differs slightly in one or more points from others of the same impression or from a previous printing of the same edition. The differences may occur in the sections, binding, or both. More than one variant may exist within a single impression. Once priority of publication has been conclusively established, such variations are referred to as issues and states. Also refers to one of two or more slightly different early texts of a literary work, for example, the plays of Shakespeare that survive in multiple versions. Abbreviated *var.* Also, one of several forms of a word retrieved when the truncated stem is used as a search term in a keywords search, for example, the terms *videocassette, videodisc, videorecording,* and *videotape* retrieved by truncating 'video,' as in video* or video$.

Variorum Edition

From the Latin phrase *cum notis variorum,* meaning 'with notes from various persons.' An edition based on scholarly comparison and interpretation of several previously published versions of the text, which also includes commentary written by various editors.

Various Dates (v.d.)

A phrase used to indicate that a set or series of volumes contains works that have different publication dates.

Varnish

The glossy coating applied to the printed surface of the paper cover or dust jacket on a new book for protection and to enhance its visual appeal. Varnish can be expensive when applied in a separate press run. A second pass is not required when varnish is added to gloss ink.

Vault

A windowless room in a library, archive, museum, or other facility reserved for housing motion picture film, usually equipped with open racks or shelves designed to hold rolls of film wound on reels or cores and stored in film cans. Temperature and relative humidity are carefully controlled inside a film vault to retard the chemical decay of film base. In media libraries, compact storage or shelving may be used to conserve space. Also used synonymously with *film archive* and *television archive..* In archives, a completely secure and fire-safe enclosure for storing valuable documents or essential records. Access is restricted to a few authorised persons and environmental controls may be maintained for conservation.

Vaulting

In archives, the storage of valuable or vital records in a completely secure and fire-safe enclosure that is used exclusively for document storage. *Electronic vaulting* is the storage of digital data off-site, offline, and out of reach of viruses, worms, and hackers.

V-Chip

A microchip installed in a television set, designed to allow parents to block access to programmes containing content considered unsuitable for children (violence, explicit sex, adult language, etc.). In 1996, Congress passed legislation requiring manufacturers of television receivers to install the V-chip in sets sold in the United States (13-inch or larger). However, according to the *Christian Science Monitor,* a survey released in July 2001 found that only 7 percent of parents with children 2-17 years old use the V-chip in their television set, either because they own an older set, do not know if their set has a V-chip, or find it difficult to use. Some 56 percent said they use the rating displayed on the screen before a programme begins to make decisions about their children's viewing.

VCR

An abbreviation of *videocassette recorder*, an electronic device designed to record onto videotape (in VHS format) signals received by a standard television receiver for playback on a television monitor. VCRs are also used to play prerecorded videocassettes (feature films, documentaries, etc.). Although VCRs are analog machines, adapters are available that enable digital data to be stored on videotape as computer backup.

Vector Data

The digital data structure in which discrete map features are represented by rows in a table of values. Shapes are defined by pairs of *x, y* coordinates, with points connecting to become lines, and lines connecting to form closed polygons (areas). Attributes are associated with each feature in the data table for a given layer of data, for example, *length* and *width* for a line representing a road, stream, coastline, or boundary. Because the size of a vector file is generally smaller than that of an image (raster) file representing the same feature, vector data is preferred for map features that have a linear component. Vector data is also easier to resize than raster data, which can become pixilated if enlarged too much.

Vellum Binding

A book bound in the dressed and polished skin of newborn animal (calf, lamb, kid, etc.), with or without tooling, left in its natural creamy white colour or painted or stained.

Vellum

A thin, fine membrane made from the unsplit skin of a newborn animal (usually a calf, but lamb, kid, and deerskin were also used), treated with lime, stretched, scraped, and polished rather than tanned, for use as a writing surface during the Middle Ages, before paper came into widespread use in Europe, and for copies of various editions (including the *Gutenberg Bible*) during the first 75 years of printing. Also used in early bookbinding as a covering material and for paste-downs. At one time the term was used interchangeably with *parchment*, but vellum is of finer quality. According to *The Bookman's Glossary* (Bowker, 1983), the finest vellum, known as uterine vellum, was made during the 13th and 14th centuries from the skins of stillborn or unborn animals and reserved for the most costly manuscripts. Because vellum is made from the entire unsplit skin, tiny marks of hair follicles are visible on one side. Highly durable, vellum has a tendency to curl towards the grain side under conditions of low humidity.

Velvet

Silk or cotton cloth with a thick, soft pile (plush), popular as a covering material in textile binding of the 16th and 17th centuries when it was often embroidered in silk and/or metallic thread.

Vending Machine

A machine designed to automatically dispense goods when the correct amount of money, or a credit or debit card, is inserted and a selection made. In libraries, copy cards are often dispensed in this way.

Vendor

A company in the business of providing access to a selection of bibliographic databases, online or on CD-ROM, by subscription (*examples*: EBSCO, ProQuest, Gale, etc.) or on a per search basis (OCLC *FirstSearch* and DIALOG), usually under licensing agreement. Providers of non-print media are also commonly referred to as vendors. In a more general sense, any individual, company, or agency, other than a publisher, that provides products and/or services to a library or library system for a fee. A distinction is normally made between book vendors (booksellers, dealers, jobbers, etc.) and serials vendors (subscription agents, continuation dealers, etc.). A vendor may also provide automated customer services such as management reports and electronic transmission of bibliographic or invoice data. The term is also used for businesses that specialise in developing and marketing library systems, such as online catalogue software and library management systems.

Venn Diagram

A graphical device in which closed circles (or ovals) are used to illustrate the logical relationship between sets of data: non-intersecting circles for sets with *no* elements in common; overlapping circles for sets with *some* but not all elements in common; and a circle within a circle for a set that is a subset of another. Invented by Johann Sturm in 1661 and named after the English logician John Venn (1834-1923) who used them from 1880 on, Venn diagrams are used in bibliographic instruction to help students visualise the results of Boolean logic in keyword searching.

Verbal Scale

Statement of equivalency.

Verbatim et Literatim

A Latin phrase meaning 'word for word and letter for letter,' precisely as written or printed. More loosely, a quotation, transcription, or translation that is faithful to the original. Also refers to a literal translation.

Verbatim

In exactly the same words as the original source or text, word for word, as in a direct quotation. It is plagiarism to quote verbatim without acknowledging the source.

Verification

The process of using bibliographic sources to ascertain that an author actually exists (or existed), or to determine the proper form of a name or the correct title of a work, usually prior to ordering or cataloguing the item for a library collection. In a more general sense, checking the truth or accuracy of any fact or statement, usually by consulting a source of authoritative information.

Vernacular Designator

A standard word or abbreviation used in cataloguing in a given language to describe or classify an item, especially a serial publication or one of its parts, for example, *fasc.* for 'fascicle' in English and 'fascicule' in French and *Fasz.* for 'Faszikel' in German. Princeton University Library provides online access to tables of *Vernacular Designators by Language* at its Web site on cataloguing documentation.

Vernacular Name

The form of a person's name used in reference sources published in his or her country of birth or permanent residence. In *AACR2*, the cataloger is instructed to use the form of name that has become well-established in English-language reference sources and to make appropriate references from other forms.

Vernacular

From the Latin *vernaculus*, meaning 'native.' In literature, works written in the daily language of a group of people, particularly the inhabitants of a specific geographic region, as distinct from the literary or official language of the same population or area, for example, the language of the novels of Thomas Hardy in which English country folk speak and act in a manner appropriate to their rural origins. In the context of the Middle Ages, a vernacular language was one spoken in a particular region, as distinct from Latin and Greek, the international literary languages of the time. The slow growth of vernacular literature in Europe was enhanced by the expansion of secular literacy following the development of universities beginning in about the 12th century.

Versal

A large ornamental capital letter written at the left-hand margin or in the text of a manuscript to indicate the beginning of a paragraph, verse, or other division. Using square capitals, rustic capitals, or uncials as models, medieval scribes exaggerated the round or vertical strokes or serifs for decorative effect. Early examples were sometimes outlined in small dots. Versals were usually written in ink of a different colour than the text (commonly in red and/or blue). The larger size meant that a versal occupied more than one line, its top usually aligned with the minuscules of the word to which it belonged.

Verse

A sequence of words arranged in accordance with established rules of metrical composition, rhyme, etc. Also, a set of lines comprising one unit in the overall pattern of a metrical composition (song, ballad, etc.) written in several sections of similar form, aside from any refrain. Synonymous in this sense with *stanza*. Also used as a general term for light poetry. In a sacred text, such as the Bible, one or more sentences forming a division of a chapter, usually numbered for reference.

Versification

The transformation of a prose work into poetic or metrical language. Also, the overall structure or style in which a poetic work is composed.

Version

One of several variations of an intellectual work, possibly created for a purpose or use other than the one originally intended. Also, a variant form of a work of unknown or uncertain authorship, such as a fairy tale or legend. Also refers to a specific translation of the Bible or any of its parts (*example: King James Version*). Abbreviated *vers*. Compare with adaptation and edition. In computer software, a specific upgrade of an operating system or application programme, usually indicated by a decimal number following the title, for example, 5.0 to indicate a significant upgrade, 5.1 a modification containing routine enhancements, and 5.11 a follow-up, perhaps to correct a minor bug in the previous version. As a general rule, there is greater risk in purchasing version 1.0 of a software programme than in purchasing subsequent versions.

Verso

From the Latin phrase *verso folio*, meaning 'with the page turned.' The back side of a book or the left-hand page of an opening in a book or other publication, usually assigned an even page number. The opposite of recto.

Vertical Exaggeration

In cartographic representation, a ratio of vertical to horizontal scale greater than 1:1, which has the effect of raising the apparent elevation of points above base level and lowering the apparent depth of points below base level. Expressed as a ratio (**5:1**, **10:1**, etc.), vertical exaggeration is often used to enhance relief on models, block diagrams, profiles, and cross sections.

Vertical File

A collection of loose clippings, pictures, illustrations, pamphlets, or other materials of an ephemeral nature that, because of size and format, are filed on edge in drawers or in a box, usually organised in folders by subject or some other classification system to facilitate retrieval. Also refers to the filing cabinet in which such materials are stored.

Very Good

A description of condition used in the book trade to indicate that a copy shows slight signs of wear, but would be acceptable to all but the most fastidious collector. Defects are noted by the bookseller. Compare with fine copy and good.

VGA

An initialism for **V**ideo **G**raphics **A**rray, a standard video adapter in an IBM PC, capable of producing resolutions of 640 × 480 pixels in up to 256 colours. VGA circuits convert the digital signals generated by the computer into analog used by CRTs and most flat-backed monitors. Superseded by SVGA.

VHS

An initialism for **V**ideo **H**ome **S**ystem, a video recording and playback format consisting of hard plastic cassettes containing half-inch videotape. Introduced by JVC in 1976 to compete with Sony's Beta format, VHS has since become the industry standard for both home and commercial use. SVHS (Super VHS) was developed to improve resolution. DVD format is gaining on VHS in library collections, particularly in public libraries.

Vide

The imperative form of the Latin verb *videre*, 'to see.' Used in the sense of 'refer to' in footnotes to direct the reader's attention to a specific passage, page, chapter, or work. Abbreviated *v.* or *vid.*

Video Clip

A short section of a longer work produced on videotape, used in a broadcast or incorporated into another work such as a Web page, usually for promotional purposes or to give the viewer a brief impression of the whole.

Video Librarian

Published bimonthly since 1986, *Video Librarian* provides over 200 reviews per issue of video-recordings in over 20 subject areas and current motion pictures available on videotape and DVD. A subscription to *Video Librarian PLUS* includes access to archives of previously published reviews, a new release calendar with links to prepublication reviews, a bi-weekly collection development column, and a searchable database of distributors. ISSN: 0887-6851.

Video Round Table (VRT)

A round table of the American Library Association (ALA), VRT provides leadership on issues related to video collections, programmes, and services in all types of libraries, including copyright, pricing, censorship, and preservation. VRT also forms alliances with the film and video production and distribution industry to promote diverse, high-quality video production.

Videocassette

A blank or prerecorded videotape permanently enclosed in a hard plastic case containing two take-up reels to which the ends of the tape are permanently attached for playback and rewinding in a device called a videocassette recorder (VCR).

Videoconference

A meeting of two or more participants conducted in real time at a distance using a video camera, microphone, and large television monitor or computer screen installed at each location, linked by satellite or digital network. *Videoconferencing* can save time and travel expense, especially in distance learning and in organisatons with geographically separate units. Also spelled *video conference.*

Videodisc

A large read-only analog optical disk usually made of plastic with a reflective metal coating on which visual images (still photographs and motion pictures) and associated audio signals are recorded for subsequent playback on a *videodisc player* attached to a television receiver and monitor. Also spelled *video disk.*

Videoreel

In *AACR2,* a term used in the physical description area of the bibliographic record to describe the physical form of a visual work recorded on videotape that is wound on one or more open reels, rather than encased in a cassette or cartridge.

Videotape

Magnetic tape on which visual images and accompanying sound are recorded for subsequent playback via television receiver and monitor, usually sold in the form of a videocassette. The industry standard is one-half-inch-wide tape (VHS).

Videotex

An interactive (two-way) telecommunication system in which a television receiver is adapted to enable computer databases to be searched over a telephone line or cable, using a menu-system or keyboard for input. Search results are displayed on the television screen. Synonymous in Britain with *viewdata.*

Viewbook

A promotional publication, usually issued annually in print or online, consisting primarily of pictures and maps of an educational institution or town, intended to introduce the campus or location visually to prospective students, residents, or visitors. The images may be photographs, photomechanical prints, or postcards. The pages of older viewbooks may be connected by accordion folds.

View-Master card

Stereograph.

Vine-Leaf Initial

An initial letter in a medieval manuscript, ornamented with a pattern of interlace or coiled vine terminating in three-pointed leaves, usually painted in red and/or blue with white shading or in gilt, a style of decoration used from the 13th century up to the second half of the 15th century.

Vinyl

The hard plastic chemical compound polyvinyl chloride (PVC) from which 12-inch wide microgroove 33 1/3 rpm long-playing records (LPs) are made. Prior to the introduction of LPs in the 1950s, 78 rpm phonograph records were made of shellac. Although vinyl plastic is flexible and unbreakable under normal use, vinyl records are easier to scratch or gouge and more prone to warping than earlier shellac records. Also used in the recording industry and by collectors as a slang term for *long-playing record*.

Virtual Library

A 'library without walls' in which the collections do not exist on paper, microform, or other tangible form at a physical location but are electronically accessible in digital format via computer networks. Such libraries exist only on a very limited scale, but in most traditional print-based libraries in the United States, catalogs and periodical indexes are available online, and some periodicals and reference works may be available in electronic full-text. Some libraries and library systems call themselves 'virtual' because they offer online services (*example: Colourado Virtual Library*). The term digital library is more appropriate because *virtual* (borrowed from 'virtual reality') suggests that the experience of using such a library is not the same as the 'real' thing when in fact the experience of reading or viewing a document on a computer screen may be qualitatively different from reading the same publication in print, but the information content is the same regardless of format.

Virtual Reality

An electronic environment created especially for computer users through the use of software that simulates the visual appearance of three-dimensional reality but lacks physical substance, used mainly for training purposes and popular entertainment.

Virtual Reference

Digital reference.

Virtual Union Catalogue

An automated system for searching the holdings of two or more discrete library catalogs together, using Z39.50 and/or other mechanisms for broadcast search and retrieval, in contrast to a centralised union catalogue in which catalogue records are gathered in a single database or physical location.

Virtual

An adjective referring to activities, objects, beings, and places that have no actual physical reality because they exist only in digital form (in cyberspace), for example, an e-mail 'box' or an electronic 'shopping cart.'

Visiting Card

A small printed or engraved card bearing a person's name and in some cases the street address, sometimes enclosed in an envelope, for presentation to the host's servant when making a formal social call and left behind to indicate that the call was made, a practice introduced in Europe in the 17th century. Some visiting cards are embellished with a portrait, coat of arms, scene, or decoration.

Visual Aid

An item, such as a motion picture, videocassette, slide, photograph, map, chart, model, specimen, etc., used by an instructor or presenter to allow the audience to view an example or representation of what is being taught. Instruction librarians sometimes bring to the classroom reference books containing information pertinent to course content to enable students to recognise them by sight.

Visual Dictionary

A dictionary in which words and phrases (grouped by subject, theme, or activity) are illustrated, usually in a line drawing on the same or the opposite page, with each term keyed to the corresponding feature in the diagram by a thin line or small reference number printed on the illustration.

Visual Resources Association (VRA)

An international organisaton established in 1982 to advance knowledge, research, and education in the field of visual information resources, VRA has a membership of information media professionals, including digital image specialists; art, architecture, film, and video librarians and museum curators; slide, photograph, microfilm, and digital archivists; architectural firms; museums and galleries; publishers and image system vendors; rights and reproduction officials; photographers and artists; art historians; and scientists. VRA sponsors an annual conference and publishes the quarterly *VRA Bulletin*.

Visually Impaired

A person whose sight makes using library materials in conventional formats difficult, if not impossible. Library services designed to meet the needs of visually impaired persons include Braille, large print, audiobooks and other recorded media, and radio reading service. In the United States, such services are available through the federally funded National Library Service for the Blind and Physically Handicapped (NLS).

Vital Records

Records essential to an agency in the ongoing conduct of its business or affairs, without which it would cease to function effectively, for example, the file of patron records used by a library in circulation transactions. For archivists, identifying and protecting vital records under every conceivable circumstance is a primary concern in records management and disaster planning.

Viz.

An abbreviation of the Latin *videlicet*, meaning 'namely,' 'that is to say,' or 'to wit,' used in text and footnotes to introduce a word or phrase added to explain more completely or precisely a previous word, phrase, or statement.

VM

Visual materials.

Vocabulary

All the words used in a language, or a list of them. Also, all the words and phrases used by a particular person, group, or profession. Also refers to a list of words in a textbook for students learning a foreign language, usually printed at the end of the text containing them or at the end of each chapter.

Vocabulary Control

In indexing, the process of creating and maintaining a list of preferred terms to indicate (1) which of two or more equivalent terms will represent a concept as the authorised subject heading or descriptor in the classification system and (2) the relations of hierarchy (broader and narrower terms) and association (related terms) among headings once they have been selected. Controlled vocabulary is recorded in a subject headings list or thesaurus that is updated as new concepts emerge and older terminology becomes obsolete. Compare with authority control.

Vocabulary Mapping

A function built into the search software of some bibliographic databases that allows the user to relate a specific search term to the appropriate subject heading(s) or descriptor(s), read a scope note explaining how the heading is used, view the hierarchical tree of headings to which it belongs, and select broader headings or narrower terms or subheadings to include in the search. Vocabulary mapping is available in large databases, such as *MEDLINE* and *PsycINFO*, which have a well-developed controlled vocabulary.

Vocal Score

The score of a musical work composed for voice (opera, oratorio, cantata, etc.) in which all the parts are shown in normal size on separate staves, with any accompaniment (ordinarily written for orchestra) reduced to two staves for performance on a keyboard instrument.

VOD

Video On Demand.

Voice Mail

A messaging system that allows a person to send, receive, and store audio messages using a standard telephone receiver. Also spelled *voicemail*.

Voice over Internet Protocol (VoIP)

Computer hardware and software designed to route telephone calls over a broadband network, such as the Internet. By converting analog voice signals into digital data packets, VoIP enables calls to be transmitted using the Internet Protocol (IP) and Real-time Transport Protocol (RTP), rather than the circuitry of the PSTN (public switched telephone network). IP telephony offers substantial cost savings over traditional long-distance calling because the user pays no surcharge on the normal fee for Internet access. Like cell phone transmission, VoIP has a higher incidence of dropped calls and generally lower voice quality. Internet telephony applications may be stand-alone or bundled with a Web browser. Synonymous with *Internet telephony, IP telephony,* and *Voice over the Internet (VOI).*

Voice-over

In motion picture, video, and television production, a narration, commentary, or prepared text spoken in the voice of a person not seen on the screen, a technique widely used in advertising. In feature films, the narrator is usually one of the characters in the drama. In documentaries, the narrator is ordinarily identified in the credits, but a celebrity narrator may be identifiable by voice alone. Also spelled *voiceover.*

VoIP

Voice over Internet Protocol.

Volume Number

The number assigned to all the issues of a periodical published during a given publication period (usually a calendar year), beginning with number one for the period (year) in which the title was first issued. If the issues are bound in one or more physical volumes, the number is printed or impressed on the spine(s). In a multivolume reference work or set, such as an encyclopaedia, the volume number appears on the spine and/or front cover and on the title page.

Volume Rights

The rights, usually negotiated with a publisher by the author or author's agent, to publish a work in volume form, including hardcover, paperback, book club, and textbook editions. Volume rights also include publication of the work in its entirety in a single issue of a periodical and reprinting, in full or in part, in an anthology.

Volumen

Latin for 'a thing rolled up.' A writing surface used in Antiquity, consisting of papyrus or vellum sheets attached end-to-end, with text handwritten in columns on one side only, in lines running parallel with the edges of the roll. The last sheet was attached to a straight stick with knobbed ends called an *umbilicus,* around which the manuscript was rolled. The rolls were stored in a box called a *capsa* or on deep shelves with a vellum label or ticket attached to one end for identification by title or contents. Synonymous with scroll.

Volunteer

A person who works for a library or other organisaton without material recompense. Library volunteers are often retirees who wish to make a contribution by remaining actively engaged in their community. They perform a variety of tasks, depending on their skills and talents, including reshelving, physical processing, mending, storytelling, landscape maintenance, etc.

VRA Core Categories

A metadata element scheme developed by the Visual Resources Association for describing works of visual culture and images that document them, to facilitate the sharing of information among visual resources collections.

VRA

Visual Resources Association.

VRT

Video Round Table.

VT100

A type of mainframe terminal developed by Digital Equipment Corporation (DEC) and introduced in 1978, which became the *de facto* industry standard, creating an environment in which other types of computers are required to use software that emulates VT100 in order to log on via Telnet to a mainframe.

Vue d'optique

A hand-coloured etching or engraving, usually a landscape, intended to be viewed through an optical system such as a Zograscope that enhanced the visual effect of linear perspective, commonly used in England and Europe in the late 1700s for peep shows. Some examples had portions of the scenes cut out and the openings backed with translucent papers, to give the impression of illumination when the print was backlit. Because the viewing device included a mirror, image and any lettering were normally reversed.

W

W3C
World Wide Web Consortium.

Wages
Money paid to an employee for the total number of hours worked in a given period (weekly, biweekly, monthly), computed at an hourly rate. Library staff employed part-time are usually paid by the hour. Compare with salary.

WAI
Web accessibility.

Wall Map
A map on any scale designed to be legible to the human eye from a distance when hung on a wall, as decoration or for practical use. Wall maps are usually mounted in a frame or suspended from a rod or hooks inserted through grommets along the upper edge. Wall maps intended for military or other field operations may be given a special coating or laminated for protection.

Wall Shelving
Single-sided shelving placed against a wall and sometimes attached to it, as opposed to free-standing shelving (usually double-sided) designed to stand on its own away from a wall or other support. Shelving of both types is manufactured in sections to allow libraries to assemble ranges of varying length.

Wallet
A style of limp leather binding in which the lower cover of the book extends beyond the sections in a flap, as wide as the fore-edge, that folds over and is fastened by a clasp or a tongue designed to fit into a slot in the upper cover.

Wallpaper
The decorative background pattern or image against which windows, menus, icons, and other visual elements are displayed and manipulated in a graphical user interface (GUI), usually created in JPEG or GIF file format. Some systems allow the user to select a wallpaper from a variety of different designs. Files of wallpaper designs are also available online from third parties. Wallpapers can be custom-

designed to display a distinctive element, such as a logo, trademark, or other symbol of institutional identity. Compare with screen saver.

Wand
Light Pen.

Wanted Poster
A broadside or poster describing one or more criminals or suspects sought by law enforcement agencies, often including one or more identification photographs and sometimes fingerprints. Some include offers of reward for information provided.

War Map
A map made for use by a nation's armed forces in the prosecution of a war, sometimes showing battle fronts and troop movements. The category also includes maps made to illustrate the course or consequences of a war, usually to the public. War maps intended for official use generally remain classified until after the war has ended. When made for use in the field, they may be printed on cloth (or some other flexible material) and treated to make them water-repellent.

War Service Library
Library War Service.

Warehouse Shelving
Library shelving with extra-deep shelves, capable of storing books 3 to 4 rows deep, used only in closed access collections to save space. According to Ruth Fraley and Carol Lee Anderson in *Library Space Planning* (Neal-Schuman, 1990), a section of warehouse shelving 30 inches deep and 36 inches wide with 7 shelves can store up to 63 linear feet of materials 3 rows deep and 84 linear feet 4 rows deep, compared with 42 linear feet for a double-faced section of standard library shelving, with the space gain outweighing additional floor space required. They note that although warehouse shelving is less attractive and not as flexible as standard shelving, it is the most efficient means of storing manuscripts.

Warping
A twist or bend in a book cover that occurs after binding or casing, severe enough to prevent the volume from lying flat, usually caused by dampness. In newly bound books, the condition may be caused by differences in the expansion and/or contraction of the materials used in the case or cover. Warping can be minimized in binding by using well-dried boards, endpapers with the grain running from head to foot, and adhesives of low water content and by proper pressing. In libraries, it is controlled by storing books in a dry, well-ventilated place.

Warrant
A written document authorising or certifying something, such as the payment or receipt of money. In law, a writ signed by the appropriate authority, authorising a specific action, such as an arrest or search and seizure. In the United

States, a warrant is presented to the person against whom legal action is to be taken. Because warrants often pertain to serious legal matters, they can be of considerable historical significance.

Warranty

A fixed period of time, specified in the sales agreement, during which the seller is obliged to repair or replace a piece of equipment that does not function properly. Once the warranty period has expired, the purchaser must pay for repairs unless a maintenance contract has been signed. As a general rule, length of warranty is an indication of the manufacturer's confidence in the product. In a more general sense, a legally binding guarantee, often providing a specific remedy if its terms are not met.

Water Tear

Paper separated along a moistened line to give the tear a soft, uneven, feathered edge as the fibres gently pull apart without breaking, a technique used in making delicate paste repairs in books and other print materials.

Water Colour

A graphic work executed in water-soluble pigment, usually applied with a brush onto a support such as vellum, canvas, or dampened paper, in a technique that predates oil painting. As the water evaporates, the pigment becomes translucent, allowing light reflected from the supporting surface to give the work the appearance of luminosity. The term includes fresco and tempera, as well as aquarelle. Watercolour was used in medieval illuminated manuscripts to brilliant effect. The medium became particularly popular in England, where its greatest masters were John Constable (example) and J.M.W. Turner (example).

Water-Damaged

Library materials that have been exposed to wet or damp conditions, usually as a result of leakage, flooding, or accident. Exposure of print materials to moisture can cause swelling, warping, staining, and subsequent contamination with mildew and mold, damage that is very difficult to repair. The leaves of publications printed on coated paper often fuse when wet, a problem that can be prevented by freezing and vacuum drying the damaged item. The University of Illinois Library provides *Tips for Saving Water-Damaged Items.*

Waterstained

The condition of a book or other printed publication that has leaves or binding discoloured by contact with water

Wax Cylinder

An early sound recording medium developed in the late 1870s by Thomas Edison in which tiny indentations were made in grooves on the outside surface of a cylinder, which could be played back as sound on a phonograph. Edison first used cylinders made of tinfoil but later switched to hard wax.

The cylinders are about 2 inches in diameter, 4 inches long, and very brittle. By 1910, the Edison Speaking Company was the only major sound recording company still making cylinders—all the other manufacturers had switched to disk phonograph records, which were less expensive to produce and could be recorded on both sides. Because the voices of some historically important people are recorded only on early wax cylinders, efforts are underway to preserve them for research.

WDL
World Digital Library.

Web
World Wide Web (WWW).

Web Accessibility
The ease with which Internet resources available via the World Wide Web can be used by people who experience difficulty in reading print, due to learning disabilities, visual impairment, or some other physical disability. In 1998, the Rehabilitation Act of 1973 was amended to include Section 508, modeled after the W3C Web Accessibility Initiative's (WAI) *Web Content Accessibility Guidelines (WCAG)* to require the information technology tools of government agencies and information services to adhere to the WAI guidelines.

Web Address
Uniform Resource Locator.

Web Browser
Client software that interprets the hypertext (HTML) code in which Web pages are written and allows documents and other data files available over the Internet to be viewed in graphical, as opposed to text-only, format (*example*: *Internet Explorer* from Microsoft). The appearance of a Web page may vary slightly depending on the type and version of browser used to view it.

Webcam
A video camera connected to a computer or computer network, enabling the computer to act as a videophone or videoconferencing station in real time. First developed in 1991, Webcams are also used in security surveillance, giving rise to concerns about privacy.

Webcast
Simultaneous transmission of live or delayed audio or video programming over the World Wide Web to all who own the equipment necessary to receive it, the Internet counterpart of broadcasting via radio or television. In a narrower sense, to send the same Web-based content (audio, video, graphics, text) to a group of Internet users, based on their individual needs or interests. The receiver must install special software known as *plug-ins* (*RealPlayer*, Apple *QuickTime*, *Windows Media Player*, etc.). Synonymous with *netcast*. Compare with webinar.

Web Citation
A written reference to a document accessed via the World Wide Web, usually including the address

(URL) of the Web page and the date of retrieval. Accepted formats vary, depending on academic discipline.

WebDewey
An enhanced version of the full Dewey Decimal Classification (DDC) database available to full members and partial users of OCLC in conjunction with the CORC online cataloguing project, *WebDewey* can be used to generate proposed Dewey class numbers for Web pages and other electronic resources. The system is also available in an abridged version.

Web Index
A search engine that organises Web sites by subject content in a hierarchy of subject categories, from the most general to the most specific. For example, links to Web sites for 'library and information science organisatons' are listed in *Yahoo!* under: Reference Libraries Library and Information Science OrganisatonsThe URL of a category in a Web index often reflects the hierarchical structure.

Weblog
A Web page that provides frequent continuing publication of Web links and/or comments on a specific topic or subject (broad or narrow in scope), often in the form of short entries arranged in reverse chronological order, the most recently added piece of information appearing first. An example in the field of library and information science is *LISNews.com,* which accepts postings from its readers. A list of library Weblog sites is maintained by Peter Scott on *Libdex.*

Webmaster
The individual responsible for managing and maintaining a Web site, often the person who designed it, whose name usually appears near the bottom of the main page or welcome screen, usually with a contact link. In libraries, the Webmaster may be the systems librarian, a 'techie,' or a person who has acquired a knowledge of HTML and Web servers.

Webometrics
cybermetrics.

WebPac
An online public access catalogue (OPAC) that uses a graphical user interface (GUI) accessible via the World Wide Web, as opposed to a text-based interface accessible via Telnet.

Web Page
An electronic document written in HTML script, stored on a Web server and accessible using Web browser software at a unique Internet address (URL), usually one of a group of related, interlinked files that together comprise a Web site. A Web page may include formatted text, graphic material, audio and/or video elements, and links to other files on the Internet.

Web Server
A system capable of providing Internet access to Web-based resources and services in response to requests from client computers on

which Web browser software is installed. A Web server includes the necessary hardware and also the operating system, TCP/IP protocols, server software, and information content of the Web sites installed on it. Web server software is designed to accept requests from users to download HTML text, image, and audio files.

Web Site

A group of related, interlinked Web pages installed on a Web server and accessible 24 hours a day to Internet users equipped with browser software. Most Web sites are created to represent the online presence of a company, organisaton, or institution or are the work of a group or individual. The main page or welcome screen, called the homepage, usually displays the title of the site, the name of the person (or persons) responsible for creating and maintaining it, and date of last update. Also spelled *Web sitee* and *web site*.

Web Widget

In computing, a small stand-alone piece of reusable application code that can be shared and embedded in any third-party HTML-based Web page without requiring additional compilation, for example, Meebo Me!, a chat box that allows Web page authors to converse in real time with site visitors. Other examples include link counters, clocks, advertising banners, daily weather reports, stock market tickers, event countdowns, etc. Web widgets are usually written in DHTML, JavaScript, or Adobe Flash. Although the host controls placement of a widget, it has no control over content. Used synonymously with *badge, snippet,* and *webjit*.

WebTV

A Microsoft trademark applied to technology that enables the user to search the Web via television, rather than a PC. A set-top box is installed containing an analog modem designed to make the connection to the Internet via a telephone line and convert data to a format that can be displayed on the television monitor, with navigation by handheld remote control device or optional keyboard. To gain access, the user must establish an account with an Internet service provider. Synonymous with *Internet TV*.

Webzine

Electronic Magazine.

Wedge-serif

A typeface with serifs that are triangular in shape, also known as latin. Wedge-shaped serifs are also found in medieval manuscripts written in Insular majuscule script from about A.D. 550 to 900.

Weekly

Issued once a week. Also refers to a serial issued once a week (*example: Publishers Weekly*). Most newsmagazines and some newspapers are published weekly (*Newsweek* and *Barron's*).

Weight

The relative thickness of a typeface, which determines how

dark it will appear on the printed page, indicated typographically by gradation (extra-light, light, semi-light, medium, semi-bold, bold, extra-bold, and ultra-bold). In selecting an appropriate weight of type for a proposed publication, the typographer considers grade of paper, type of ink, and method of printing. Most books are printed in medium type, with bold or semi-bold used for headings and emphasis.

Weighting

Use of an algorithm to predict the relevance of documents retrieved in a search, usually based on the frequency of search terms and their location in the bibliographic record (in title, descriptors, abstract, or text), often expressed as a percentage. Weighting allows scored records to be presented to the searcher in ranked order.

WESS

Western European Studies Section.

Western European Studies Section (WESS)

Established in 1973, WESS is the section of the Association of College and Research Libraries (ACRL) within the American Library Association (ALA) representing librarians who are professionally involved in the selection, acquisition, organisaton, and use of information sources originating in or related to the countries of Western Europe. WESS aims to facilitate the enhancement of library services in support of study and research in Western European affairs from ancient times to the present.

Western

A work of fiction (novel, short story, etc.), motion picture, or television programme or series in which adventure is the primary theme; the narrative is secondary to the setting (the 19th-century American West); and the characters are typically cowboys, frontiersmen, outlaws, ranchers, miners, settlers, indigenous peoples, etc. In series westerns, the hero is often a lawman. In movie westerns, the hero usually wears a light-coloured Stetson and the villain a black hat. As Diana Tixier Herald notes in *Genreflecting: A Guide to Reading Interests in Genre Fiction* (Libraries Unlimited, 2000) that, 'The appeal of this genre is worldwide, based on a dream of freedom in a world of unspoiled nature, a world independent of the trammels of restraining society.' The audience for western fiction is predominantly male.

Wet Gate Printing

A method of printing motion picture film in which the original film is passed briefly through a chemical solution just prior to exposure that fills in any scratches and abrasions, especially on the base side, to prevent them from showing on the new film stock. A wet gate can be incorporated into either a film printer or a telecine used to transfer images on film to videotape. In *liquid gate printing*, the film moves through a liquid-filled glass cell at time of exposure, filling in any scratches and preventing refracted light from reproducing them on the fresh stock.

WGSS

Women and Gender Studies Section.

Wheel Binding

A style of leather binding developed during the 18th century by Scottish binders in which the centre of the cover is embellished with a circular design in the shape of a wheel, with spokes radiating from a central point. The style may have evolved from fan binding, popular throughout Europe during the 17th century.

Whipstitching

A binding method in which the sewing thread is passed over and over the spine, often used in early pamphlets.

White Letter

A term used in early printing for roman type, as opposed to gothic or *black letter*.

White Line

In printing, a line of spacing equal in depth to a line of printed matter, used before and after headings, long quotations, etc., to set them apart from the text.

White-Vine Initial

An initial letter in a medieval manuscript, decorated with an interlace pattern of vines stems made to appear light in colour by applying paint of contrasting colour to the surrounding background while leaving the vine unpainted, a technique that makes the bare surface of the underlying support (parchment, vellum, or paper) an important design element.

Wide Area Network (WAN)

A communication network covering an extensive geographic area, such as a country, region, province, or state. Compare with local area network.

Widow

A dangling word or phrase or line shorter than one-third the specified line length, at the end of a paragraph, especially when it falls at the head of a column or page of text matter, considered awkward by typographers and eliminated in typesetting whenever possible.

Width

The dimension of a book or other bound item from spine to fore-edge, usually less than its height, the exception being volumes square or oblong in shape. In library cataloguing, the height of a book is given in the physical description area of the biblio-graphic record in centimeters but not the width. Also refers to the horizontal dimension of a section of single- or double-sided shelving. Most library shelving is sold in sections 36 inches wide.

Wi-Fi

An abbreviation of *wireless fidelity*, a trademark that may be used with products certified by a non-profit, industry-wide consortium called the Wi-Fi Alliance as belonging to a class of wireless local area network (WLAN) devices based on the IEEE 802.11 standards of interoperability. Today, virtually all laptop and palm-sized computers and many personal computers, video game consoles, smartphones, printers, and other peripherals include an IEEE 802.11 device, enabling them to connect to the Internet within range of a wireless network connected to the Internet.

WIMPS

An acronym for 'windows, icons, mouse, pull-down menus.' Synonymous with graphical user interface.

Wind Rose

A star-shaped graphic device used on an early map or chart to orient the reader to the four cardinal directions (north, east, south, and west) associated with the winds that were observed to issue from them prior to the development of the compass in the late 13th century. North was traditionally represented by the *fleur de lis* and east, the direction of Jerusalem, by the Maltese cross In modern usage, a graphic used in meteorology to show the amount of time the wind blows in each compass direction at a specific geographic location

WIPO

World Intellectual Property Organisaton.

Wire Coil

A continuous length of metal wire threaded through holes punched along the binding edge of the leaves of a book or notebook in spiral binding. Flexible hard plastic is also used for this purpose.

Wire Photograph

A photograph that has been scanned and converted to electronic signals for transmission via telegraph or telephone wires, then reformed into an image at the receiving end. The first halftone photograph was transmitted by Western Union in 1921. The Associated Press introduced its AP Wirephoto service in 1935.

Wire Service

News service.

Wireless Handheld Devicev

A durable, lightweight computer small enough to be held comfortably in the hand, designed to be used in a wireless network for applications requiring mobility. Some handhelds have phone and two-way pager functionality. Synonymous with *handheld terminal*, *mobile terminal*, and *portable terminal*.

Wireless Local Area Network (WLAN)

A local area network that links electronic devices via electromagnetic airwaves, rather than by wire or cable, usually providing connection to an Internet service provider through an access point (router). WLANs enable users to remain connected while moving around within the area of coverage—usually a home, office, or public facility.

With All Faults (W.A.F.)
A term used by booksellers, book dealers, and auctioneers to inform prospective buyers that an item is offered for sale *as is* and may not be returned if found to be in defective condition.

Withdrawal
The process of deleting all references in a library catalogue to an item that has been permanently removed from the collection without being replaced by another copy of the same edition. The item is usually stamped 'withdrawn' to avoid confusion in the disposition process. Also refers to the item *withdrawn.*

Witnessv
In the context of bibliography and textual criticism, a manuscript or incunabulum regarded by scholars as evidence of authority for a text. A *codex unicus* is a text for which only one witness exists. In binding, a book with the fore-edge so lightly trimmed that some leaves are left rough.

Wizard
An interactive utility available in some computer applications, usually in the form of a context-sensitive dialog box that provides step-by-step assistance in completing a complex task, as distinct from a general help menu accessible via the toolbar, from which the user may select as needed. Wizards can usually be turned 'off' if found intrusive.

Women and Gender Studies Section (WGSS)
The section of the Association of College and Research Libraries (ACRL) within the American Library Association (ALA) formed to discuss, promote, and support cross-disciplinary women's studies collections and services in academic and research libraries, including bibliographic instruction, liaison with teaching faculty, and information retrieval in the field.

World Digital Library (WDL)
In November 2006, the Library of Congress announced receipt of a $3-million 'no strings' gift from *Google* to begin digitising significant primary source materials from national and other major research libraries around the world, to make them freely available via the Internet in multilingual format. The concept was first proposed by Librarian of Congress James H. Billington in June 2005 in a speech to the plenary session of the U.S., National Commission for UNESCO. The World Digital Library is modeled on LC's American Memory project.

World Intellectual Property Organisaton (WIPO)
A specialised agency of the United Nations with headquarters in Geneva, WIPO is responsible for administering 21 international treaties concerning the protection of intellectual property under copyright, patent, and trademark law for the benefit of its 177 member nations.

World Library and Information Congress
The annual conference of the International Federation of Library As-

sociations and Institutions (IFLA), the world summit of libraries and librarians, held in a different member country each year, with the host country responsible for local arrangements (exhibits, receptions, tours, plenary programme, etc.) in close cooperation with the international headquarters of IFLA. The 69th congress held in Berlin in August 2003 was attended by 4500 people.

World Wide Web (WWW)

A global network of Internet servers providing access to documents written in a script called Hypertext Markup Language (HTML) that allows content to be interlinked, locally and remotely. The 'Web' was designed in 1989 by Sir Timothy Berners-Lee, working at the CERN high-energy physics lab in Geneva. Mark Andreeson, a student at the University of Illinois, later devised a simple point-and-click system called *Mosaic* that subsequently evolved into the *Netscape* Web browser. Abbreviated *Web.*

WYSIWYG

What You See Is What You Get (pronounced 'wizzy-wig'), an exact correspondence between text and/or graphics as displayed on a computer screen and its appearance when printed, difficult to achieve in reality because the resolution of monitor and printer rarely match.

X

Xerography
From the Greek *xeros* and *graphos*, meaning 'dry writing.' A method of reproducing text and/or images in which dry resinous toner transferred from an electrostatically charged plate is thermally adhered to a sheet of paper or some other copying surface inside a photocopier (originally called a *xerox machine*). The result is a photocopy or *xerox copy*. Xerography is a form of reprography.

X-Height
The mean height of the lowercase letters of a typeface that have neither ascenders nor descenders, sometimes used instead of point size as an indication of type size. The x-height letters of the roman alphabet are: a, c, e, m, n, o, r, s, u, v, w, x, and z. The tops and bottoms of some letters such as the 'c' and 'o' may extend slightly above the mean line and below the base line. Also spelled *ex-height*.

XML
Extensible Markup Language.

X-Rated
A motion picture or videorecording containing material considered suitable for adults only, usually because it contains material considered pornographic. The term is also applied to print publications containing adult material (magazines, photographs, etc.).

x-ref cross-reference.

XSL

Extensible Stylesheet Language.

Xylograph
Text and/or image printed from a woodblock. The blockbooks of the 15th and 16th centuries are a prime example. Xylographic illustration was also used in manuscripts and press-printed books of the same period, sometimes hand-tinted.

Xylography
Printing done from blocks of wood, especially by the early process of wood engraving, concurrent with the early development of printing from movable type. The results, known as *xylographica*, often contain more illustration than text.

Y

YA book
young adult book.

YA
An abbreviation of *young adult*, an adolescent aged 12-18, usually in the ninth to twelfth grade.

Yahoo!
An acronym for *yet another hierarchically officious oracle*, a worldwide directory of Web sites developed in 1994 by two Stanford University engineering students to organise Web content in a hierarchical system of subject categories. *Yahoo!* also provides other Web-based services (news, weather, travel, e-mail, shopping, games, etc.). It uses a smaller database than most other Web search engines, but searches in *Yahoo!* usually have high precision because the Web sites it lists are selected by human beings rather than robot software. Jonathan Swift coined the term 'yahoo' in *Gulliver's Travels* (1726) to refer to an imaginary race of coarse, brutish creatures in human form. Mark Twain later applied it to any boorish person.

YALSA
Young Adult Library Services Association.

Yapp Binding
A form of limp or semi-limp leather binding with rounded corners and bent-in edges that overlap the sections, sometimes by as much as half the thickness of the text block, named after William Yapp, the 19th-century bookseller who designed the style for pocket bibles sold in England. Geoffrey Glaister notes in *Encyclopaedia of the Book* (Oak Knoll/British Library, 1996) that a similar style of binding with tooled edges was used in the mid-16th century. Synonymous wth *yapped binding*, *yapped edges*, and *Yapp edges*. Compare with circuit edges.

Yawning Boards
Covers that curve away from the text block of the book instead of lying flat against it, a condition usually caused by warping.

Yearbook
An annual documentary, historical, or memorial compen-dium of

facts, photographs, statistics, etc., about the events of the preceding year, often limited to a specific country, institution, discipline, or subject (*example*: *Supreme Court Yearbook* published by Congressional Quarterly). Optional yearbooks are offered by some publishers of general encyclopaedias. Most libraries place yearbooks on continuation order and shelve them in the reference collection. Yearbooks of historical significance may be stored in archives or special collections. Also spelled *year book*. Compare with annual.

Yellow Pages
The portion of a telephone directory or trade directory following the white pages in which the names, phone numbers, and mailing addresses of commercial enterprises are listed, usually alphabetically by subject or in a classified arrangement, so named because the section is printed on yellow paper. Yellow pages are also available online (*example*: *SuperPages.com* from Verizon) and for specific professions (*Librarian's Yellow Pages*).

Yellowback
An inexpensive popular novel bound in a shiny yellow paper or board cover with a picture printed on the front, usually a woodcut in three colours, a type of publication that originated in England in the 1850s and was used until the end of the century for inexpensive reprint editions.

Yellow Press
A popular name for newspapers and periodicals of the early 20th century that published news stories of a vulgarly sensational nature, comparable to the modern tabloid. Synonymous with gutter press.

Yellowing
A colour change that occurs in the condition of certain grades of paper with the passage of time, particularly those made from unbleached or groundwood pulp, one of the reasons most libraries convert newspaper back files to microfilm or microfiche. The problem can be averted in libraries by purchasing materials printed on acid-free permanent paper.

Young Adult Book
A book intended to be read and enjoyed by adolescents 12 to 18 years of age. Also refers to a book intended for adults but considered suitable by reviewers and librarians for mature ninth- to twelfth-grade readers. Public libraries usually maintain a separate section for young adult literature managed by a librarian who specialises in YA services, including collection development.

Young Adult Library Services Association (YALSA)
A division of the American Library Association (ALA) founded in 1930, YALSA has a membership of librarians responsible for evaluating and selecting books and nonprint materials for young adults

(age 12 to 18) and for promoting and strengthening library services for young adult readers. YALSA publishes the journal *Young Adult Library Services*.

Young Adult Services
Library services intended specifically for adolescent patrons (ninth through twelfth graders), including collection development, programming, and readers' advisory. Public libraries usually have a room or section devoted specifically to young adult materials, managed by a librarian who specialises in providing services for this age group.

Young Reader's Choice Award (YRCA)
An annual literary award established in 1940 at the suggestion of the late Harry Hartman, a Seattle bookseller, to promote reading for enjoyment by children and young adults. Nominations are taken by the Pacific Northwest Library Association (PNLA) from the children, teachers, parents, and librarians of Alaska, Idaho, Montana, Oregon, Washington, British Columbia, and Alberta. To be nominated, a book must have been published in the preceding 3 years and printed in the United States or Canada. The award is given to one title in each of three divisions: junior, middle, and senior. Only children in grades 4-12 who live in the Pacific Northwest are eligible to vote. Voting takes place from March 15 to April 1.

Z

Z39.50
A client-server protocol established as a NISO standard that allows the computer user to query a remote information retrieval system using the software of the local system and receive results in the format of the local system, often used in portal and gateway products to search several sources simultaneously and integrate the results.

Zero-Base Budgeting (ZBB)
Financial planning that starts from zero at the beginning of each new budget cycle, with no assumptions carried over from previous experience, a method used in both the public and private sectors. In ZBB, every expense must be justified in each new cycle.

Zig-Zag Book
A book made by folding a continuous strip of paper backward and forward accordion-style. When the pages are sewn at the back fold, the strip is printed on one side only. When both sides are printed, the folds are left unsewn to allow the volume to be opened to its full length. This form of book is called an orihon when made from a manuscript or printed document originally produced as a roll. Also spelled *zigzag book*. Synonymous wuith *accordion book*. Compare with concertina.

Zig-Zag Guard
In binding, a continuous single-piece guard produced by folding a sheet of strong paper or linen accordion-style, used in photograph albums and other guard books, in large blankbooks for sewing the folios, and in conservation bookbinding for resewing the sections. Also spelled *zigzag guard*. Synonymous with *continuous guard*.

Zincograph
A lithographic print made from a suitably prepared zinc plate—less expensive than using lithographic stone.

Z ine
Derived from 'fanzine' (a contraction of 'fan magazine'), pro-

nounced 'zeen.' The term came into use during the 1980s to refer to a small, low-circulation magazine or newspaper, self-published out of passion for the subject rather than for personal gain, usually produced with the aid of desktop publishing software and high-quality photocopy machines. Zines represent the convergence of amateur publishing hobbyists, high school underground newspapers, the literary small press, political radicalism, and do-it-yourself popular culture. They are usually not available by subscription, often appear irregularly or infrequently, and may have a lifetime of only one or two issues. Some are available online via the World Wide Web. Selected zines are evaluated in the reference serial *Magazines for Libraries*.

Zip

To compress a data file using PKZIP software or some other utility capable of compressing data into PKZIP format. When such a file is restored to an uncompressed format, it is said to have been *unzipped*.

Zip Disk

A 3.5-inch removable magnetic disk cartridge developed by Iomega, capable of storing 100MB or more of data, much more than a standard floppy disk, at relatively low cost. A special Zip drive must be installed on a microcomputer to allow a Zip disk to be used.

Zip Drive

A disk drive developed by Iomega that uses a 3.5-inch removable Zip disk capable of storing 100MB or more of data at relatively low cost, used for storing very large files and collections of files. The drive usually comes with software that catalogs the contents of the disk and provides file security.

Zoo-Anthropomorphic Initial

A figure initial in a medieval manuscript or early printed book composed wholly or in part of one or more animal/human hybrids, often a human head on an animal body, or vice versa.

Zoomorphic Initial

A figure initial in a medieval manuscript or early printed book composed wholly or in part of forms recognisable as animals or imaginary beasts. Zoomorphic initials are common in the *Book of Kells*.

Bibliography

Ahluwalia, J.: *Annual Review of Information Science and Technology*, New Delhi: Indian Society for Information Science, 2007.

Bardhan, P.: *Advances in Librarianship*, Mumbai: Academic Press, 2009.

Batra, G.: *Indian Libraries,* Delhi: Indian Library Association, 1999.

Betty-Carol Sellen and Arthur Curley: *The Collection Building Reader*, New York: Neal-Schuman, 1992.

Carolyn Horton: *Cleaning and Preserving Bindings and Related Materials*, Chicago: American Library Association, 1967.

Chadha G. K.: *Anglo-American Cataloging Rules*, Chicago: American Library Association, 2002.

Christopher de Hamel: *The British Library Guide to Manuscript Illumination: History and Techniques*, Toronto: University of Toronto Press, 2001.

Christopher Morris: *Academic Press Dictionary of Science and Technology*, Christopher Morris: Academic Press, 1992.

Elizabeth Unger Mangan: *Catalogue of Illuminated Manuscripts: Glossary*, Chicago: American Library Association, 2003.

Frances C. Wilkinson and Linda K. Lewis: *The Complete Guide to Acquisitions Management*, Westport, CT: Libraries Unlimited, 2003.

Heartsill Young: *The ALA Glossary of Library and Information Science*, Chicago: American Library Association, 1983.

James Bettley: *The Art of the Book: From Medieval Manuscript to Graphic Novel*, London: V&A Publications, 2001.

Jane Greenfield: *ABC of Bookbinding*, New Castle, New York: Oak Knoll Press, 1998.

Jean Peters: *The Bookman's Glossary*, New York: R. R. Bowker, 1983.

Jessica L. Milstead: *ASIS Thesaurus of Information Science and Librarianship*, Medford, NJ: Information Today, 1998.

John Carter: *ABC for Book Collectors*, New Castle, Delaware: Oak Knoll Press, 1995.

John Feather: *A Dictionary of Book History*, New York: Oxford University Press, 1986.

John P. Dessauer: *Book Publishing: A Basic Introduction*, New York: Continuum, 1989.

Larry Millsap and Terry Ellen Ferl: *Descriptive Cataloging for the AACR2R and the Integrated MARC Format: A How-to-Do-It Workbook,* New York: Neal-Schuman, 1997.

Manly Banister: *Bookbinding as a Handcraft*, New York: Sterling Publishing Co., 1975.

Matt T. Roberts and Don Etherington: *Bookbinding and the Conservation of Books: A Dictionary of Descriptive Terminology*, London; New York: Phaidon, 2001.

Nat G. Bodian: *Bodian's Publishing Desk Reference*, New York: Oryx Press, 1988.

P.J.M. Marks: *The British Library Guide to Bookbinding: History and Techniques*, Toronto: University of Toronto Press, 1998.

Patricia Jean Wagner: *The Bloomsbury Review Booklover's Guide*, Denver: Bloomsbury Review, 1996.

Stella Keenan: *Concise Dictionary of Library and Information Science*,